SHATTERING SILOS

Shattering Silos

Reimagining Knowledge, Politics, and Social Critique

LAMBERT ZUIDERVAART

McGill-Queen's University Press
Montreal & Kingston · London · Chicago

© McGill-Queen's University Press 2022

ISBN 978-0-2280-1157-6 (cloth)
ISBN 978-0-2280-1158-3 (paper)
ISBN 978-0-2280-1362-4 (ePDF)
ISBN 978-0-2280-1363-1 (ePUB)

Legal deposit third quarter 2022
Bibliothèque nationale du Québec

Printed in Canada on acid-free paper that is 100% ancient forest free (100% post-consumer recycled), processed chlorine free.

Funded by the Government of Canada / Financé par le gouvernement du Canada

Canada Council for the Arts / Conseil des arts du Canada

We acknowledge the support of the Canada Council for the Arts.

Nous remercions le Conseil des arts du Canada de son soutien.

Library and Archives Canada Cataloguing in Publication

Title: Shattering silos : reimagining knowledge, politics, and social critique / Lambert Zuidervaart.
Names: Zuidervaart, Lambert, author.
Description: Companion volume to: Religion, truth, and social transformation and art, education, and cultural renewal. | Includes bibliographical references and index.
Identifiers: Canadiana (print) 20220171912 | Canadiana (ebook) 20220171955 | ISBN 9780228011583 (paper) | ISBN 9780228011576 (cloth) | ISBN 9780228013624 (ePDF) | ISBN 9780228013631 (ePUB)
Subjects: LCSH: Knowledge, Theory of—Political aspects. | LCSH: Knowledge, Theory of—Social aspects. | LCSH: Political science—Philosophy
Classification: LCC BD .Z85 2022 | DDC 320.01—dc23

This book was typeset by True to Type in 10.5/13 Sabon

For Nicholas Wolterstorff

Contents

Preface ix

Introduction: Truth and Politics 3

1. Philosophy, Truth, and the Wisdom of Love 20
2. Holistic Alethic Pluralism 31
3. Distantial Ways of Knowing: Toward a New Epistemology 53
4. Social Domains of Knowledge: Technology, Art, and Religion 69
5. Transformational Social Critique and a Politics of Hope 87
6. Reformational Philosophy Revisited 104
7. *The Tree of Life*: Hegel, Malick, and the Postsecular Sublime 126
8. Toronto to Berlin and Back Again 147
9. Revolution Isn't What It Used to Be 172
10. Pursuing Truth in a Post-Truth Society 187

Publication Information 207

Notes 209

Works Cited 241

Index 253

Preface

This is the third volume presenting my work in and about reformational philosophy, a nearly 100-year-old tradition described in the book's introduction. Whereas the previous two volumes – *Religion, Truth, and Social Transformation* (2016) and *Art, Education, and Cultural Renewal* (2017) – collect essays that span more than three decades, the current book arises from work done since 2015. By making this recent work more widely available, *Shattering Silos* serves to introduce various philosophical contributions and concerns from the reformational tradition. It also takes up responses to the first two volumes and extends the lines of thought those volumes lay out. This extension goes both backwards and forward, uncovering intellectual origins to specific ideas, and looking ahead to topics I hope to pursue in future years.

This volume refuses to set up rigid boundaries among knowledge, politics, and social critique. Knowledge, I argue, occurs within various social domains, and the contours of these domains and their roles in contemporary life are subject to political struggle. So too, the architectonic critique of society that I advocate draws on many domains of knowledge including, yet exceeding, the arts and sciences. Moreover, this critique casts politics as a striving for truth in the broadest sense. Through such interweaving of knowledge, politics, and social critique, philosophy can help challenge and redirect an allegedly post-truth society.

Five chapters in this book stem from the efforts of Dean Dettloff when he was a doctoral candidate in philosophy at the Institute for Christian Studies (ICS) in Toronto. Working as a research assistant at ICS's Centre for Philosophy, Religion and Social Ethics, Dean arranged an extensive online book symposium to coincide with the publication of *Religion, Truth, and Social Transformation* in the spring of 2016. The symposium featured blog commentaries on every chapter by one or more of my colleagues and (former) graduate students. My responses originally occurred in four blog posts. Writing these responses provided an opportunity to clarify, modify, deepen, and reconsider the ideas presented in *Religion, Truth, and Social Transformation*. In this way the symposium provided a wonderful forum for "communal scholarship," to which scholars at ICS have long aspired. Now the responses appear, lightly revised, in chapters 5 and 6. I thank the Centre for Philosophy, Religion and Social Ethics for permission to republish these materials here.

A year later, on his own initiative, Dean arranged to interview me several times. The first interview discussed my life's work. It took place on 13 March 2017, one day after a celebratory gathering in Toronto to mark my retirement from the faculty of ICS. Two months later, the day after I gave a valedictory address at ICS's annual convocation, Dean conducted a second interview, about politics this time. It was podcast one week later. Then, a year or so later, he followed up with a third interview, conducted via Skype, about my current work on the idea of truth. Dean subsequently undertook the laborious task of transcribing all three interviews, so that together he and I could edit them, adding titles, headings, and endnotes. The three interviews appear in the current volume as chapters 8, 9, and 10, respectively. I am very thankful for Dean Dettloff's engaged interactions with my work, his superb ability to organize occasions where this work could be discussed, and his uncanny knack for asking excellent questions. I also thank Joe Kirby for preparing the index to this volume.

The other five chapters stem from recently published essays. Chapter 1 is a lightly revised version of the aforementioned 2017 valedictory address, as published by the journal *Christian Scholar's Review*. It points to "Holistic Alethic Pluralism," an article I had published in the journal *Philosophia Reformata* one year earlier, which now appears in revised form as chapter 2. A few months after giving the valedictory address, I wrote two new essays about knowledge, to fill in the epistemological background to my holistic and pluralist conception of truth. Subsequently published in *Philosophia Reformata*, they appear here, with permission from the publisher Brill and slightly revised, as chapters 3 and 4. The other chapter – chapter 7 – was written for a collection of new essays on postsecular cinema published by SUNY Press.

Revised for the current volume, it describes and carries out what I call redemptive art criticism, in which claims about knowledge, politics, and social critique intersect. Details about the sources of all ten chapters appear in "Publication Information" at the end of this book. I am grateful to the editors and publishers listed there for permission to incorporate these materials into the current volume. I also want to acknowledge with gratitude the generous publication grants this book has received from the Andreas Center at Dordt University and the Priscilla and Stanford Reid Trust.

The interview in chapter 8 mentions a 1977 ICS summer seminar in aesthetics, organized by my mentor Dr Calvin Seerveld, where I presented a paper titled "Musical and Musicological Knowledge." This was my first attempt to address a scholarly audience about the emerging conceptions of knowledge and truth that have permeated my work ever since. Among the audience members who applauded this attempt was Professor Nicholas Wolterstorff, a prominent analytic philosopher whom I had just met for the first time. His books would subsequently play crucial roles in my own development as a young scholar and professor, including *Reason within the Bounds of Religion* (1976), *Art in Action* (1980), and *Until Justice and Peace Embrace* (1983).

Eight years later, when I left The King's University in Edmonton, Alberta in 1985 to join the Philosophy Department at Calvin College (now Calvin University) in Grand Rapids, Michigan, Nick and I became faculty colleagues. He was a well-known and widely respected senior faculty member at Calvin who, having studied there in the early 1950s, had joined Calvin's Philosophy Department in 1959. I, by contrast, arrived as a relatively unknown junior faculty member reimported, so to speak, from Germany, the Netherlands, and Canada. At the time I was trying to turn my dissertation on Adorno's aesthetics into a book. Nick was unfailingly generous in his reading of this work, and he regularly encouraged me to bring it to completion. Were it not for his support, I might never have finished *Adorno's Aesthetic Theory* (MIT Press, 1991), my first academic book.

Such support from a senior colleague has proved invaluable over the years. It continued long after Nick left Calvin in 1989 to join the faculty at Yale University and right into his retirement years after 2002. Although he and I approach philosophical topics from quite different angles – he as a Harvard-trained analytic philosopher shaped by Scottish Common Sense Realism, and I as an ICS-trained continental philosopher indebted to German Idealism and its aftermath –

we have always clicked, both as persons and as scholars. For more than forty years I have learned from Nicholas Wolterstorff what it means to be an intellectually rigorous, religiously attuned, and socially engaged philosopher. Indeed, my regarding knowledge, politics, and social critique as closely interlinked owes much to his work. With deep gratitude for Nick's inspiring example and his generous support, I dedicate this book to him.

SHATTERING SILOS

Introduction:
Truth and Politics

> Is it of the very essence of truth to be impotent and of the very essence of power to be deceitful? And what kind of reality does truth possess if it is powerless in the public realm? Is not impotent truth just as despicable as power that gives no heed to truth?
>
> Hannah Arendt[1]

The questions Hannah Arendt raised to begin her 1967 essay "Truth and Politics" have acquired new urgency in an allegedly post-truth society. Now, however, the issues are not simply how to speak truth to power and whether political speech unavoidably distorts the truth. Just as urgent is the question whether truth itself can survive the onslaught of post-truth politics, with its daily attacks on science, the news media, and the public sphere. Whereas Arendt cautioned philosophers to steer clear of political power, for fear that politics would corrupt philosophical truth, today's philosopher must directly resist the politicians in power, lest they destroy truth itself.

To resist, however, philosophers need to shatter the silos of their own profession: epistemology here, value theory there; metaphysics here, social critique there; academics here, politics there. It is time to discover anew, as Theodor Adorno recognized, that all philosophy, including a theory of knowledge and truth, is social philosophy.[2] Its point is to take up the challenges of society as a whole. Today these challenges include politically motivated attacks on philosophy's very soul, on the love of wisdom and the pursuit of truth. If philosophers do not break out of their self-prescribed silos, they will be unable to counter such attacks.

1. SHATTERING SILOS

Perhaps the most restrictive silo, or at least the one that proves most resistant to internal criticism, occurs in philosophical reflections on truth itself, a silo reinforced by much of contemporary epistemology. For many philosophers, the nature of truth and its importance have become topics for increasingly refined and technical debates. These debates concern the ability or inability of sentences, statements, beliefs, and propositions to be true, as well as either the need for or the irrelevance of objects or facts or states of affairs to make such "truth bearers" true – what, in the remainder of this book, I label *propositional truth*. Although such debates about propositional truth have implications for whether and how to resist politically motivated attacks on truth, the terms that frame the debates, and how the debates are conducted, keep contemporary philosophical truth theory safely – albeit dangerously – isolated from the political arena.

Arendt was well aware of these issues, even though, in my view, her essay "Truth and Politics" does not overcome such isolation. It also fails to resolve a tension between her affirming the enduring strength of truth and her recognizing the enormous power of political leaders to ignore and suppress it. The essay employs two concepts of truth, not one. Arendt labels them *philosophical truth* and *factual truth*. The two sorts of truth differ primarily in how they come to be established. Whereas philosophical truth – the truth of general understanding – is established by the solitary philosopher, factual truth – the truth of what is or what has happened – is established by the testimony of many people. Because Arendt associates the political realm with plurality, factual truth intrinsically belongs to the political realm, she says, as do the opinions that people advance and discuss in public.

Factual truths are not mere opinions, however, no more than a philosophical truth is. Nevertheless, a favourite device for political tyrants is to treat them as all the same, such that every truth claim becomes a matter of mere opinion, and deliberate lies in the service of political violence come to seem innocuous. That is why, as Arendt astutely notes, the political liar, when "lacking the power to make his falsehood stick, does not insist on the gospel truth of his statement but pretends that this is his 'opinion,' to which he claims his constitutional right."[3]

Yet Arendt holds that, in the end, both philosophical and factual truth can outlast political attacks: "Persuasion and violence can destroy truth, but they cannot replace it." Truth can outlast political attacks by being upheld from a standpoint "outside the political realm" by the "existential modes of truthtelling" of the solitary philosopher, the isolated scientist or artist, the impartial historian or judge, and the independent fact-finder, witness, or reporter.[4] It is precisely in upholding the impartiality of truth – its "non-political and, potentially, even anti-political nature"[5] – that Arendt thinks the political relevance of truthtelling professions and institutions such as philosophy and the academy lies.[6]

By locating philosophy's political relevance in its upholding the "nonpolitical" character of truth, Arendt's essay tends to reinforce the contemporary isolation of philosophical truth theory from the political arena. In a political environment where truth itself is under attack, however, it is doubtful that such isolation is philosophy's strength. Rather, the isolation of philosophical reflections on truth from the current political arena gives tacit permission for political demagogues to ignore philosophy while trying to destroy its spirit.

Historically, reformational philosophy, like Adorno and Critical Theory, has challenged such isolation. From its earliest stirrings in the work of Abraham Kuyper (1837–1920), to its initial articulation in the writings of Herman Dooyeweerd (1894–1977) and Dirk Vollenhoven (1892–1978), to more recent rearticulations by second- and third-generation thinkers, reformational philosophy has insisted that theories of knowledge and truth are not spiritually neutral. As Dooyeweerd put it in the first article published by the journal he and Vollenhoven founded in 1936, "philosophical theoretical thought is not self-sufficient *in its own domain*."[7] Accordingly, any philosophical account of what knowledge and truth are and why they matter presupposes a stance, either implicit or explicit, on the direction in which human life and society should be headed. If that is so, then I would claim that epistemology and truth theory belong, at least implicitly, to a more encompassing social philosophy, such that they cannot be politically neutral either.

Before elaborating on this claim, however, let me make some preliminary remarks about reformational philosophy. As is explained in the introductions to two previous volumes,[8] reformational philosophy stems from a late-nineteenth-century revival of Dutch Calvinism led by the theologian, educator, and political leader Abraham Kuyper.[9] The Kuyperian tradition, as it has come to be known, views human life as belonging to a good creation that, although damaged and misdirected, can in its entirety be redeemed. For a Kuyperian, to be a Christian is to work toward the redemption of creation, including culture and society, and this requires organized collective efforts in education, labour, politics, and many other social domains.

Hence the Dutch Kuyperian movement spawned its own political party, business and labour organizations, and faith-oriented schools, culminating in the Vrije Universiteit Amsterdam or Free University or, as it is currently known, the VU Amsterdam. Founded in 1880, the VU Amsterdam was the first independent faith-oriented university in the Netherlands, free from both state and church control. Kuyperians who immigrated to North America continued such efforts, giving significant impetus to faith-oriented schooling as well as university education (especially Calvin University, Dordt University, and Trinity Christian College in the United States and the Institute for Christian Studies, The King's University, and Redeemer University in Canada) as well as organizations in other domains (such as the Center for Public Justice in Washington DC and Citizens for Public Justice in Ottawa).

Abraham Kuyper died in 1920, shortly after the First World War ended, but his legacy lived on. A few years later, in 1926, two young Kuyperian scholars who also happened to be brothers-in-law took up strategic positions at the VU Amsterdam. Dirk Vollenhoven became the university's first full-time philosopher, and Herman Dooyeweerd joined the law faculty, where he became Holland's leading legal theorist. In the ensuing years, Vollenhoven and Dooyeweerd forged a comprehensive philosophy both inspired by a Kuyperian vision and conversant with the latest trends in academic research and European philosophy.[10] Their philosophy came to be known as reformational philosophy, rooted as it was in a revival of Reformed (i.e., Calvinist) Protestant Christianity that aimed to renew life and society.

Reformational philosophy traveled to North America in the 1950s and 1960s, thanks both to graduates of Calvin College who pursued doctoral studies at the VU Amsterdam and Dutch Kuyperians who emigrated to Canada after the Second World War and quickly established their own faith-oriented schools and organizations. The Institute for Christian Studies (ICS), a graduate school for interdisciplinary philosophy affiliated with the Toronto School of Theology at the University of Toronto, emerged from the confluence of these two streams. Since opening its doors in 1967, ICS has been the leading centre for reformational philosophy in North America.[11]

As one can quickly tell from the graduate programs and research emphases at ICS, the tradition of reformational philosophy is intrinsically interdisciplinary, and it aims to address central issues of life and society. Three themes unify this tradition. One is that all of creation, including human culture and society, in all its legitimate and worthwhile diversity, exists in response to a loving Creator. A second is that, in principle, structural differentiation in society is good, for it enables distinct social institutions, whether academic, economic, political, or religious, to have their own legitimate tasks and contribute in their own way to human flourishing. A third theme is that the deep unity to human life, in all its diversity, consists in the spiritual direction of our responses to the divine call to love.

Although articulated in different ways by various reformational thinkers, together these three themes make for an inherently interdisciplinary philosophy, one that combines radical holism and normative pluralism, all with a view to transforming life and society. When the current volume discusses the more technical details of writings by Dooyeweerd and Vollenhoven or by second-generation philosophers such as Calvin Seerveld (born 1930) and Hendrik Hart (1935–2021), as it occasionally does, these themes continue to resound, almost like a three-voice ostinato. They resist philosophy's construction and maintenance of self-prescribed silos. They also propel my claim that, in belonging to a more encompassing social philosophy, epistemology and truth theory cannot be politically neutral.

2. JUSTICE, POWER, AND POLITICS

Political nonneutrality does not require that philosophical accounts of knowledge and truth be overtly partisan, either endorsing or opposing specific political positions. Nor, as Arendt recognized, does it mean philosophers should attempt to acquire formal positions of political power. They should not, for example, "be tempted, like Plato, to win the ear of some philosophically inclined tyrant, and ... erect one of those tyrannies of 'truth' which we know chiefly from the various political utopias, and which ... politically speaking, are as tyrannical as other forms of despotism."[12] Rather, epistemology and truth theory are politically nonneutral in the sense that what we say knowledge and truth are and why we say they are important have unavoidable implications for the views we hold about the nature of good government and the role of political participation. If, for example, we characterize knowledge in such a way that it can only be the possession of a privileged elite (Plato's philosopher kings, for example), then it is unlikely that our epistemology will support representative governance or widespread participation in the affairs of state. Further, an elitist epistemology will more readily lead to outright rejection of political democracy than will an epistemology that characterizes knowledge as a common possession or perhaps as not a possession at all.

Even though, with their insistence on spiritual nonneutrality, reformational philosophers have long recognized that philosophy is not politically neutral, they, unlike Arendt, have seldom addressed the relation between truth and politics.[13] The current volume aims to help fill this lacuna.[14] Arendt's worries about how truth and politics relate arise both because the dispassionate pursuit of truth can seem utterly impotent in the face of overwhelming political power and because the ruthless pursuit of political power can run roughshod over any appeal to truth. If, however, these are not two separate pursuits – if in some sense even the pursuit of political power is properly in the service of truth – then these worries, if not alleviated, could be recast. For this, however, we would need different conceptions of politics and of truth from those Arendt employs.

Politics, of course, is a protean term, and it has many usages. For the purposes of this introduction, let me assign it three overlapping meanings: struggles for liberation among and within communities, groups, and organizations; participation in informal networks of communication and influence about matters of public concern; and activities within formal structures of governance for legally stipulated jurisdictions. These three meanings roughly cover what could be called new social movements (e.g., gender politics), the public sphere (e.g., news media), and the state, respectively – with *state* understood expansively enough to cover not only local, regional, and national governments, but also international and suprastate organizations of legislation, administration, and jurisprudence. What unites all three meanings, in my view, is that they involve both power struggles aimed at achieving justice and justice struggles based on relative positions of power. Whether oppressed minorities fight for their rights or nonprofit agencies publicly advocate for new environmental regulations or political parties try to pass and enforce tax legislation, all of them engage in politics in the intended sense: they try to gain or employ enough power to promote what they consider to be a just end, and they try to shape that just end in such a way that it can be achieved.

On this construal, politics is not simply about power. It is equally about justice. So too, the concern for justice is never nonpolitical, not even within philosophical attempts to say what justice is and why it matters. The concern for justice always either includes or implies a stance on the proper ways to achieve justice and on proper forms and uses of power. Accordingly, politics is a doubly normative enterprise where, in principle, struggles for power confront questions about both the legitimacy of power and its appropriateness to the ends of justice and where, again in principle, struggles for justice confront questions about both the scope and the achievability of the justice sought.

Such double normativity implies in turn that, properly construed, truth and politics are not at odds. Rather, *politics itself is a social domain of truth*: not only is the pursuit of truth intrinsic to politics as the empowered struggle for justice but also truth as a whole unfolds in part via political efforts. To show how politics can be a social domain of truth, let me briefly introduce my general conception of truth.

As I explain later and in other writings,[15] I conceive of truth in general as a dynamic correlation between two poles, between (1) human fidelity to societal principles and (2) a life-giving disclosure of society, where "life-giving disclosure" means that which furthers the interconnected flourishing of all creatures. This dynamic correlation occurs in specific and specifiable ways within different social domains of knowledge and truth, including, but not limited to, art, science, and religion. Politics is another of these social domains. It is an arena in which people can be faithful to societal principles and can contribute to life-giving disclosure.

Justice is the leading societal principle for politics as a social domain of truth; liberation from oppression is the most important way in which politics can contribute to life-giving disclosure, to the interconnected flourishing of humans and other creatures. Justice is not the only societal principle that solicits human fidelity in politics, however. Solidarity and resourcefulness also come to mind. So does a fundamental principle guiding the pursuit and exercise of political power, namely, that such power must indeed serve the ends of justice. I call this fundamental principle or guideline the expected justifiability of power. Political power that violates it cannot be legitimate or appropriate. Nevertheless, despite the relevance of these other principles, including the justifiability of power, the societal principle of justice must take the lead in politics.

Reconceived along these lines, politics is a social domain of truth. It is a domain in which fidelity to the societal principle of justice, pursued on the basis of justifiable power, can dynamically correlate with the liberation of oppressed groups, communities, and populations, such that society becomes more conducive to the interconnected flourishing of all creatures. In other words, justifiably em-powered and liberating pursuits of justice characterize politics as a social domain of truth.

Obviously, many political struggles do not live up to this characterization. There is political untruth just as much as there is political truth. The crucial point to notice, however, is that the expectation of truth is *intrinsic* to politics. Hence, in answer to the Arendtian questions that opened this chapter, one can say that truth is not *essentially* impotent, nor is political power *essentially* deceitful. Instead, political power is one of the ways in which truth can unfold, provided such power is both justifiable and in the service of justice. Moreover, the reason why political power that "gives no heed to truth" is "despicable"[16] is not simply because what Arendt calls philosophical truth and factual truth deserve to be heard and followed, but especially because such political power, no matter how strong and pervasive, is *politically untrue*: it cannot be justified, and it does not serve the ends of justice.

Still, one wonders what to make of a politics that *is* thoroughly deceitful in the specific sense that Arendt feared, a post-truth politics in which leading politicians, including the former president of the United States of America, bully, lie, and prevaricate, ignore scientific evidence, celebrate "alternative facts," and attack mainstream news media as "fake news." Was not Arendt right in 1967 to signal "the relatively recent phenomenon of mass manipulation of fact and opinion," and did she not correctly call upon the professional truthtellers to maintain their "curious passion ... for intellectual integrity at any price"?[17] To both questions, I would answer yes, indeed.

Yet it is crucial to keep in view the *political* reason why post-truth politics is despicable and why intellectual integrity is required. The reason is simply this: political deceit undermines political truth, whereas intellectual integrity supports it. In the absence of factual accuracy, for example, we cannot really address questions of justifiable power, achievable justice, and genuine liberation; in the absence of intellectual integrity, we cannot achieve the level of factual accuracy needed to sort these matters out. In its deceitfulness, post-truth politics guts the body politic: it eviscerates any passion for achievable justice, and it cuts off any commitment to that justifiable power known in a constitutional democracy as the rule of law. Post-truth politics is politically false; philosophical truth theory needs to show why and how it is. A theory of truth cannot be politically neutral.

3. TRAJECTORIES OF TRUTH

The chapters in this volume offer new ways to think about truth and politics. The book begins and ends with discussions of what truth is and why it matters. Whereas the first chapter explores the relevance of ancient wisdom traditions for contemporary reflections on truth, the second and last chapters show how my responses to these traditions interact with leading topics and figures in analytic and continental philosophy. Tucked between these bookends lie two chapters on the epistemological background to my holistic and pluralist conception of truth (chapters 3 and 4); three that indicate how holistic pluralism concerning knowledge and truth affects conceptions of politics, philosophy, and social critique (chapters 5, 6, and 7); and two (chapters 8 and 9) on the biographical origins and political ramifications of the expansive social philosophy – including epistemology and truth theory – described in previous chapters.

Chapter 1 asks what truth means in a supposedly post-truth society. Historically, philosophy in the West has portrayed itself as a truth-seeking love of wisdom. How it seeks truth, however, and the truth it seeks, put Western philosophy at odds with religious wisdom traditions that also claim to seek the truth. In this chapter I explore what ancient Jewish and Christian wisdom traditions might contribute to a new philosophical conception of truth. Commenting on selected passages from Hebrew and Christian scriptures, I suggest that, in the first instance, truth in these wisdom traditions does not mean factual accuracy or the correctness of assertions. Instead, it means blessed faithfulness in relationship to others. Understood in this way, truth is not primarily propositional, and the love of wisdom is not primarily a philosopher's vocation. Rather, truth is a way of life to which everyone is called.

This understanding of truth puts such wisdom traditions at odds with the mainstreams of philosophical truth theory in the West. Tracing Western philosophical conceptions of truth to their pre-Socratic origins in a godlike search for what is uncreated and indestructible, the essay shows why standard philosophical notions of propositional truth cannot do justice to the broader meaning of truth in the Jewish and Christian scriptures. Truth in this broader sense must be lived out, not simply asserted, and it requires us to seek the good, to resist evil, and to live in hope.

That broader sense of truth directly informs my own attempts to formulate a new conception of truth, which I introduce in chapter 2 under the label *holistic alethic pluralism*. On that conception, truth is to be lived, and when we do make assertions, their correctness needs to belong to our living the truth. To live the truth is to be faithful to societal principles such as justice and solidarity in ways that contribute to the interconnected flourishing of all creatures. Propositional truth – the focus of so many philosophical truth theories today – is important, but its importance is indexed to the more comprehensive faithfulness and creaturely disclosure to which everyone is called. This understanding of truth has ramifications for knowledge, politics, and social critique, as discussed in the chapters that follow.

Chapter 2 lays out my research program on the idea of truth. First it describes challenges to the idea of truth in contemporary philosophy and gives reasons why a robust conception of truth is needed. Next it presents two overriding concerns – ontological and axiological – that such a conception should address. In addressing these concerns, I argue, one needs to take up three sets of issues: relations between propositional truth and the discursive justification of truth claims; distinctions and connections between propositional and non-propositional truth; and the sorts of cultural practices and social institutions within which truth occurs. My detailed response to these issues, as sketched in the last section of the chapter, is to propose a holistic, normative, and structurally pluralist conception of truth.

Intrinsic to this conception is the recognition that there are diverse societal principles, such as solidarity, resourcefulness, and justice, that call for human fidelity. Because there are diverse societal principles, there also are diverse ways in which we can be faithful to societal principles as well as diverse ways in which we can contribute to a life-giving disclosure of society. Yet, on the proposed conception, all these ways belong to truth as a whole. Hence the conception is both pluralist – recognizing distinct domains of truth – and holistic – insisting that all the distinct domains belong to the same truth as a whole.

If such holistic alethic pluralism is to make sense, then one also needs to show that there are diverse ways of acquiring and testing knowledge, ways that are distinct from one another yet equally legitimate and equally able to contribute to knowledge as a whole. This hypothesis – I call it *holistic epistemological pluralism* – has been a distinctive emphasis of reformational philosophy over several generations. The next two chapters ask what that hypothesis comes to, and how to make it plausible.

Chapter 3 explores a new theory of knowledge proposed in the late 1970s by Australian philosopher and educator Doug Blomberg. After locating his work in a tradition of holistic pluralism with regard to knowledge, I introduce the notion of distantial knowing, Blomberg's key innovation. He uses this notion to identify and describe multiple ways of acquiring normative insight. These ways, which include aesthetic, economic, and political knowing, are not theoretical, but they open up concrete experience. Although in agreement with Blomberg's emphasis on the integrality and multidimensionality of knowledge, I argue that he does not adequately demonstrate that various nontheoretical paths to normative insight are indeed *distinctive* ways of knowing.

Building on the previous chapter, chapter 4 asks whether and how to distinguish different sorts of knowledge within a unified conception of knowledge as a whole. It begins with the thesis that knowledge, in its deepest meaning, is not a thing to possess but a complex relationship to inhabit. It encompasses human knowers, practices of knowing, the knowable, known results, guiding principles, and procedures of confirmation. Within this complex relationship, humans attain insight of various sorts within different social domains of knowledge. Justified true belief, which many epistemologists have equated with knowledge, is part of knowledge as a whole, just as propositional truth is part of truth as a whole. Yet it is only a part, and it is not decisive for characterizing knowledge either as a whole or in its different social domains.

To show why this is so, I first briefly describe artistic knowledge and scientific knowledge, indicating how they are distinct from each other and yet both genuinely sorts of knowledge. Then I examine two other social domains of knowledge at greater length, namely, technology and religion. Knowledge, chapter 4 concludes, takes on distinct contours within different social domains: some of them, like art and technology, provide pre-propositional insight; others, like religion, offer insight that is post-propositional. Yet all of them contribute to knowledge as a whole.

Next the book takes up some sociopolitical implications of such holistic pluralism in epistemology. Prompted by a 2016 blog symposium on the book *Religion, Truth, and Social Transformation*, chapter 5 responds to commentaries about my work on social philosophy, politics, and social critique. The first half of the chapter replies to questions concerning the political roles of religion and my call for an architectonic critique of contemporary society. I explain that the predominance of the capitalist economy and administrative states in contemporary Western societies, while problematic, needs to be faced head on by those who want to envision a society where all social institutions honor the societal principles of resourcefulness, justice, and solidarity, and where all creatures can flourish. Moving toward such a society requires what I call *differential transformation* within and among society's macrostructures (economy, state, and civil society).

The second half of chapter 5 goes into greater detail about the politics of hope that an architectonic critique suggests. This politics puts a heavy emphasis on agencies of change within civil society, and it orients itself toward a disclosure of society in the future. Such a future orientation leads to questions about whether a politics of hope fosters complacency toward those who really suffer. In reply, I propose that the hope required offers no assurance. Rather, it urges us to resist societal evil, the source of so much suffering, even though we seem unable to remove it. Because societal evil nests, to a large extent, in mutually reinforcing dynamics within and across societal macrostructures, the politics of hope needs to aim at differential transformation on a global scale. Such a politics is neither reformist nor revolutionary, I suggest – a topic taken up at greater length in chapters 8 and 9.

My emphasis on differential transformation also raises questions about the politics of science. Viewing scientific knowledge and truth as one social domain within knowledge and truth as a whole, I call for a *normative* integration of science with societal systems. For the sciences should help redirect societal systems toward genuine resourcefulness and justice and should not simply reinforce the normatively deficient agendas of turbocapitalism and the administrative state. In order to achieve such redirection, science also needs a stronger integration – both normative and structural – with civil society. Stronger integration along such lines would require ongoing and lively exchanges between scientists and citizens both at universities and in other civil-societal organizations.

Architectonic social critique and a politics of hope raise questions about what philosophy itself is like and how it should contribute to a life-giving society. Chapter 6 takes up such metaphilosophical questions by discussing the critical retrieval of insights from earlier generations of reformational philosophy. The first half of the chapter responds to questions concerning my appropriation of second-generation contributions, especially those of Hendrik Hart and Calvin Seerveld.

One such question concerns the scope of philosophical inquiry. Although philosophers influenced by Richard Rorty and the later Ludwig Wittgenstein might be sceptical of any philosophy that aims to understand all of "reality" or "being" or "existence," I agree with Dooyeweerd and Vollenhoven that philosophy is a "totality discipline": it properly studies all of creation. Yet this does not license philosophy to issue "totalitarian" claims to absolute knowledge. One could say that art and religion, which G.W.F. Hegel regarded as vehicles of absolute truth, mark thresholds between what philosophy can and cannot grasp. In my own terms, artistic truth and religious truth are not the same as either scientific or philosophical truth. Nevertheless, when artistic truth and religious truth give rise to linguistic validity claims and people challenge these claims, then the participants in art and religion who raise the claims need to engage in rational discourse about them. For if, specifically, we were to exempt religious validity claims from rational discourse about them, then we would clear a path for both bad theology and religious dogmatism.

Related wariness about dogmatism surfaces in my emphasis on immanent criticism with metacritical intent, which I recommend as an approach to the work of other philosophers. Underlying the emphasis on immanent criticism is a desire to practice solidarity with fellow philosophers. The point is not to ignore deep-going differences about knowledge, politics, and the direction of human life and society, but rather to find life-giving insights amid and beyond the differences. That makes even the historiography of philosophy a creative and redemptive enterprise.

The desire to practice solidarity provides a unifying theme in the second half of chapter 6, where I take up issues in my critical retrieval of first-generation reformational philosophy. The section begins by explaining why I reject Dooyeweerd's notion that a "supra-temporal heart" lies at the core of human existence. My primary objection is that the notion supports Dooyeweerd's problematic emphasis on the "antithesis" as a thorough-going conflict between two spiritual communities. This antithetical construal of spiritual struggle tends to parochialize truth and to undermine social solidarity. Dooyeweerd's insistence on supra-temporality also helps generate self-referential incoherence in his transcendental critique of theoretical thought, problematic intuitionism in his modal theory, and his essentialism concerning structures of individuality – all of which I have discussed before[18] and which I return to in chapter 6. Yet questions about social solidarity are an even stronger concern, especially for considerations of truth and politics.

The strength of this concern shows up in commentaries on two chapters about truth in *Religion, Truth, and Social Transformation*. One commentary asks whether my critique of the spiritual antithesis in Dooyeweerd's conception of truth implies that I embrace theological universalism: the idea that, in the end, everyone will be redeemed. And the other suggests that my own attempt to articulate a new conception of truth makes a strong argument for inclusion, for solidarity with other human beings. Without taking a position on theological universalism, chapter 6 insists that one can distinguish between spiritual truth and spiritual falsehood without turning this into a conflict between two (or more) spiritual communities. I also explain how, by emphasizing inclusion in my conception of truth, I try to remain faithful to the spirit of the reformational tradition, which grounds all spiritual struggles, including their expressions in conflicts over truth and politics, in the generosity of God's love for all of creation.

This spirit of generosity, together with a refusal to compartmentalize knowledge, politics, and social critique, leads to a specific way to interpret and evaluate the arts.[19] I call this approach *redemptive art criticism*; chapter 7 illustrates what it involves. There I reclaim insights from Hegel's account of the sublime to help make sense of Terrence Malick's film *The Tree of Life*. I argue that this Hegel-inspired approach illuminates not only Malick's body of work but also the film's sociohistorical setting and its film-critical context. Hegel, like reformational philosophy, refuses to compartmentalize. In turn, postsecular art of the sublime like Malick's provides an important reason why, referring back to Hegel, we need to reconceive the relations among religion, art, and philosophy. Indeed, to develop adequate interpretations for postsecular art, we should reclaim from Hegel an understanding of art, religion, and philosophy as complementary pursuits of comprehensive truth.

The interviews in the final three chapters elaborate the themes already discussed, providing an informal overview of what motivates my scholarly work and how it aims to contribute to a transformation of philosophy and society. Chapter 8 explores the personal and intellectual roots to my current work on truth and politics. It recounts an intellectual odyssey both through Dooyeweerd and reformational philosophy and through Adorno and Critical Theory, beginning with the author's experiences as a graduate student in Toronto and Berlin. I explain that the topic of truth has been on my horizon since I began graduate studies at ICS with Hart and Seerveld during the early 1970s. What began as an interest in artistic truth, especially in music, expanded, via my dissertation work on Adorno in Berlin during the later 1970s, into questions about truth in society as a whole.

The chapter also discusses how research on Hegel, Karl Marx, and Critical Theory has affected my approach to reformational philosophy, leading, for example, to my pursuing immanent criticism with metacritical intent and rejecting Dooyeweerd's understanding of the spiritual antithesis. Yet I retain reformational philosophy's holistic pluralism and its commitment to making a redemptive difference in society. Politically, this commitment can lead to tensions between more reformist and more revolutionary approaches to large-scale changes in society. I indicate how my own emphasis on differential transformation, which, strictly speaking, is neither reformist nor revolutionary, negotiates a sociopolitical conflict between Adorno and Jürgen Habermas in order to address macrostructural issues that reformational philosophy has ignored. I also reflect on how Adorno's research in the 1930s and 1940s on American popular culture and social psychology remains highly relevant for understanding and addressing post-truth politics in the United States. That leads to concluding reflections on the political and academic settings that shaped my own work on cultural politics and artistic truth in the 1990s and beyond.

Questions about politics take centre stage in the next chapter, chapter 9. It opens with a discussion of post-truth politics. I suggest that intellectuals, with their understandable opposition to old-style positivism, are partially responsible for the ease with which political leaders like Donald Trump dismiss the need for factual accuracy and correct assertions. That's why, politically, we need a good philosophical account of factual truth and its importance. Countering post-truth politics will also require both continual resistance within civil society and an architectonic critique of what I call *societal evil*. I explain that this notion, which stems from my reading of Adorno and Horkheimer's *Dialectic of Enlightenment*, refers to life-destroying patterns so deeply entrenched in society that they are hard to recognize, to take responsibility for, and to resist – for example, patterns of ecological destruction and economic exploitation.

Asked whether my call for differential transformation is simply reformist after all, I explore obstacles to political revolution that Marx himself would have recognized, and that Adorno and Horkheimer certainly saw. I also point to scriptural sources of my hope for a better society and of my normative expectations for what such a society would be like. This leads to an extended discussion about whether there is or can be a Christian Left today and about how North American Kuyperians divide politically between more conservative and more progressive tendencies. Then the chapter concludes with brief reflections on why, to challenge post-truth politics, intellectuals and activists should think globally while acting locally.

The final chapter (chapter 10) returns to the central topic with which this book begins: the idea of truth, and its traditional sources within Western culture. Now, however, I reflect on a more recent history that led to contemporary divides between and within analytic and continental truth theories. I also show how my work tries to bridge these divides. Specifically, I explain how my idea of truth – as a dynamic correlation between fidelity to societal principles and a life-giving disclosure of society – tries to incorporate the best insights in the analytic tradition, Critical Theory, and Heideggerian thought. Describing propositional truth as one sort among several within truth as a whole, I point to a structural isomorphism both *between* propositional truth and other domains (such as artistic truth and religious truth) and *from* each of these domains to the structure of truth as a whole. This structural isomorphism is the key to holistic alethic pluralism.

I believe such an approach can help counter the academic hyperspecialization that hinders scholars from either speaking truth or speaking of truth in an allegedly post-truth society. My approach also allows one to propose a substantive concept of scientific truth, based on a robust account of propositional truth. Given the repeated dismissals of scientific findings and rational arguments by post-truth politicians who, I argue, are fundamentally anti-truth, it is crucial to make a convincing case for the distinctiveness and importance of scientific truth.

Also crucial is to sort out the historical roots to current conceptions of truth. In that connection, chapter 10 suggests that both the Greek philosophical tradition and the Abrahamic wisdom traditions connect truth to fidelity and disclosure, the two concepts highlighted in my own conception. Whereas the Greek philosophical tradition emphasizes faithfulness to what is real, biblical wisdom traditions emphasize faithfulness in relationship to the other. Similarly, while the Greeks call for a disclosure of being or reality, the biblical traditions call for a disclosure of life and creation. Having articulated the notions of fidelity and disclosure in distinctive ways, these two strands in Western culture lead, respectively, to an emphasis on propositional truth – as is characteristic of analytic philosophy – and to an emphasis on holistic truth – that is more characteristic of some continental philosophy. Holistic alethic pluralism tries to interweave worthwhile elements of both strands, for the sake of truth-seeking scholarship, truth-telling politics, and the common good.

I

Philosophy, Truth, and the Wisdom of Love

The love of wisdom needs the wisdom of love. Let me say what this means and why it matters. I begin with a poem by Miriam Pederson titled "Hold Your Horses."[1]

> Lasso truth
> like a run-away steer
> and you will find its veins
> running cold.
>
> Approach it like a lover
> with a ribbon for her hair
> and truth, in time,
> will lean in your direction.

Or, as I have put it more prosaically, the love of wisdom needs the wisdom of love.

Since ancient times, philosophy in the West has described itself as pursuing the truth out of love for wisdom. In its origins, Western philosophy is not simply an academic discipline or professional occupation. It is, in the words of Pierre Hadot, a way of life or a spiritual exercise, and it offers a path to truth that challenges other ways in which people love wisdom and pursue truth.[2] This puts philosophy in tension with robust wisdom traditions attached to the world's religions, such as Hinduism, Buddhism, Confucianism, Taoism, Judaism, Islam, and the religions of Indigenous peoples.[3]

Christianity, too, includes a wisdom tradition, one that flows from Judaism and does not easily combine with Greco-Roman philosophy.[4] Hence the strong contrast in I Corinthians between Greek wisdom and Christ as "the wisdom of God" (1 Cor. 1:18–25), a theme echoed in the letter to the Colossians, which finds "all the treasures of wisdom and knowledge" hidden in Christ (Col. 2:2–3).[5] In the early days of Christianity, it was not readily apparent how the wisdom of the Greeks and the wisdom of Christ should relate, no more than it is obvious today how one can honour the Christian wisdom tradition while philosophically pursuing the truth. The very words in which Western philosophy has described its vocation – truth, love, wisdom – are spiritually loaded terms; in the Jewish and Christian scriptures, these terms do not mean what many philosophers have taken them to mean. So Christian philosophers must reconceive the meaning of these terms in line with their religious wisdom tradition and with the scriptures that provide its decisive touchstone.

I want to explore what this might require for an understanding of truth. After commenting on some biblical passages, I shall suggest that a philosophy in line with the Jewish and Christian scriptures should understand truth as a way of life rather than simply a set of assertions, as something enacted rather than merely claimed.[6] Then I shall discuss three endeavours through which we can live (the) truth: by seeking the good, by resisting evil, and by living in hope. I shall conclude by connecting all three endeavours with the call to love.

WISDOM, TRUTH, AND LOVE

In a remarkable confluence of central biblical concepts, Psalm 85 links truth with love, justice, and peace. Translations often hide these links, for it is hard to render ancient Hebrew in contemporary English. Yet Psalm 85 prominently employs the term *emeth*, the central concept of truth in the Jewish scriptures, and it portrays truth as meeting up with steadfast love (*chesed*) in the messianic condition. When God promises peace to God's people (v. 8), and when God's glory (*kabod*) comes to dwell on Earth (v. 9), then, says Psalm 85, love and truth will meet; justice and peace will kiss (v. 10). The Hebrew word for peace is *shalom*. This means much more than concord or an absence of conflict. Shalom is a condition of complete fulfillment where all creatures flourish – a condition I call "interconnected flourishing." Psalm 85 envisions a glorious day when justice and *shalom* embrace, when steadfast love and truth converse. In that day truth will spring up from the earth, and justice will shine from the sky (v. 11).

Now, if you have a standard Western philosophical concept of truth, you might well wonder what truth could possibly have to do with love, justice, and shalom. The standard Western concept ties truth to factual accuracy and to the correctness of assertions. On one common construal, a statement is said to be true when it corresponds to the facts. But if that's all truth comes to, then it would seem bizarre to envision a day when love meets truth.

In the Jewish scriptures, however, the primary meaning of truth (emeth) is not accuracy or correctness. Instead, emeth means faithfulness, and it pertains both to God and to human beings. To be true, in the first instance, is not simply to be correct but to be faithful in relationship to others. God is true in faithfully carrying out God's Word of promise for creation, and human beings are true when their dealings are faithful to the conditions of God's promise. That is why Calvin Seerveld says truth in the scriptures means "God's blessing presence is in evidence" in human life.[7]

When Psalm 85 imagines truth and love sitting down together, for a *koffieklets*, so to speak, it points to a society where people, in their everyday dealings, are so faithful to God's Word of promise that God's lovingkindness completely envelops them, like gentle mist on the very soil from which their faithfulness springs.[8] In principle, there is no tension between love and truth, nor, as Nicholas Wolterstorff has shown, between love and justice.[9] Without traces of such truth and love, such faithfulness and lovingkindness, there would be neither justice nor shalom; with truth and love present in their fullness, justice and peace do embrace. In other words, when people are true in response to God's lovingkindness, they live in justice with one another, and the world they inhabit flourishes. Then, as Psalm 85 says, God "will indeed give what is good," and Earth "will yield its harvest" (Ps. 85:12, NIV).

To live in this way is to listen to the voice of wisdom, "she who danced when earth was new," in the words of Ruth Duck's hymn text "Come and Seek the Ways of Wisdom." To live in the truth is to "follow closely what [Wisdom] teaches, for her words are right and true. Wisdom clears the path to justice, showing us what love must do."[10] Here, in one succinct stanza, Dr Duck crystallizes what the Jewish wisdom tradition[11] has to say about truth and love and wisdom, the central themes in Western philosophy's self-description. Her hymn text resonates with Proverbs 3, where, as in Psalm 85, love and truth meet. In Proverbs 3, Lady Wisdom urges her child to keep lasting love (chesed) and truth (emeth) close, to bind them around its neck and inscribe them on its heart (v. 3). And the promise that accompanies such wise instruction points again to justice and shalom: "you will find favor" with God and others (v. 4), follow the right paths (v. 6), and receive bodily refreshment (v. 8).

The brilliant second stanza to Duck's hymn rightly connects all of this with the prologue to the Gospel of John (John 1:1–18). There Jesus, as God's Word of promise "made flesh among us," embodies a Wisdom "full of glory, truth, and grace."[12] The word "glory" (*doxa*) in John's gospel recalls the glory (kabod) of God come to dwell on Earth in Psalm 85. Moreover, as Hendrik Hart observes, John's description of Jesus as "full of grace and truth" (John 1:14) is "almost certainly a direct 'quote' of the Old Testament pair '*chesed* and *emeth*'" – Psalm 85's "love and truth" – which together "proclaim God as full of love, compassion, mercy, forgiveness, faithfulness."[13] Jesus, then, is the very incarnation of God's blessing in whom love and truth meet, even as Jesus embodies the wisdom that teaches us how to find God's blessing.

John's prologue illuminates Jesus' response to Thomas in John 14. After Jesus tells his disciples he is going to prepare a place for them in his Father's house, and they know the way there, Thomas exclaims: "We do not know where you are going. How can we know the way?" (v. 5) According to John, Jesus replies: "I am the way, and the truth, and the life. No one comes to the Father except through me" (v. 6). Heard in the echo chamber of the Jewish scriptures and the prologue to John, this reply proclaims Jesus himself as the very incarnation both of God's blessing and of the wisdom that shows how to find this blessing. To find their way to God's house of blessing, to God's glory on earth, to the promised messianic condition, the disciples will need to walk in Jesus's way. They must follow his teachings. They are to live as he lived. What this way comes to is the life of love: the life of loving God above all and our neighbours as ourselves, in response to a God who creates everything out of love – *creatio ex amore*, to quote James Olthuis.[14]

In Jesus, then, the decisive themes of Western philosophy – truth, love, and wisdom – intersect. In intersecting there, however, they fundamentally redirect philosophy.[15] For in Jesus, as in the Jewish scriptures, truth is not primarily propositional, and the love of wisdom is not simply an intellectual pursuit. Instead, truth is a way of life to which wisdom points everyone. Our challenge now is to decipher what such redirection means for how philosophers understand the idea of truth.

2. SEEKING THE GOOD

Parmenides, a pre-Socratic poet-philosopher, carved out the channels where the mainstreams of Western truth theory have flowed.[16] Parmenides aligns truth with being that does not change. For Parmenides, to be wise is to know what does not change. Philosophy, as the love of wisdom, is a godlike search for what is "uncreated and indestructible," what is "complete, immovable, and without end."[17] Most people, however, do not seek unchanging truth: Parmenides regards them as swept up in what comes and goes, what lacks immutable being, what, strictly speaking, amounts to nothing. They do not love wisdom but folly; they have opinions without knowledge; they embrace falsehood and the lie. Between these two paths – between a godlike search for immutable being and truth, and all-too-human ignorance amid changing appearances – Parmenides sees no bridge or middle way.[18] Moreover, only the philosopher can follow the esoteric way of unchanging truth.

The Jewish and Christian wisdom traditions turn such an esoteric conception of truth upside down. Affirming that God created everything good, and recognizing temporal change and interconnections as intrinsic to created goodness,[19] they do not align truth with unchanging and self-sufficient being. Nor do they connect wisdom with knowing immutable truth. Instead, Judeo-Christian "truth" has to do with blessed faithfulness *within* relationships and *amid* change, and "wisdom" pertains to instruction for faithful living, for lives of loving God and neighbour. *All* human beings, including philosophers, are called to live in and live out the truth.

This implies in turn that truth and goodness intersect.[20] To live the truth is to try to do what truth requires – to do what contributes to blessed faithfulness. And to do what truth requires is to embrace and promote that which is good. To live the truth, then, we must seek the good.

To resist the truth, by contrast, is to ignore or refuse what truth requires – to block blessed faithfulness. Such ignorance or refusal goes hand in hand with an embrace of that which is evil. Indeed, persistent and deep-seated falsehood feeds into what Seerveld calls "the Lie."[21] The Lie is much more than a simple fib, much more than intentionally saying something inaccurate or incorrect in order to deceive.[22] The Lie completely and deliberately twists all that is good in order to promote evil.[23]

In 2016 the Oxford Dictionaries chose the term "post-truth" as the International Word of the Year, noting that "use of the word *post-truth* ... increased by approximately 2,000% over its usage in 2015." The adjective "post-truth" refers to "circumstances in which objective facts are less influential in shaping public opinion than appeals to emotion and personal belief." It suggests the concept of truth "has become unimportant or irrelevant."[24]

The Oxford Dictionaries announced their choice just one week after the surprise election of Donald Trump to be president of the United States. Politically, it did seem we had entered a time when factual "truth" had become insignificant: a time when Kellyanne Conway, Trump's Counselor, could characterize obvious falsehoods as "alternative facts"; when Scott Pruitt, a climate change denier, could be appointed head of the U.S. Environmental Protection Agency; and when the president himself regularly tweeted blatant lies, seemingly without serious repercussions. Truth in the standard Western sense of factual accuracy and correct assertions seemed to have become politically passé. Anyone who knows what authoritarian and totalitarian regimes are like would find this trend worrisome.

Even more worrisome, however, would be tendencies toward a world that is beyond truth in the scriptural sense of blessed faithfulness. In such a scripturally "post-truth" world, it would not matter whether we seek to live the truth and whether our cultural practices and social institutions enable us to embrace what is good. It would not matter whether we promote justice or pursue oppression, whether we show solidarity toward others or practice hatred, whether we respect or rape the Earth. In fact, the very distinction between good and evil would fade away. This is the larger worry of an allegedly post-truth world, namely, that in dismissing the importance of correctness and accuracy, people will simultaneously lose their desire to seek the good, thereby tolerating societal evil and embracing the Lie. The term "post-truth" signals more than a political quandary. It points to a deeply spiritual crisis in society.

3. RESISTING SOCIETAL EVIL

Within this crisis, those who want to live the truth by seeking the good must also challenge falsehood by resisting evil. In the first instance, to challenge falsehood in an allegedly post-truth world means not only refusing to give up a distinction between factual truth and factual untruth but also holding everyone accountable to standards of accuracy and correctness. We certainly should not allow politicians, business leaders, or academic administrators to get away with regularly dishing out what American philosopher Harry Frankfurt calls bullshit.[25] Rather, we should dispute their duplicity, even as we call out those who ignore the evidence, distort the facts, and deliberately lie; these are egregious offences, and they unravel the fabric of a democratic society.

In addition to challenging factual untruth, however, to live the truth requires us to resist evil in all of its other manifestations. Here I would distinguish evil for which each of us is individually responsible from evil for which we have collective responsibility. I am especially concerned about collective evil that has become so entrenched in our cultural practices and social institutions that we find it hard both to take responsibility for it and to resist it. I call such entrenched collective malevolence "societal evil." A society's ongoing destruction of the Earth, oppression of the poor, and hostility toward so-called aliens are prime examples of societal evil.[26]

The call to live the truth as blessed faithfulness requires us to resist societal evil. But it also requires us to recognize the limits to our own resistance, limits in a double sense: first, individual and organized efforts to resist societal evil can do only so much[27] and, second, viable resistance must embody the spirit of truth, the spirit of blessed faithfulness. This second limitation is crucial. Deeply entrenched societal evil has a pervasive spiritual direction: the direction of the Lie, the direction of what completely and deliberately twists the good. Only in the spirit of blessed faithfulness can the spirit of societal evil be truly resisted,[28] for only as we cling to the good can we stand up to the Lie.

I am not suggesting we should be naïve about the violence we face. Yet, as Canadian singer-songwriter Bruce Cockburn recognizes, to be true, our resistance must not embody the spirit of what we resist, such that we become "grim travellers":

> Bitter little girls and boys from the Red Army Underground
> They'd blow away Karl Marx if he had the nerve to come around
> They're just grim travellers in dawn skies
> See the beauty – makes them cry inside
> Makes them angry and they don't know why
> They're grim travellers in dawn skies[29]

If we put on the opaque mask of grimness, we will not see the dawn sky. We will not see the good that calls us to resist. We do not need grimness. Instead, we need an articulate sense of the good we seek, as well as a spirited critique of the evil we resist.

That is where true philosophy, as a hopeful love of comprehensive wisdom,[30] can help. On the one hand, philosophy can help us sort out the diverse goods in our lives and spell out those that matter most for society as a whole. Here I have in mind shared societal principles such as justice, resourcefulness, and solidarity that can guide not only the lives of individuals and communities but also the cultural practices and social institutions in which all of us participate. In a contemporary setting, such principles are what call for human faithfulness; when honoured, they carry a Word of promise.

On the other hand, philosophy can also help us take the measure of societal evil by providing a critique of society as a whole, what, following Abraham Kuyper, one can call an architectonic critique.[31] Such a critique is enormously difficult, and, to a large extent, it has fallen out of philosophical fashion. Yet it is essential for wise resistance. We need to understand how the current organization of society both blocks and permits blessed faithfulness. We also need to detect the sore spots where suffering gathers and where social transformation can begin. Philosophy that pursues comprehensive wisdom about the contemporary world can help in both respects.

4. LIVING IN HOPE

Earlier I said Psalm 85 portrays truth and love as meeting up "in the messianic condition." I also suggested that, according to the Gospel of John, Jesus's disciples will need to walk in his way in order to find a path to "God's house of blessing." Such phrases introduce a theme of hope for the future quite foreign to the mainstreams of Western truth theory.[32] Scriptural truth talk contains an ongoing interplay between the current call to blessed faithfulness and the eschatological promise of a faith-fulfilling blessedness still to come – the promise of a new heaven and a new Earth (Rev. 21:1–4) where justice and peace embrace (Ps. 85:10), where the wolf lies down with the lamb (Isa. 11:6), where God, in love and truth, is "all in all" (Eph. 1:23).[33] This promise means that God, first and foremost, is a God of love, and Jesus is the very embodiment of God's love. For those who would follow Jesus, to live the truth is to walk along the pathways of love, love for God and neighbour, in hope for God's future, despite our own fragility and failure, and amid the societal evil that surrounds us. To live in such hope, we must remain ever open to the Spirit of truth, which can take us in surprising new directions.

Hope for a future where love and truth meet has ripple effects in the present, both in our seeking the good and in our resisting evil. Living in such hope, we can neither regard our current dealings and practices and institutions as fully "in the truth" nor despair over the depth and power of societal evil. This implies, in turn, that contemporary philosophy needs to be more than a love of comprehensive wisdom that helps us sort out societal principles and articulates an architectonic critique. For philosophy's love must be a *hopeful* love: it must remain open to a promised future whose surprises surpass philosophical comprehension.

That is why, in my own attempt to reconceive the idea of truth, I would insist on the eschatological openness of both societal principles and what I call the "life-giving disclosure of society." Human beings are called to be faithful to societal principles such as justice and solidarity, and these principles are embedded in human history. Yet societal principles also remain open to a future where, right now, we can scarcely imagine what justice and solidarity will mean and require. So too, human beings, in their fidelity to societal principles, are called to promote a society where "human beings and other creatures come to flourish in their interconnections."[34] Yet we need to relativize our efforts, recognizing how the society we hope for lies beyond our striving, and how our fidelity to societal principles does not suffice to bring it about.

Hence I would describe truth as a *dynamic* correlation between human fidelity to societal principles and a life-giving disclosure of society.[35] In light of the Jewish and Christian wisdom traditions, I would also insist that there is more to truth – more to blessed faithfulness – than our current fidelity and disclosure can achieve. And this "more" challenges the prevailing Western concept of truth as a static correspondence between assertions and facts. For there is always more to truth, more even to factual truth, than a static correspondence can capture. Hope for the future must be part of a biblically attuned conception of truth, including factual truth. Although this seriously complicates any attempt to provide a theory of factual truth, such complications deserve philosophical attention.[36]

5. THE CALL TO LOVE

I have not tried to provide a theory of factual truth in this chapter. Instead, I have explored biblical underpinnings for the broader conception of truth within which I intend to offer a theory of factual truth.[37] On this broader conception, truth is to be lived rather than merely asserted, and our assertions of truth need to belong to our living (the) truth.[38] To live the truth is to be faithful in relation to God and others. Such faithfulness is summarized in the call to love God above all and our neighbours as ourselves.[39]

In contemporary society, the contours of this call to love show up in historically embedded and eschatologically open societal principles such as justice and solidarity. When we are faithful to such principles, we experience the blessing of a loving God. This blessing occurs via a life-giving disclosure of society. In contemporary society, then, truth amounts to a dynamic correlation between human fidelity to societal principles and a life-giving disclosure of society, with both the fidelity and the disclosure sustained by hope for God's future. In the end, there is no such truth without love, for love and truth must meet.

To live (the) truth is to seek the good: solidarity, justice, interconnected flourishing; to resist evil, especially what alienates and oppresses and kills the Earth's creatures; and to live in hope for a future where justice and peace embrace. There's no place for the Lie in God's future. But there *is* a place for everyone who walks along the pathways of love, following God's Word of promise "made flesh among us," the way and the truth and the life.

God's future calls to everyone, in the voice of Wisdom incarnate, inviting them to a feast of love and joy. And, in the sixteenth-century words of George Herbert, truthful responses to Wisdom's call will sing back their own invitation:

Come, my Way, my Truth, my Life:
Such a Way, as gives us breath:
Such a Truth, as ends all strife:
Such a Life, as killeth death.

Come, my Light, my Feast, my Strength:
Such a Light, as shows a feast:
Such a Feast, as mends in length:
Such a Strength, as makes his guest.

Come, my Joy, my Love, my Heart:
Such a Joy, as none can move:
Such a Love, as none can part:
Such a Heart, as joys in love.[40]

2

Holistic Alethic Pluralism

From its beginnings in the work of Herman Dooyeweerd and Dirk Vollenhoven, reformational philosophy has taken issue with the mainstreams of Western philosophy and has proposed comprehensive alternatives. A distinctive feature to these alternatives is to ground both epistemology and social philosophy in a robust ontology. Nowhere do the potential contributions of this ontological emphasis show up more strikingly than in the arena of truth theory. Yet truth theory also poses some of the greatest challenges to a viable and intelligible reformational contribution. The reasons for this are complex, but they have to do both with contemporary doubts about the idea of truth and with entrenched conceptions of truth as being primarily or solely propositional. The challenge, then, is to develop an approach to the idea of truth that shows why contemporary doubts are misplaced and entrenched conceptions are inadequate.

In this chapter I present the main lines of a research program aimed at meeting this challenge.[1] First I describe doubts about the idea of truth in contemporary philosophy and give reasons why, nevertheless, a robust conception of truth is needed. Next I present two overriding concerns – one ontological and one axiological – that such a conception should address. Then I discuss three sets of issues that a contemporary approach needs to take up in order to address these concerns. My detailed response to these issues, as sketched in the last section of the essay, is to propose a holistic, normative, and structurally pluralist conception of truth, one that I call holistic alethic pluralism.

1. TROUBLING TRUTH

The idea of truth is in trouble. Prominent contemporary philosophers have questioned whether it is a substantive idea. They doubt that it deserves the emphasis Western philosophy traditionally has given it or that it should play a central role in intellectual endeavours. Some have asked whether we even need it. Their questions both reflect and reinforce broader trends in Western society, where many people wonder whether it is either possible or necessary to pursue truth. "That's just your opinion" waits as a ready response to anyone who claims to know or speak the truth. Likewise, when someone's truth claim is challenged, a defensive "That's my truth" all too quickly gets trotted out. Moreover, many people seem to think "truthiness" – the appearance of truth, not necessarily its substance – is all one can hope to achieve in a public setting, and truthiness, not truth, is all one needs to achieve. If you think truth is a substantive and socially significant idea, as I do, you face formidable opposition both within the gilded halls of professional philosophy and in the more ramshackle arena of public opinion.

Four positions in recent philosophy cause the most trouble for a substantive and socially significant idea of truth. The first stems from what I call scientism. By scientism I mean the claim that the sciences – especially the natural sciences – are the primary way, and perhaps the only way, to attain real knowledge. Historically, scientism implied a high regard for truth and its pursuit. Traditional scientism considered finding the truth to be the primary goal of science, and it regarded science as the best way to attain truth. Hence traditional scientism held truth in high esteem. In recent years, however, one strand of scientism – what I call neo-scientism – has adopted quite a different stance. Neo-scientism continues to valorize scientific knowledge. But it argues that, precisely because of the empirical explanations that science gives us, truth is unimportant. Stephen Stich, for example, after rejecting the view that true beliefs are intrinsically valuable, suggests they also are unlikely to be instrumentally valuable in the pursuit of other goals such as "happiness or pleasure or desire satisfaction." Not only can we not tell empirically which of several "true" beliefs about a particular object is better than another, but also the consequences of having a true belief might be worse than not having it or having a false belief about the same object.[2] Hence true beliefs are not very reliable, nor is truth an important standard for cognitive evaluation.

A second truth-troubling position is that of deflationism. The deflationist holds that when we say something is true, we do not employ a genuine predicate: either "is true" has no extension (i.e., there is nothing to which it applies) or it does not express a real property. According to the deflationist, our claiming that a sentence, assertion, or proposition is true does no significant work. Consequently, there is little need to provide a theory of what truth is or why it is important. Disquotationalism, a prominent version of deflationism, even suggests that "truth talk" itself is largely unnecessary. In the words of Willard Quine, "To ascribe truth to the sentence ['Snow is white'] is to ascribe whiteness to snow ... Ascription of truth just cancels the quotation marks." Hence we do not need to say such a sentence is true. We could "just utter the sentence."[3]

A third position, radical contextualism, holds that the validity of truth claims is relative to the social and cultural contexts in which claims get made. Hence there is no objective truth, in the modern sense of "objectivity," nor is objective truth the goal of inquiry, whether scientific or otherwise. Richard Rorty is the most forceful recent proponent of radical contextualism. In an essay criticizing Crispin Wright's book *Truth and Objectivity*, for example, Rorty argues there is no practical difference between assessing a claim's truth and assessing its justification. When we say a claim is true, we are simply saying it is justified, and when we say a claim is justified, we are saying it is justified for the audience to which the claim is addressed. Rorty's project concerning truth is "to change the rhetoric, the common sense, and the self-image" of his own Western intellectual community.[4] Specifically, he questions the universal validity that philosophers traditionally have assigned to claims made in the name of truth.

These first three truth-troubling positions arise, for the most part, from issues and debates internal to the discipline of philosophy. The fourth, by contrast, arises from philosophically informed critiques of Western society. It has to do with the ideological roles fulfilled both by conceptions of truth and by claims to truth. This position has many versions, which one can find throughout contemporary critical theory, broadly construed.[5] The most prominent version occurs in the literature surrounding the work of the French poststructuralist Michel Foucault. Although Foucault's own conception of truth shifted during his lifetime, and although his writings on truth often are ambivalent, a prominent position in the Foucaultian literature portrays truth as no more than an ideological tool within struggles for power.[6] The result is to regard truth claims as power moves and as primarily rhetorical rather than logical, such that the question whether a truth claim is *valid* becomes the question whether it is *effective* in a struggle for power. I call this position the political instrumentalizing of truth – or politicization, for short. It instrumentalizes truth with respect to power, and it has the effect of undermining the significance of truth.

Together, these four positions – neo-scientism, deflationism, radical contextualism, and politicization – dramatically trouble the idea of truth. They cast doubt on the importance of truth in academic work, on the substantive character of truth as an idea, on the validity of claims made in the name of truth, and on the significance of truth in contemporary society.

But why should one think the idea of truth is substantive and socially significant? Haven't the positions already mentioned thoroughly undermined the credibility and appeal of any philosophical attempt to conceptualize truth as a robust idea? When it comes to truth, why not simply embrace the cultural *Zeitgeist* and go with the philosophical flow? Let me offer four reasons for resistance. They are historical, societal, academic, and discipline-specific.

First, historically, the idea of truth has been a primary orienting principle in Western culture since ancient times. The pursuit of truth has been one of the highest aspirations for intellectual leaders; the exposure of falsehood, one of their chief tasks. Truth also is a central theme in Judaism, Christianity, and Islam, the three religious traditions that have so pervasively shaped Western societies and continue to influence cultures around the world. Simply to give up on a robust idea of truth would be to turn one's philosophical back on this historical legacy, thereby ignoring philosophy's own historically shaped self-understanding as a rigorous endeavour to make sense of the world in which we live.

Second, regardless of what some philosophers say and what many nonphilosophers seem to think, it would not be easy to give up the idea of truth in the institutions of contemporary society. Despite a public cultural climate of doubt concerning truth, and amid widespread despair about the effectiveness and legitimacy of social institutions, people still act inside these as if truth is a viable and important idea. We expect our friends and colleagues to be truthful, and we take offence when they are not. We continue to hold journalists to standards of correctness and accuracy, and we consider them accountable when they deliberately fabricate their reports and knowingly misrepresent what has happened. In our courts of law, we still ask witnesses to "tell the truth, the whole truth, and nothing but the truth," and we penalize those who evidently commit perjury. We do not always just shrug and smile when politicians and government officials dish out what Frankfurt has memorably labeled "bullshit."[7] In all of these settings – in friendships, the workplace, journalism, law, and politics – and in many others besides, the idea of truth provides a normative background for contemporary social institutions, and people continue to act accordingly, often in conflict with their overt opinions about truth.

Third, in the academic world, the idea of truth sets the stage for fundamental debates about why scholars do their work and whether their work is worth doing. If finding truth is not the point of scholarly inquiry, then what is, and why would that be worth pursuing? Similarly, if truth is not a viable and important idea within the academy, why do conflicts over realism and anti-realism have such staying power in mathematics and the natural sciences? Why do worries about relativism and anti-relativism continue to pervade the humanities and social sciences? It would be very difficult to understand and address such issues and debates if an idea of truth were not at stake in them.

In the fourth place, the idea of truth has been and continues to be central to the tradition and discipline of philosophy itself. From its earliest glimmerings among the pre-Socratics until today, Western philosophy has regarded itself as a search for truth. It also has tried repeatedly to say what truth comes to and why it deserves our attention. To deflate this idea, or to treat it as merely a rhetorical device, would have wide ramifications for philosophy itself. The search for an adequate idea of truth is part and parcel of the search for an adequate philosophy.

In all of these ways, then – historically, societally, academically, and philosophically – the idea of truth matters. Indeed, the stakes in theoretical debates about truth are high. Moreover, many philosophers today recognize this, as is evidenced by the growing stream of monographs and anthologies about truth during the past few decades.[8] The trouble with truth is not that it is thin and insignificant. The trouble, instead, is that too many philosophical conceptions of truth are either insufficiently robust or robust in the wrong way. They do not adequately show why and how truth is a substantive and socially significant idea. In fact, when properly understood, the idea of truth can create trouble for truth-troubling positions.

As first steps toward such a conception, let me next comment on the matters of truth and why they matter (section 2). Then I introduce three sets of issues a sufficiently robust conception of truth needs to address (section 3), and I conclude by previewing a research program in this arena (section 4).

2. TRUTH MATTERS

Two issues lie at the centre of philosophical concerns about truth: what truth is, and why truth is important; or, what matters truth comprises, and why truth matters. In the language of traditional philosophy, the first issue pertains to the "nature" of truth. The second has to do with truth's "value." As soon as one identifies these issues in traditional language, however, one runs into objections from contemporary truth theorists. Some deny that truth has a nature. Others question truth's value. Still others both deny that truth has a nature and question its value.

I, too, doubt that truth has a nature, as "having a nature" has traditionally been understood: I doubt that truth possesses an essential property or an essential set of properties for which necessary and sufficient conditions can be stated. Yet my reasons for doubting this are nearly the opposite of the reasons given by others who raise questions along these lines. Contra primitivism (e.g., Donald Davidson), the problem with defining truth's nature is not that *truth* is so basic a concept that it defies further specification. Nor, contra deflationary accounts (e.g., W.V.O. Quine), is the problem that when we say something is true, we fail to employ a genuine predicate. Rather, truth is such a protean and complex idea that what it is about resists being reduced to an essential set of properties, and the uses of the truth predicate are so variegated that it can have differing extensions and can express various distinct properties. Instead of being too basic to be specified, the idea of truth is so dynamic and complex that it requires multiple specifications. In the words of Theodor Adorno, the idea of truth is a "constellation."[9] Like a Wittgensteinian open concept, it resists being reduced to a real definition, to a statement of necessary and sufficient conditions for anything to be true. The philosophical challenge this idea poses is to develop a sufficiently complex circumscription, one that carefully identifies areas of commonality among the various matters labeled as "true" but does not attempt to spell out a limited set of necessary and sufficient conditions for whatever can be true.[10]

I also question whether one should say truth has or is a "value." My reservations here do not concern whether truth is important: I think truth is very important indeed, both in philosophy and in daily life. Rather, I find the language of valuation singularly inappropriate for expressing why truth matters. In contemporary usage, which reflects dominant tendencies in a consumer capitalist society, when people say something is a value or has a value, they often mean it is something they prefer to a certain degree or something they would prefer in the right set of circumstances. This usage turns values into consumer preferences, such that the "value" in question is important to the extent that it is preferred. The upshot of such usage, when applied to truth, is that people portray the importance of truth as a matter of personal or communal preference. This, it seems to me, gets things precisely backwards. It is not the case that truth is important because it is preferred. Instead, truth is preferred – or at least it should be preferred – because it is important. On my view, truth is important because it guides human thought and action along fruitful paths and provides an ongoing horizon of orientation for cultural practices and social institutions.

So, I do not say that the central concerns of philosophical truth theory pertain to the "nature" and "value" of truth, as these terms are commonly understood. Rather, they pertain to what truth is and why it matters – on the understanding that one can circumscribe what truth is but cannot neatly capture it in a real definition, and that one should say why truth is important but should not treat it as a mere value. Further, these two concerns overlap and intersect: one's "definition" of truth holds implications for how one understands its importance, and one's "valuation" of truth helps shape one's circumscription of what truth is. Hence it is no accident that philosophers who do not think truth is a substantive idea also have serious doubts about the importance of truth. Nor is it surprising that philosophers who regard truth claims as merely rhetorical have little to say about what truth actually is. The two central concerns, and how one responds to them, overlap and intersect.

For convenience, let me give each concern a label. Questions about what truth is can be said to express an *ontological* concern; questions about why truth matters, an *axiological* concern, where "axiological" pertains to the study of whether something is good, to what extent, and in which respects. One can group a large range of questions under each label, however, and truth theorists disagree about which of these questions is more important than others. Consequently, depending on a theorist's own emphasis, one can classify the various types of truth theory in different ways.

Looking at some attempts to classify truth theories can shed light on the two main concerns and on how they intersect. In *Theories of Truth*, for example, Richard Kirkham aims to identify exactly which problem various truth theorists try to solve. Accordingly, he distinguishes among three "projects" – the metaphysical project, the justification project, and the speech-act project – and he suggests that only the metaphysical project can yield a theory of truth. This scheme of classification allows him to regard Bertrand Russell, Brand Blanshard, Charles Sanders Peirce, and Alfred Tarski as all pursuing variations of the same project, even though they commonly are distinguished as offering correspondence, coherence, pragmaticist, and semantic theories of truth, respectively. On Kirkham's classification, all four of them pursue the metaphysical project, which is "to identify what truth consists in, what it is for a statement (or belief or proposition, etc.) to be true."[11] He sees the main divisions as lying between such theorists, who try to spell out the necessary and sufficient conditions for a statement or proposition's being true (the metaphysical project), and those who try to say either what feature(s) would justify a truth claim (the justification project) or what it means to employ the truth predicate in ordinary language (the speech-act project).

Michael Lynch proposes a different way to map the same landscape. In his comprehensive anthology of primarily Anglo-American truth theories, Lynch divides the field between those who affirm and those who deny that truth has a nature.[12] He divides the affirmers into alethic pluralists (e.g., the later Hilary Putnam), who say truth has more than one nature, and alethic monists, who say it has only one nature. He further subdivides the alethic monists into those who affirm that truth is "at least partly epistemic" (pragmatist, verificationist, and coherence theorists) and those who deny this (correspondence, primitivist, and identity theorists). By "having a nature" Lynch means truth is a definable property or set of properties. Hence his anthology ranges across a continuum from robust affirmative theories, which "assume that truth is an important property that requires a substantive and complex explanation," to theories that reject this:

specifically, a continuum from realist correspondence theories (e.g., Russell and J.L. Austin) to anti-realist deflationary theories (e.g., P.F. Strawson and Quine). Lynch appears to locate his own functionalist theory, a version of alethic pluralism, toward the middle of this continuum, in line with what he describes as "a growing consensus among some philosophers that neither traditional robust theories nor deflationary theories are right."[13]

Despite the different emphases Kirkham and Lynch bring to their classification schemes, and despite the different questions about truth these schemes highlight, both schemes are primarily motivated by an ontological concern about what truth is. Correlatively, they tell us little about why and how the various theories consider truth important. The latter, axiological concern, by contrast, receives primary emphasis in an anthology assembled by José Medina and David Wood that gives greater attention to European philosophy. Medina and Wood include none of the realist correspondence theories with which Lynch's anthology begins. They begin instead with questions posed by Friedrich Nietzsche and William James concerning why we "value" truth. From there the anthology goes into debates about the objectivity, universality, and potentially nonpropositional character of truth, and then it considers the relations of truth to disclosure, testimony, and power. Rather than treat truth as a property whose nature either can or cannot be explained, their anthology explores the "normative space" of truth – whether and why we "value" truth. Theories of truth, on their account, do not so much address ontological questions about what truth is as they open up *"ethical, political,* and *historical questions."*[14]

Yet, if one reads the selections in this anthology – writings, for example, by Søren Kierkegaard, Edmund Husserl, Martin Heidegger, Emmanuel Levinas, Jacques Derrida, and Hannah Arendt – one can see that their accounts of whether and why truth is important either assume or state positions about what truth is. Similarly, if one works through the selections in Lynch's anthology, one can discover that their accounts of what truth is either assume or state positions about whether and why truth is important. Such duality of attention is unavoidable, it seems to me, given the inherent complexity of truth and the multiple roles of truth in human life.

My own approach aims to take seriously both sides of the continental divide in contemporary philosophy, both the analytic and the continental traditions. I resist any attempt to parcel out ontological and axiological concerns to one side or the other, as if the analytic tradition raises exclusively ontological questions or as if the contributions of the continental tradition are somehow restricted to axiological questions. Nevertheless, I do agree with Linda Martín Alcoff that, although the topic of truth provides a potential "bridge between analytic and continental philosophical traditions," each tradition has had trouble seeing this potential. Continental philosophers have had trouble because of the "normative concern" that motivates their critiques of knowledge and of epistemology, Alcoff says. Their concern makes them wary of attempts to define what truth is. Analytic philosophers have had trouble seeing truth as a bridge because, according to Alcoff, they take a nonnormative approach to truth. This approach leaves their epistemology "immature" concerning "the intersections of epistemology with social and political issues."[15]

I would add, however, that normative considerations (axiological ones, in my vocabulary) are in fact present in the analytic tradition, just as the continental tradition contains significant attempts to say what truth is. Hence, in addressing both ontological and axiological concerns, I aim to do so with a view to theories on both sides of the so-called continental divide. Further (and this is my main point), ontological and axiological concerns about truth intersect, such that an adequate account of what truth is has significant implications for why truth is important, and vice versa.[16]

3. KINDS AND DOMAINS OF TRUTH

Three sets of issues open a path to take up both sorts of concerns in this tradition-crossing way. One pertains to the relations between propositional truth and the justification of truth claims. A second has to do with the distinctions and connections between propositional and nonpropositional truth. And the third set of issues pertains to the sorts of practices and institutions within which truth occurs. This section introduces each set of issues, before the concluding section summarizes a research program that would address all three.

3.1 Truth and Justification

A dominant debate in recent truth theory concerns the relation between propositional truth and the discursive justification of propositional truth claims. The debate divides truth theorists into two camps, according to whether or not they think the truth of a proposition depends on whether someone is or could be justified in believing or asserting the proposition. Theorists who affirm that propositional truth depends on discursive justification to some significant degree have what is called an epistemic conception of truth. Theorists who deny this have a nonepistemic conception.

To a large extent, this debate over truth and justification maps directly onto a second debate over alethic realism and anti-realism. Whereas alethic realists claim that the truth of a proposition depends on whether things in the world are as the proposition says they are, alethic anti-realists claim that it depends on other factors instead, such as how well the proposition coheres with other propositions (coherence theories) or how well the proposition works in theory or practice (pragmatic theories). Because demonstrating how well a proposition coheres or works requires discursive justification, alethic anti-realists typically have epistemic conceptions of propositional truth, just as alethic realists typically have non-epistemic conceptions of propositional truth.

The debate over whether truth is epistemic raises both ontological and axiological questions concerning truth, justification, and the relation between them. If the truth of a proposition simply depends on whether it is discursively justified or justifiable, why do people regularly treat propositions as true without regard for their (potential) justification? Is there something about the truth of propositions that exceeds their discursive justifiability? Conversely, if the truth of a proposition never depends on whether it is discursively justified or justifiable, why do people regularly challenge propositional truth claims and ask us to back them up with good arguments? Is there something about the process of discursive justification that affects the truth of a proposition? In both cases, the question "why" pertains to not only what truth and justification consist in but also why they are important. As was indicated earlier, an adequate theory of propositional truth needs to say both what truth is and why it is important. But it also needs to say what discursive justification is and why it is important. Moreover, the theory should specify the relation between propositional truth and discursive justification and should explain why this relation is important.

A first step in this direction is to recognize that the notion of "propositional truth" is a catchall for three distinct but closely interconnected concepts: the reliability of beliefs, the correctness of assertions, and the accuracy of propositions.[17] It is because so many beliefs are reliable in practice – in ordinary experience and conduct – that people regularly treat the propositional content of these beliefs as "true" – i.e., sufficiently accurate – without regard for their potential justification. Ordinarily, for example, we do not go around justifying or expecting others to justify the belief that the sun is shining or the grass is green. We find these beliefs to be reliable in practice, and we take their propositional content to be accurate enough for the purposes of daily life.

Yet most people also recognize that not all of their beliefs are reliable, and ones that were reliable or seemed reliable can turn out to be unreliable. Moreover, we often discover the unreliability of our beliefs when we make assertions and others question our assertions. When such questions arise, one can either give up one's assertion, repeat or rephrase it, or give reasons for making the assertion. Once one begins to give reasons, one enters the process of discursively justifying the asserted proposition as being true – i.e., as being accurate. Such discursive justification sheds light on the purported reliability of the belief in question and on the correctness claimed for the assertion.

Hence we can learn something about our beliefs and their reliability through the process of discursive justification. The potential for such learning is one important reason why people challenge our propositional truth claims and why we try to support these with good arguments. In this sense, the justification or justifiability of a proposition has an intimate connection with the proposition's accuracy and thereby with the correctness of an assertion and the reliability of a belief. Indeed, the debate over whether propositional truth is epistemic points toward both the multidimensional character of so-called propositional truth and the specific role that discursive justification plays in our attaining propositional truth.

3.2 Propositional and Existential Truth

To this point I have focused on propositional truth and have suggested that this concept needs to be internally differentiated. Even if they granted the need for internal differentiation, however, many philosophers would question the need to specify a certain type of truth as "propositional." They would question this because it seems to imply there could be other types of truth that are not propositional. These philosophers might disagree among themselves about whether beliefs, sentences, statements, assertions, or propositions are the primary "bearers" of truth. Nevertheless, they would agree in limiting truth, properly so called, to such conceptual and linguistic matters. For these philosophers, the idea, for example, of a nonpropositional artistic truth, which I have proposed elsewhere, would be a nonstarter. They have what I call "propositionally inflected" conceptions of truth.[18]

Yet there are clear historical precedents for thinking nonpropositional matters can be true or false. Aristotle, for example, suggests that Greek tragedy (and, by extension, perhaps other "imitative" or representational arts) can be true, insofar as its function is to give insight into the kinds of things that could occur under certain circumstances.[19] Anselm regards the truths of statements, of thought, of action, of passion, and of sensing as all being varieties of truth as "rectitude" (*rectitudo*), which he directly links with justice as "rectitude of [the] will preserved for its own sake." He also tends to subsume sensing and language usage under "action," such that truth pertains in the first instance to what people do and how they interrelate, not to what they believe and say.[20] So too, as is well known, Hegel ranks the arts and religion alongside philosophy as the cultural pinnacle of knowledge and truth. They are forms of "absolute spirit," he says, and what gives the arts and religion their truth capacity is not propositional.[21] All three of these philosophers, and many others besides, regard nonpropositional matters as true or false, even though they do not deny or reject propositional truth.

Further, if one pays attention to ordinary language, one notices many uses of "true," "truly," and "truth" that are difficult or impossible to reduce to propositional truth. People speak of "true friends." They admire companions who are "true to their word." They say something "rings true" when it matches their experience. Also, in line with a modern ideal of ethical authenticity, they say they want to be "true to themselves."[22] What should we make of such usages? Are people simply sloppy in their use of language? Are they employing concepts that are so different from the concept of propositional truth that truth theorists do not need to include these other concepts in their accounts of truth? Or is there enough commonality among such usages and concepts that a theory of truth should encompass all of them and explain how they are interrelated?

One's response to such historical precedents and language usages proves decisive for the scope of one's theory of truth. If one dismisses them, or if one has a prior commitment to the solely propositional character of truth proper, then one does not need to account for what

I call existential truth. Nor does one need to say how propositional truth, in its differentiated forms, relates to existential truth. Instead, one can take what I call a monothetic stance toward the topic of truth. Whatever one says about what truth is and why truth is important will presuppose the thesis that there is only one kind of truth, and that kind is propositional. Much of the literature on truth in the analytic tradition is monothetic in this sense, no matter how robust or deflationary the accounts given, and even when the accounts embrace a form of alethic pluralism.

The obvious alternative to a monothetic stance is to take historical precedents and variegated usages seriously, to ask whether truth is more than propositional, and to consider whether some truth is nonpropositional. Conceptions that raise these considerations tend to take what I call a stereothetic stance toward the topic of truth. Unless these conceptions deny that any truth is propositional – an extreme position that would fly in the face of both historical precedents and ordinary language – they need both to account for propositional truth and to show how it is related to other forms of truth. Much of the literature on truth in the continental tradition takes a stereothetic stance, although I believe the tradition has rarely succeeded in explaining the relation between propositional and existential truth.[23]

Because these two contrasting stances, monothetic and stereothetic, are so deeply entrenched in how different truth theorists delimit their field of investigation, it is very difficult to provide convincing arguments, across this divide, about the notion of existential truth. What looks like equivocation from one side can look hermeneutically astute from the other. Perhaps, however, there is room for agreement about some aspects of language usage. I suspect most philosophers would agree that when we call someone a "true friend," we do not mean that she or he is true in exactly the same way a true proposition is true. A true friend is someone who really cares about you, someone you can count on "through thick and thin," and someone you love to be with.[24] It would be odd to say any of this about a true proposition. Yet one can wonder whether there is enough continuity between our assigning "true" to propositions and "true" to friends that one can say the two usages share a common meaning. Further, is there an idea of truth that would encompass both the truth of propositions and the truth of friends – indeed, more broadly, both propositional truth and all truth that is not propositional? If so, what would that idea be?

Without taking up the broader question here, let me comment on the usages of "true propositions" and "true friends." The common meaning these two usages seem to share lies in notions of dependability and fidelity. Part of what we mean when we say either propositions or friends are true is that we can depend on them. We can depend on true propositions to provide the accurate insight we need, for example, and we can depend on true friends to stand by us when we need them. So too, we understand true propositions to be "faithful" in a certain sense, faithful "to the way things are," just as we regard true friends as people who are faithful to who we really are. Moreover, when I call an acquaintance a true friend, I am not simply saying they are "true to type" – i.e., that this person measures up to the standards for friendship. I also am saying that this person is true to me – they are true as *my friend*, not simply true to what friendship is, but dependable and faithful *toward me*. There is more to my calling an acquaintance a true friend than there is to my saying of our favourite feline, for example, "Measha is a true cat" – i.e., that Measha is true to her feline type. Perhaps, then, the notions of dependability and fidelity point us toward a wider idea of truth encompassing not only the truth of propositions and the truth of friends but also additional types of apparently nonpropositional truth that ordinary language usage signals.

By itself, such analysis of linguistic usage cannot provide a knockdown argument for why one should take a stereothetic stance toward truth in general. Someone committed to a monothetic stance could reply that propositional accuracy, for example, remains the core concept of truth, while notions such as dependability, fidelity, and the like are at best analogies of propositional truth. In any case, I think paying close attention to variegated truth talk, if I may call it that, at least raises questions about how to account for existential truth, much of which appears to be nonpropositional, and how to understand the relation between apparently nonpropositional truth and truth that is clearly propositional in character.

In this context I mean by *existential truth* all the ways in which people pursue and experience truth. Existential truth has to do with truth as it is lived and not simply believed, as it is practised and not simply asserted, as it is carried out and not simply claimed. Taking a stereothetic stance, I assume that people can and do pursue truth in art and religion, for example, and not only in science and philosophy, and that propositional truth is neither the quintessence nor the goal of such artistic and religious pursuits. I also assume that people can and do experience truth in pre-linguistic and preconceptual ways – hence, in pre-propositional ways – and that one cannot adequately explain what they experience by reducing it to propositional matters. Moreover, I believe that a sufficiently robust account of propositional truth needs to explore how propositional pursuits of truth link up with nonpropositional pursuits and how pre-propositional experiences of truth inform an awareness of propositional truth.

A more detailed account of propositional truth than I have given here would make clear, however, that this distinction between propositional and existential truth is preliminary and potentially misleading. For *propositional truth is itself a mode of existential truth* – an important and distinct mode, to be sure, but neither external to existential truth nor, in principle, opposed to existential truth. In other words, propositional truth is among the ways in which people live and practice the truth. What I have mentioned as nonpropositional pursuits and pre-propositional experiences of truth are intrinsic to differentiated and holistic engagements with truth, to which propositional truth itself belongs. Accordingly, the preliminary distinction between propositional and existential truth will need to be subsumed into a distinction among pre-propositional, propositional, and post-propositional kinds of (existential) truth.

3.3 Social Domains of Truth

In the background to this expansive conception of truth lies a social ontology of the domains within which truth occurs. Derived primarily from the philosophies of Dooyeweerd and Vollenhoven,[25] this social ontology distinguishes among interpersonal interactions, cultural practices, and social institutions. A conversation between two or more people, for example, would be an interpersonal interaction. If it occurred at a music concert or art exhibition, this interaction would take place in the context of the cultural practices of art making and art interpretation and within the frame of art as a social institution. Cultural practices and social institutions themselves belong to a larger societal formation whose structure and dynamic inflects their character and possibilities. All of these matters – cultural practices, social institutions, and a societal formation – have emerged historically, and they continue to change as history unfolds. Accordingly, unlike many truth theories that focus on sentences, speech acts, and propositional claims, and thereby limit their attention to certain actions and interactions, my conception of truth tries to acknowledge the larger social and historical fabric within which truth-relevant conduct and interpersonal relations occur.

This approach assumes that human knowledge is both internally differentiated and socially embedded. Here I depart from standard epistemological accounts that try to capture what knowledge is in formulations such as "justified true belief." I do not deny that justified true belief is an important component of knowledge. As is explained in chapter 4, however, I am not convinced that this formula, and others like it, can do justice to the diverse ways in which people come to know and in which they test and revise what they know. For example, I know Joyce, my life partner for more than forty years, and I know her very well. Yet I would be hard pressed to render this knowledge as a set of justified true beliefs, as would anyone else who has intimate knowledge of another person. Further, I do not think the appeal to this usage of "to know" involves an equivocation, as if one were using the same word to designate two logically unrelated concepts. It is not like trying to subsume the concept of a riverbank under the concept of a commercial bank simply because one can use "bank" to designate either concept.

Here one faces a decision like the one posed with respect to variegated usages of "true" and its cognates. Either one can insist that knowledge proper reduces to what standard epistemologies describe, or one can seek a more expansive conception of knowledge that embraces ordinary, but philosophically non-standard, usages of "know" and its cognates. Not surprisingly, my proposed conception of truth exemplifies the second, expansive approach. I take it that people acquire, test, and revise their knowledge in a vast array of interpersonal interactions, and they do so within the contexts and frames provided by various cultural practices and social institutions. Sharing a meal, healing the sick, tending a garden, protesting an injustice, and watching a video, for example, all are ways in which people acquire knowledge regarding themselves, others, and the world they inhabit. What they acquire in these ways cannot be reduced to justified true beliefs.

It is especially important, it seems to me, to understand how cultural practices and social institutions help make the acquisition, testing, and revision of knowledge possible. Few philosophers would doubt that the practices of science or, more broadly, of professional teaching and research are practices of knowledge. Most probably also would recognize that the institution of schooling, from pre-school through university, significantly frames such practices via professional expectations and standards, procedures of evaluation and accreditation, and patterns of governance and funding. Despite notable contributions from feminists and social epistemologists, however, not enough philosophers bring such institutional framing into their accounts of scientific knowledge. Even fewer would seriously entertain the suggestion that scholarship and schooling are only two among many matrices of cultural practices and social institutions within which the process of knowledge occurs.

My own working pluralist hypothesis, presented more fully in chapters 3 and 4, is that most if not all of the main social institutions in a differentiated modern society, along with the cultural practices they frame, configure distinct social domains of knowledge. This implies they are social domains of truth as well. By calling them social domains of truth, I intend to suggest two things. First, the main social institutions, along with their correlated cultural practices, are distinctive ways in which knowledge and truth occur. Second, the knowledge and truth that occur within them take on the distinctive character of the institutions and practices within which they occur. Hence, for example, the type of knowledge and truth one can find within artistic practices and the social institution of art is characteristically distinct from the type of knowledge and truth one can find within the practices and institution of religion. Both of these types, in turn, are characteristically distinct from scientific knowledge and truth. So too the knowledge and truth attainable in the political domain are characteristically distinct from those which one can attain in the domain of kinship, friendship, and intimate life partnerships.

This is not to deny that different types of truth belong to a larger whole, nor is it to forget that overlaps, mixtures, and cross-fertilizations occur among the various types. Yet I want to test the hypothesis that there are different social ways of knowing and different social domains of truth. If this hypothesis can be borne out, it will shed light both on distinctions among pre-, post-, and propositional truth and on the relations among them, for in each social domain one or another of these three kinds of truth will prevail. The hypothesis also will help ensure that a general conception of truth is sufficiently comprehensive to account for truth in all its dynamic complexity.

4. RESEARCH PROGRAM

The attempt to propose such a conception will begin with a notion that dominates in contemporary truth theories, namely, the concept of propositional truth. My proposal will first examine what it is for a proposition to be true and will work out the distinction, already mentioned, among reliability, correctness, and accuracy. This distinction requires an equally differentiated account of the "facts" that are said to make propositions true, at least on certain truth theories. That account will lead to a preliminary indication of why the relation between propositions and facts is important.

The next step is to provide a more complete account of what the truth of propositions consists in. I shall do this in terms of a relationship between achieving a certain type of insight and pursuing a specific type of validity with respect to such insight. My account will claim that the truth of propositions consists in a correlation between accurate insight and inferential validity. This relationship is important because it allows us to discover and test the purported soundness of our practical beliefs and assertions.

Then I shall take up the topic of justification and its relation to propositional truth. First I shall propose an account of justification that points past the impasse between epistemic and nonepistemic conceptions of truth, with special attention to the debate between Hilary Putnam and William Alston.[26] Then I plan to refine this account by introducing a distinction between the justification of propositional truth claims and their corroboration. Whereas the justification of truth claims hinges on questions of validity, which we normally address within discursive argumentation, the corroboration of a truth claim hinges on the quality of an insight, and it requires some indication that what we claim is or can be borne out in practice. As pragmatic truth theories recognize in their own way, the corroboration of truth claims provides a bridge between propositional truth, properly so called, and the wider expanses of existential truth to which propositional truth belongs.

Because of this bridge, one can ask whether there are varieties of propositional truth beyond the three already mentioned – i.e., beyond reliability, correctness, and accuracy – and if so, how they are interrelated. This, I take it, is a leading concern of alethic pluralists with respect to propositional truth. Indeed, the rise of alethic pluralism in analytic philosophy in response to the impasse between deflationism and traditional correspondence theories provides another bridge between propositionally inflected truth theories and more stereothetic approaches. This is especially so of the pioneering work done by Crispin Wright, Michael Lynch, and Douglas Edwards.[27] After discussing some proposals along these lines, especially in the work of Michael Lynch,[28] I shall argue for a more radical kind of alethic pluralism, within which one can locate propositional alethic pluralism. The more radical alethic pluralism, as already indicated, posits differences between propositional and nonpropositional truth, and it links these differences with the different sorts of cultural practices and social institutions within which truth occurs. In other words, I shall propose a social-ontological pluralism with respect to truth, one that simultaneously insists on a holistic unity across legitimate differences. There is an underlying unity to truth as a whole, I shall argue, and this unity is manifested within and across the differentiated types and domains of truth. I call this position holistic alethic pluralism.

What does such a holistic and pluralist conception of truth come to? I shall suggest that truth as a whole, and within each of its domains, amounts to a relationship between normative validity and life-giving insight. More precisely, truth consists in a dynamic correlation between human fidelity to societal principles, on the one hand, and a life-giving disclosure of society, on the other. Here I understand "dynamic correlation" both as a structure and as a process. Moreover, as both structure and process, it points in a certain direction. I shall argue that this directional structural process shows up in the various social domains of truth, but in characteristically distinct ways. Whereas, for example, it shows up in the arts as a dynamic correlation between aesthetic validity and imaginative disclosure, it shows up in the sciences as a dynamic correlation between theoretical validity and evidence-based accuracy. Yet there is an isomorphism across different domains of truth, such that all of them are domains of the same truth as a whole. This conception allows propositional truth to emerge as one important kind of truth, important both for its distinctive contributions and for its role with reference to other kinds and domains of truth, but not either the only kind or the most important.

Building on this general conception of truth as dynamic correlation, I then plan to lay out a similarly general conception of the authentication of truth. The question here concerns how truth is borne out. I shall argue that truth is borne out by people bearing witness to it, and they bear witness to it by doing what truth requires. Authentication is the process of bearing witness to truth by doing what truth requires. I also shall argue that the justification and corroboration of propositional truth are not external to the process of authentication. Rather, they are intrinsic to it, such that one can understand justification and corroboration as specific, institutionally framed ways to bear witness to truth by doing what it requires. If successful, this approach can socially recontextualize the discursive practices that truth theorists and epistemologists often discuss in isolation, without regard to their social relevance.

A similar concern about social recontextualization will motivate a subsequent discussion of science and truth. I intend to take issue not only with those who deny that truth is an important goal for scientific pursuits but also with those who think science provides the highest or even the sole mode of truth. I shall argue instead for a conception of scientific truth that both retains its overriding importance for science and relativizes it to truth as a whole, which exceeds and precedes scientific truth.[29] This will allow me to argue that the sciences and, more broadly, the academic enterprise, need to contribute to the common good, precisely by way of pursuing scientific truth within a social context and practicing what I call socially ethical scholarship.[30]

This argument, like the general conception of truth it presupposes, raises questions about the relation between truth and goodness. Do these two ideas end up being the same idea, or are there important distinctions and relations to be maintained between them? I plan to take up questions along these lines with a focus on democratic politics. In a democratic polity, I shall suggest, truth requires the pursuit of social justice together with the promotion of liberation, especially for the sake of those who suffer the greatest injustice and impoverishment. This in turn requires citizens who "speak truth to power" and a vital public sphere where suffering is voiced and priorities adjudicated. The achievement of social justice and freedom would be the political good, which is never attained once and for all but is always already underway. Political truth is what calls us to seek the political good. So too, in general, truth calls us to seek goodness; to the degree that we achieve the good, we have done what truth requires. Although not identical, then, truth and goodness thoroughly intermesh.

Moving on from science and politics, I shall then examine the types of truth available in the practices and institutions of art, religion, and philosophy – the three domains of culture that Hegel placed at the pinnacle of truth. Although opposed to the Hegelian idea of "absolute spirit," I, like Hegel, shall argue that each of these domains has a special role to play in the unfolding of truth as a whole: art, via cogent imaginative disclosure; religion, via faithful and worshipful disclosure; and philosophy, via a dialectical propositional disclosure of life and society. I also shall suggest that falsity in these domains, while noticeable within them, is both a telling index of societal evil and a contributing factor. Here too, as in the case of science, the practices of art, religion, and philosophy need to contribute to the common good.

The last stage of the research program will ask how philosophy should contribute. Specifically, how should philosophy help people "live (the) truth"? As the previous chapter indicates, I believe there are three ways to live (the) truth. One is to find ways to that which is good. A second is to engage in redemptive critique of that which is evil. A third is to remain open to a complete reorientation of one's own life and communities, if that is what truth requires. Philosophy can contribute to this in two ways, I shall argue: first, by engaging in a thorough critique of contemporary society as a whole; and second, by both learning from the social-ethical insights people gain from living the truth and reflecting with them on how to pursue such practical wisdom.

To strive for propositional truth is a crucial step along the lifeways of truth. Yet the path itself, and the horizon that beckons, are much more than propositional pursuits, by themselves, can provide. Propositional truth, then, is important but not all-important, and philosophy, as the love of wisdom, needs to show why this is so. Showing this is what reformational philosophy can offer in the contested arena of contemporary truth theory.[31]

3

Distantial Ways of Knowing: Toward a New Epistemology

In the doctoral dissertation he finished in 1978, the Australian philosopher and educator Doug Blomberg proposes a new approach to school curriculum at the primary and secondary levels.[1] His dissertation argues for what Blomberg calls an "integral curriculum." He bases this argument on a holistic and pluralist model of knowledge derived from Herman Dooyeweerd, Calvin Seerveld, and other reformational thinkers. Around the same time, Hendrik Hart, the leading reformational systematic philosopher in Canada, completed a two-volume syllabus that proposes a similarly holistic and pluralist epistemology,[2] in preparation for a subsequent book that would lay out an "integral ontology."[3] Although Hart's syllabus does not cite Blomberg, and Blomberg's dissertation does not cite Hart,[4] both clearly desire to offer a new theory of knowledge attuned to the Hebrew and Christian scriptures and more expansive than standard epistemologies. This desire characterizes much of the English-language reformational movement in the years surrounding the deaths of Herman Dooyeweerd in 1977 and Dirk Vollenhoven in 1978.

Four decades later one wonders what to make of these attempts to articulate a holistic and pluralist epistemology. Were they on the right track? Do they still hold potential for carrying out an "inner reformation" of schooling and the academic enterprise? What challenges would face contemporary efforts to provide a suitably holistic and pluralist conception of knowledge?

I plan to take up such questions in two stages. In the current chapter I revisit Doug Blomberg's early work and explore issues pertaining to the role of "analytic knowing" within knowledge as a whole. Then, building on this exploration, the next chapter tries to show how a suitably comprehensive conception of knowledge can account for both the differences and the connections among distinct social domains of knowledge, including, but not limited to, art, science, and religion.

The current chapter proceeds as follows. First I locate Blomberg's dissertation in a reformational tradition of holistic pluralism with respect to knowledge. Next I present his innovative conception of distantial knowing and explore a related distinction between normative insight and concrete understanding. Then I explore three issues raised by Blomberg's conception: (1) the role of analytic or logical knowing in postanalytic or postlogical ways of knowing, (2) the question of normative awareness within concrete experience, and (3) how the relation between cultural practices and social institutions contributes to distinct types of knowledge. These issues, especially the first and third, provide focal points for the next chapter, on social domains of knowledge.[5]

1. HOLISTIC EPISTEMOLOGICAL PLURALISM

The turn toward a simultaneously holistic and pluralist account of knowledge is not simply an innovation of the "Toronto School" of reformational philosophy. Although the best-known discussions of epistemology by Dooyeweerd do not propose multiple, modally differentiated ways of knowing, one can discover this hypothesis in writings by Vollenhoven and other reformational contemporaries. For example, one finds references in Vollenhoven's early writings to psychical knowing as a *knowing of* (*weten van*) distinct from analytic *knowing that* (*weten dat*),[6] as well as occasional mentions of *faith-knowledge* (*geloofskennis*) in his later writings,[7] although nothing like the full-blown accounts he gives of analytic or logical knowing in both early and later writings.

Similarly, in a seminal essay translated for a 1971 Festschrift honouring the theologian Cornelius Van Til, J.P.A. Mekkes clearly distinguishes conceptual understanding (or "thought" or "the analytical function") from (ethical) loving as a different kind of knowing to which conceptual understanding makes a submerged contribution. Mekkes also suggests there are several other ways of knowing: "I do not experience explicitly the analytical function of my loving ... so long as it truly *concerns* loving. This entire act is a conscious *unity*, from beginning to end, in which nevertheless pre-eminently knowing must reach its high point. To this *knowing* our function of distinguishing ('thought') makes an implicit contribution by way of founding it ... I become acquainted with loving by way of *loving* the one who is loved, just as I become acquainted with right by doing right ... in situations where justice is at stake, with nature in its operation and necessary forming, etc. This holds for all of our life, for all of our knowing of this life, that is, of the creation."[8]

So too, in his introductory text on philosophy, K.J. Popma forthrightly distinguishes "strictly analytic knowledge" from "the various types of knowledge that are connected with [*samengaan met*] supra-analytic functions: a sense of language [*taalbesef*], a sense of justice [*rechtsbesef*], faith-knowledge [*geloofskennis*], aesthetic knowing (and knower)." He suggests that these range from "psychically" to "pistically" qualified types of knowledge, and he specifies scientific or theoretical knowledge as the analytically or logically qualified type.[9]

Indeed, in a lucid essay on epistemology devoted primarily to Dooyeweerd and Vollenhoven, René van Woudenberg argues that reformational philosophers typically begin with an inventory of what humans can know and then note that there are different *sorts* of knowledge, such as the knowledge of competence (*vaardigheidskennis*), the knowledge of acquaintance (*vertrouwdheidskennis*), and propositional knowledge (*informatie-kennis*), as well as different *modi* of knowing, such as those Popma distinguishes. Van Woudenberg acknowledges that this "inductivist" approach, which begins with questions about the extent of knowledge, will not satisfy "methodist" philosophers, who begin with questions about the criterion of knowledge, about what can count as knowledge. Nevertheless, it has the advantage of trying to do justice to what people experience as knowledge.[10]

In light of these precedents, one can regard the Toronto School's holistic epistemological pluralism as a deepening of insights already suggested by Dutch colleagues and students of Dooyeweerd. When one compares Blomberg's dissertation and Hart's syllabus with Dooyeweerd's reflections on epistemology, however, especially in Part II of the second volume to *A New Critique of Theoretical Thought*,[11] three departures from Dooyeweerd stand out. First, both Blomberg and Hart put a much heavier emphasis than Dooyeweerd does on Hebrew wisdom traditions as sources of insight into knowledge, ones that conflict with the Greek traditions that have so strongly shaped Western philosophy and theology. Where Dooyeweerd appeals to cosmological self-consciousness and the biblical ground motive of creation, fall, and redemption as keys to understanding both "naïve experience" and "theoretical thought," Blomberg and Hart go directly to Old Testament wisdom literature for insight into what knowledge involves, as well as to its New Testament elaboration, especially in the writings traditionally attributed to the Apostle John. Their direct appeal to the scriptures and biblical interpretation gives a new articulation to what it means to develop a philosophy of knowledge "in line with scripture," to use Vollenhoven's phrase.[12]

Second, although Blomberg and Hart retain Dooyeweerd's emphasis on the "Gegenstand relation" as what distinguishes theoretical work in the sciences and the academy from everyday knowledge, they modify his emphasis in ways that challenge the traditional divide between theory and practice.[13] These modifications allow them to embed theoretical work in the practices and institutions of everyday life, and to do so more directly and substantially than Dooyeweerd could have allowed.

Closely related to such embedding, in the third place, are the attempts by both Blomberg and Hart to treat knowledge as a "totality concept" (Hart) that comes to expression not only propositionally and theoretically but also in a wide array of other "ways of knowing" (Blomberg). Hence, according to Blomberg, we need to go beyond Dooyeweerd's claim that various modal functions are implicit in naïve experience and become explicit when we engage in theoretical thought. Rather, experience as a whole is made up of multiple distinct but interrelated ways of knowing, of which theoretical work is just one.[14] One effect of such pluralistic holism about what counts as knowledge is to deprivilege the roles of (theoretical) reason and science[15] in human life and society – especially, for Blomberg, in schooling and education. As Blomberg notes with characteristic modesty, by expanding Dooyeweerd's schema he tends "to downplay somewhat the significance of theoretical thought in the opening of the horizon of human experience."[16]

2. DISTANTIAL KNOWING

The key innovation Blomberg's dissertation introduces, after he shows why Dooyeweerd's epistemology does not go far enough, is the notion of *distantial knowing*. Blomberg derives this notion from a clue that Calvin Seerveld offered in his lectures on the arts and literary criticism in the early 1960s.[17] There Seerveld expands Dooyeweerd's bi-level epistemology – naïve experience and theoretical thought – to make room for a third and distinct kind of knowledge. Seerveld calls this third kind "imagination" or "imaginative knowing," and he suggests that it involves taking aesthetic distance from "the perceptive action of naïve experience." Yet, like theoretical knowledge, imaginative knowledge starts from such experience (from "the *habitus* of ordinary perception"), and it "rests in the same bed" of transmodal intuition as "theoretical knowledge and everyday knowledge" do.[18]

Whereas theoretical knowledge takes distance from ordinary experience by one's shifting into a Gegenstand relation, however, imaginative knowledge takes distance by one's shifting into what Seerveld calls "the *Hineinlebenshaltung*." This is a stance or attitude in which one tries to "live into" the "multiple meanings, peripheral nuances and tributary connections" of a situation or event or object and to "catch all these meanings symbolically together" as they present themselves aesthetically. Unlike the scientist's theoretical attitude, which disrupts ordinary experience by singling out a modal field for precise analysis, guided primarily by logical considerations, the artist's imaginative stance disrupts it by highlighting and intensifying the multiple meanings of what we ordinarily experience, guided primarily by aesthetic considerations.[19] In other words, whereas distance-taking theoretical knowing involves a logically qualified act or process, distance-taking imaginative knowing involves an aesthetically qualified act or process.

Although Blomberg points out several puzzles in Seerveld's conception of imaginative knowledge, he says it opens the door to a still wider hypothesis: perhaps there is a distinct way of distantial knowing for *every* "normative aspect" of human experience, not only logically qualified theoretical knowing and aesthetically qualified imaginative knowing (Blomberg uses the term "aesthetic knowing") but also "techno-cultural knowing, lingual knowing, social knowing, economic knowing, jural knowing, ethical knowing and confessional knowing."[20]

According to Blomberg, distantial knowing is distinct from both "concrete experience" and "religious knowledge." It opens up concrete experience, and it receives direction from religious knowledge. Moreover, distantial knowing occurs in different ways, each way qualified by a different modal aspect and focused on the norm(s) for that aspect. To illustrate, economic knowing is a way of distantial knowing in which businesspersons, for example, reflect on their concrete experience with a view to what ought to happen economically. Their reflections might be enriched by an economist's "theoretical articulation of economic principles," but the businesspersons are not engaged in theoretical reflection.[21]

The differences between theoretical thought and other ways of distantial knowing are crucial for Blomberg's integral curriculum model, which rejects the traditional focus on merely academic study and promotes a more "practical" approach. Unlike theoretical thought, he says, all the other modes of distantial knowing, being either techno-cultural or post-techno-cultural, involve an intention to form or shape *what is* by reflecting on *what ought to be*. Because of such purposive reflection, these other modes of distantial knowing are praxis-oriented in ways that theoretical knowing is not. Whereas distantial nontheoretical knowing objectifies the world in order to transform it – positing norms such as economic stewardship and public justice in the process – distantial theoretical knowing simply tries to uncover "norms as they have been positivized." According to Blomberg, "it is not the task of science to change the world."[22] Instead, "theory is the handmaiden of both concrete experience and the nontheoretical [distantial] ways of knowing, for theoretical insight alone is powerless to transform the world."[23]

Blomberg's account of distantial knowing relies heavily on Dooyeweerd's account of the opening process whereby the meaning of each modal aspect becomes disclosed as its anticipatory moments come to expression. For example, Dooyeweerd says the attribution of guilt in a legal context presupposes an opening of the juridical aspect in anticipation of the ethical modal aspect.[24] Just as, according to Blomberg, the anticipatory disclosure of the analytic aspect finds expression only within theoretical thought – and "not within the closed structure of pre-theoretical thought"[25] – so the other (postanalytic) ways of distantial knowing bring to expression the specific anticipatory or opened meaning of the modal aspects that give them their distinct focus. And that helps explain why these ways of knowing, while not characteristically analytic and certainly not theoretical, nevertheless take distance from concrete experience: "It seems reasonable to suppose that *each way of knowing rises above the indeterminately multi-aspectual character of naïve experience as a particular aspect in its opened meaning becomes the focus of human knowing, and by the very fact of providing a specific, modal focus to knowing, distances this qualifying aspect of the act of knowing from the systatic coherence of naïve experience*."[26]

On the one hand, then, we have concrete experience, which is multi-aspectual, holistic, and oriented "to the structures of individuality in their multi-aspectual functioning."[27] On the other hand, we have various ways of distantial knowing, including theoretical thought, that are modally focused and that open up the concrete experience in which they are embedded and from which they take distance. One aim of a school curriculum, says Blomberg, should be to nurture students in *all* of these ways of distantial knowing and thereby to open up their concrete experience, for "the school should be concerned with the opening of knowledge in all its dimensions."[28]

3. NORMATIVE INSIGHT AND CONCRETE UNDERSTANDING

Although my brief digest cannot do justice to a nearly 600-page dissertation, perhaps I have summarized enough to pose questions that remain relevant for contemporary attempts to spell out a holistic and pluralist epistemology. The first and obviously most pressing question concerns how to characterize knowing and knowledge. In various places Blomberg's dissertation describes knowledge as norm-related. Knowledge is "a response to the norms which God established," he writes, and it amounts to "insight into these norms." In addition, because the norms "are diverse," Blomberg thinks it follows that "there are many forms of knowledge."[29] Why this follows is not clear, however: theoretical thought is said by Blomberg (and Dooyeweerd) to give us (theoretical) insight into many diverse norms – aesthetic, lingual, logical, social, etc. – yet this does not entail that there are many forms of theoretical knowledge, does it? Moreover, "insight into norms" seems to characterize specifically distantial knowing in Blomberg's account; he does not typically use this phrase to characterize what he calls religious knowledge and the everyday knowledge of concrete experience. So it appears that he regards all knowledge as responding to God's norms but only distantial knowledge as providing insight into these norms.

This is borne out in "Toward a Christian Theory of Knowledge," an essay published two years after Blomberg completed his dissertation, where he connects knowledge with responsible acting and seems to introduce a distinction between *insight* and *understanding*. Blomberg begins this essay by saying "we can only really speak of 'knowledge' when an integral subjection to the norms for human acting is involved." He also describes knowledge as the relationship of human knowers, in their acts of knowing, to "the knowable," a relationship that is subject to the central "religious" call "to love God and neighbour through service in the creation."[30] According to Blomberg, the human knower is a self in relation to God or to some substitute for God, such that self-knowledge requires knowledge of God, and vice versa. In his Dooyeweerdian vocabulary, this implies that the human knower is fundamentally a religious creature and, because of this, knowledge in its most comprehensive sense "is properly an integral understanding of self, world and God."[31] The human knower achieves such integral understanding both through "concrete experience or everyday knowledge" and through "distantial knowing." Everyday knowledge involves direct "contact" with other creatures and "recognition" of the coherent relations among them. It is "rich, immediate, integral, concrete."[32] Distantial knowing, by contrast, involves taking distance "from what is, in order to envision and to implement what ought to be."[33]

In further describing the various ways of distantial knowing, Blomberg uses such terms as "focus on" and "formulate" (theoretical knowing), "having insight" (techno-cultural), "intuiting the norms" (lingual), "understanding" (social), "perceiving" (economic), "seeing how" (aesthetic), "apprehending" (jural), "knowing what is demanded" (ethical), and "comprehending" (confessional).[34] These terms do not appear to carry any specifically modal meaning. Rather, Blomberg seems most concerned to distinguish the norm-recognizing *insight* that accompanies all distantial ways of knowing from the *concrete understanding* that we have when we simply talk with someone, for example, or when we buy and sell commodities. Achieving distantial insight requires creative searching for what can and what ought to be, but concrete understanding does not,[35] although the results of such searching can and must enrich concrete understanding: "Whereas concrete experience involves a resting in the order of creation, distantial knowing involves a reaching out to give positive expression to potential that is as yet unrealised in the individual as communal horizon. Whilst concrete experience involves accepting what is given, distantial knowing involves asking what might be."[36]

The creative character of distantial knowing does not mean, however, that it constitutes the cognitive object in a Kantian fashion or creates its meaning. Rather, "the knowable" – any creature insofar as it can be known – comes to human beings "as revelation," Blomberg says; it reveals God, it reveals itself, and it reveals how humans should respond to it. Accordingly, human knowing should respect the "God-given individuality" of knowable creatures and the "peculiar place" God has given them in creation. It should also aim "to lead each creature to more fully display its potential to glorify God."[37] Hence the knowable is neither a simple given nor a mere construct. It exists within a web of relationships with other creatures, including human beings, and it reveals itself in a relational manner.

To summarize: Blomberg holds that all human knowing and knowledge are religious: i.e., they occur in response to God's call to love. At its core, human knowledge is supposed to be an integral understanding of God and creation, including the human self – integral in the sense that it respects the integrity of all creatures in their mutual interrelations. Such integral understanding occurs in the interplay between the immediacy and concreteness of everyday knowledge, characterized by subject-oriented concrete understanding, and the distance and creativity of distantial knowing, characterized, when it succeeds, by law-oriented normative insight. In this way Blomberg blunts Dooyeweerd's sharp divide between naïve (pretheoretical) experience and theoretical thought. He also relativizes the law-seeking capacities of theoretical work, by ranging it alongside eight other distantial ways of gaining insight into the norms for human action.

4. ANALYTIC KNOWING

There is much in Blomberg's early epistemology that I applaud. I, too, regard knowledge and knowing as responses to God's call to love and as properly respecting the integrity and interrelatedness of all creatures – even though I prefer to use the term *spiritual* rather than *religious* to characterize this central core to knowledge.[38] I am less convinced, however, about the distinction between everyday knowledge and distantial knowing. I also wonder whether Blomberg has done justice to the uniqueness and social significance of theoretical work. Although I do not plan to lay out these concerns in great detail, let me show why they arise. They revolve around the role analytic or logical practices play in postanalytic or postlogical ways of knowing.

When I read Blomberg's general descriptions of distantial knowing and his more detailed accounts of specific ways of distantial knowing, it is not clear that he has identified *distinctive* ways of knowing. Distantial knowing in general, and each way in particular, all seem to come down to a reflective awareness of the relevant norms within a certain situation, relationship, or organization. So far as I can tell, there is nothing specifically "economic" about a consumer or businessperson's understanding that economic transactions and organizations should be stewardly or resourceful. Nor is there anything specifically "aesthetic" about the insight artists or audiences attain into the "central [normative] meaning of the aesthetic aspect," which Blomberg, following Dooyeweerd, describes as "harmony or coherence,"[39] and which others, following Seerveld, might describe as "imaginative cogency."[40] Yet Blomberg seems in each case to think there is something modally specific, using terms like "stewardous economic insight" and "aesthetic insight" for such instances of reflective norm-related awareness.[41] I doubt that such insights are in fact specifically economic or aesthetic in character. Their being insights into the norms for economic or aesthetic matters does not make them characteristically "stewardous" or "harmonious."

Now it may be so that, for the most part, one needs to participate in the relevant practices and institutions in order to arrive at such norm-related reflective insight in daily life: that one needs, for example, to engage in economic transactions to attain such insight into the norm of stewardship or resourcefulness or must take up the practices of art making and art interpretation in order to gain such insight into the norm of imaginative cogency. Yet this does not mean that economic insight is itself stewardous or that aesthetic insight is itself harmonious (Blomberg) or allusive (Seerveld). The insight in each case is simply a reflective awareness of the relevant norms for specific practices and institutions, and it is not specifically economic or aesthetic in character.

Blomberg's attempts to characterize different ways of knowing as distinct in their modal qualifications remind one of the argument in James Olthuis's dissertation that ethical judgments and evaluations are ethically qualified acts "in which the (always-present) analytical function comes to the fore in a manner and with such emphasis that it 'determines' or 'specifies' the distinctive individuality of the act." They are ethically qualified and analytically founded acts, Olthuis says, just as aesthetic judgments are aesthetically qualified and analytically founded, and economic valuations are economically qualified and analytically founded.[42] Although he gives greater prominence than Blomberg does to the role of analytic practices in the acquisition of normative insights, Olthuis's approach raises a similar issue: What is specifically ethical or aesthetic or economic about ethical evaluations, aesthetic judgments, or economic valuations? To evaluate a deed as unethical is simply to identify it as not responding properly to an ethical norm. The evaluator does not thereby engage in typically ethical practices but rather carries out an analytic action within or with regard to an ethical situation.

To say this, however, would strike Olthuis in 1969 as collapsing practical judgments into theoretical judgments: like Blomberg, he tends to equate "opened" analytic practices with theoretical ones. Indeed, he contrasts pre-theoretical judgments such as a parent's advice to a child or a person's judging something as a good buy – which would be "ethically and economically qualified judgments uttered in respectively ethical and economic situations" – with the theoretical judgments of an ethicist about the ethical aspect or an economist about buying habits – which would be "scientific (analytically qualified) judgments."[43] In resisting the traditional privileging of theoretical thought, also in Dooyeweerd's work, Olthuis, like Blomberg, tries to turn what are plainly analytic matters into nonanalytically qualified practices.[44]

How then, should one modally characterize the norm-related insights that arise in various differentiated types of practices and institutions? If they are not economic when they arise in economically qualified transactions and businesses and are not aesthetic when they occur in aesthetically qualified art practices, what are they? My hypothesis, in agreement with Dirk Vollenhoven and Hendrik Hart, is that they are all analytic or logical – not theoretical, but nonetheless the attainments of ordinary analytic/logical practices in which we make distinctions, identify matters, and come to understand connections. We can label the entire constellation of such practices as *thinking* or *thought*, or as *analytic knowing*, to use a term suggested by Vollenhoven's *Isagôgè Philosophiae* and found in Hart's syllabus.[45] This is not to propose that thinking or analytic knowing is the only way in which we (come to) know the norms or, in my own terminology, the societal principles that pertain to economic, aesthetic, and other types of practices and institutions. But it is to propose that, insofar as the knowing in question is a matter of reflective awareness, it typically occurs in our thinking about our practices and institutions and our trying to sort out in thought what makes for better and worse ways to conduct business, make art, and the like. Moreover, as both Blomberg and Hart suggest, such norm-related thinking ordinarily occurs *within* the relevant practices and institutions, as what Hart calls "practical thought."

So far as I can tell, Blomberg equates opened-up analytic knowing with theoretical thought. Hence, in rightly trying to relativize the role of theoretical thought in human life and to remove it from the pedestal to which the Greek philosophical tradition raised it, he cannot do justice to the role of ordinary thinking – analytic knowing – within social life. For he also tends to equate all nontheoretical thought with analytic functioning *in its closed condition*. Because norm-related insight requires a certain openness to possibilities and implications, and because Blomberg does not want to make theoretical thought the pivotal source of such openness, he posits modally distinctive ways of distantial knowing. It would be simpler, and more plausible too, to say instead that in the ongoing conduct of life, people ordinarily come to norm-related insights by way of practical analytic knowing, by coming to know in a practically analytic way what makes for better and worse practices and institutions.

5. MEDIATED EXPERIENCE

This approach allows me to address a second worry I have about Blomberg's account. A side effect to his emphasis on distantial knowing is that concrete experience or everyday knowledge comes across as "naïve" in a problematic way: it seems to be reduced to an immediacy that is bereft of normative insight. Indeed, Blomberg regards all of "naïve experience" or "concrete experience" – to which, presumably, nontheoretical thought belongs – as "coterminous with all modes of experience in their closed dimensions." That's why he needs to find, in addition to theoretical thought, other ways of knowing that can open up concrete experience. "Disclosed (opened) functioning" is, he says, "a special, extraordinary way of acting into the world; it is the way that one acts when acting 'creatively,' when one is extending the boundaries of experience."[46] Not only does this construction – concrete experience on the one side, and norm-related distantial knowing on the other – seem to reinscribe the neoKantian fact/value divide that Blomberg, like Dooyeweerd, hopes to circumvent, but also it does an injustice to the normative awareness built into the most ordinary and even underdeveloped human experience. From an early age human beings are aware of normative expectations attached to the most basic activities: eating and drinking, walking and talking, playing and sleeping. Such activities have better and worse times and better and worse ways to do them. Even the small child becomes aware of this, always, of course, in a specific sociocultural setting.

We do not need distantial knowing any more than we need theoretical thought in order to have such normative awareness – it is intrinsic to quite ordinary experience. No experience, no matter how "concrete," is devoid of such normative awareness. All experience is culturally and societally mediated, caught up in the practices and institutions that make human life possible in better and worse ways. In that sense, no human experience is immediate in the way that Blomberg describes concrete experience. Nor does any experience simply "accept" the given in a passive way.[47]

Perhaps recognizing that the supposed naïveté of experience is problematic, together with other reasons, has led Blomberg to prefer the phrase "ways of wisdom" to "ways of knowing" in his more recent writings. Wisdom, as he describes it, is a matter of historically grounded "normative dispositions." We are accountable to "a multiplicity of norms ... in any given situation," and wisdom's greatest concern "is not with how we think or say we might act but how we indeed tend to act ... Wisdom's interest is in tendencies to act in normative ways ... not mainly in the ability to enunciate what the principles of proper action might be."[48] Here tendencies to act become more prominent than insights into norms.

That opens a doorway to understanding concrete experience as a continual "realization of value"[49] and not as an immediate and passive acceptance of the given. Although Blomberg continues to talk about an "integral curriculum" as one that begins from concrete experience and nurtures it, he now uses the term "primary experience" and describes this not in terms of immediacy and passivity but in terms of the "timed bodiliness" of all experience and the concrete, interrelated, and multifunctional wholes with which primary experience is "in touch," from a position of "engagement and trust."[50] So too, the curriculum aims not so much to *open experience* as to *nurture wisdom*. Schools, the later Blomberg says, should be primarily concerned not about what students (come to) know but about who they are and who they come to be: "schools are not to be in the 'knowledge business,' but in unrelenting pursuit of wisdom, the formation of character. Knowledge does not yield wisdom; information does not guarantee formation."[51] Despite my reservations about juxtaposing wisdom and knowledge like this, and about the potential moralism of an emphasis on character formation, I can see how such formulations release Blomberg from the fact/value divide apparently embedded in his earlier distinction between concrete experience and distantial knowing.

If my questions about the notion of distantial knowing are on the right track, however, and if Blomberg himself has significantly modified this notion in favour of a new emphasis on wisdom, then what is left of the original impetus to distinguish multiple ways of knowing? Is there anything worth retaining in this regard? I believe there is. In order to say what, however, I need to mention one more issue raised by Blomberg's 1978 dissertation. In Dooyeweerd's terminology, the issue has to do with relations among modal functions, human acts as modally qualified structures of individuality, and cultural realms or "radical types." In my own vocabulary, it has to do with relations among cultural practices and social institutions. Let me explain.

6. PRACTICES AND INSTITUTIONS

Blomberg's dissertation takes the cue for his innovative conception of distantial knowing from Seerveld's discussion of imagination as a distinct sort of knowledge, one that involves a distance-taking stance quite different from the distancing Gegenstand relation in theoretical thought. If one carefully examines Seerveld's examples for such "imaginative knowing," one notices that nearly all of them stem from the arts as a cultural realm or social institution. Hardly any of them come from ordinary nonartistic aesthetic activities such as playing a game or decorating one's home. His examples include a dramatist's exploring and presenting a family's social dynamics, a painting by Henri Matisse, a Puccini opera, literary works by Shakespeare, Mark Twain, and James Joyce, etc. This suggests that the distancing Seerveld has in mind – or at least what he illustrates in this context – is not the "aesthetic distance" one might experience on a befogged ship at sea.[52] He does not propose – or at least he does not illustrate – a distantial way of *aesthetic* knowing, as Blomberg suggests. Rather, Seerveld proposes and illustrates imaginative knowing as a peculiarly *artistic* way of knowing. It occurs when one is busy within a cultural realm – the arts – where, according to Seerveld's systematic aesthetics, the products are *multidimensional*, and they are *aesthetically qualified and techno-formatively founded*.

So Seerveld's discussion leaves wide open the question whether anything that deserves the terms *knowing* and *knowledge* occurs in ordinary aesthetic activities that are *not* caught up in the making and interpreting of art. To complete his paralleling of imagination with theoretical thought, Seerveld would have had to examine both the relation between what Vollenhoven calls scientific and nonscientific knowing,[53] on the one hand, and the relation between artistic and nonartistic aesthetic knowing, on the other – if indeed there is any nonartistic aesthetic knowing.

Not noticing this complication in how to read Seerveld's proposal, Blomberg simply equates artistic knowing with aesthetic knowing and then uses this equation as a launching pad for proposing other ways of distantial knowing. But that approach avoids the question whether *all* "opened-up" normative acts (or practices, in my vocabulary) are cognitive ones, or *only* those that are caught up in the internal workings of differentiated cultural realms or social institutions. Moreover, do practices as such contribute knowledge, or would this be better attributed to the institutions that frame practices? For example, should we say that a particular artist working on a particular artwork seeks and proffers (imaginative) knowledge? Or should we say instead that all art making and art interpretation take place within a social institution – the arts – and it is this institution, rather than any particular practice, that provides a specific type of knowledge and, correlatively, a specific type of truth – artistic truth?

As elaborated in Blomberg's dissertation, the conception of distantial knowing does not address such questions. Yet I think they are crucial if one wants to propose a holistic and pluralist epistemology where *knowing* and *knowledge* are not weasel words or signs of equivocation. These questions are also important if one wants to find robust nontheoretical counterparts to what Dooyeweerd calls theoretical thought, which occurs, for the most part, within the social-institutional framework of the sciences, the academy, and advanced research. By addressing such questions, perhaps one can retrieve the correct impetus to Blomberg's innovative conception of distantial knowing.

In the current chapter I have suggested that Blomberg's holistic and pluralist epistemology has both precursors among the first generation of reformational philosophers and counterparts in the second generation, including Hart, Olthuis, and Seerveld. So far as I can tell, however, no one else writing in the 1970s worked out such a detailed account of modally distinct ways of knowing and demonstrated its implications for curriculum and schooling. This is one of his most important contributions to the reformational movement and, more broadly, to the world of education. While acknowledging the importance of Blomberg's account, I have also identified issues in it concerning analytic knowing, ordinary experience, and social institutions. These are the issues I take up in the next chapter, aiming, like my friend and esteemed colleague Doug Blomberg, to continue the inner reformation of scholarship and schooling.[54]

4

Social Domains of Knowledge: Technology, Art, and Religion

Ever since the earliest writings of Herman Dooyeweerd and Dirk Vollenhoven, reformational philosophy has pointed toward a holistic and pluralist conception of knowledge. Whether in Dooyeweerd's distinction between theoretical and pre-theoretical thought or in Vollenhoven's distinction between analytic and supra-analytic knowing, reformational philosophy has suggested that there is more to knowledge than standard epistemologies recognize. Knowledge includes ways of knowing that both support and surpass what standard epistemologies capture.

As the previous chapter shows, this suggestion became the working hypothesis for Doug Blomberg's innovative attempt in the late 1970s to use reformational epistemology to spell out an "integral curriculum" for primary and secondary schooling.[1] Distinguishing eight ways of "distantial knowing" in addition to theoretical thought, Blomberg claimed that schools should promote all of them as ways both to open up concrete experience and to give expression to religious knowledge. The previous chapter argues that, despite the innovative potential of Blomberg's multiple ways of knowing, he has not convincingly distinguished nontheoretical distantial knowing from ordinary analytic knowing. This argument leaves unanswered, however, whether and how one should distinguish different types of knowledge within a unified conception of knowledge as a whole. Answering requires an ongoing critical retrieval of insights from Blomberg and other reformational thinkers.

1. COMPLEX RELATIONSHIP

To continue this critical retrieval, let me begin with a strong thesis indebted to Dooyeweerd, Vollenhoven, Blomberg, and Hendrik Hart: In its deepest meaning, knowledge is not a thing to possess but a relationship to inhabit. Moreover, this relationship is complex, involving those who know (human knowers),[2] the process whereby they come to know (the knowing), that with respect to which the process proceeds (the knowable), the result of this process (the known), the principle or principles that can guide the knowers toward the result, and a confirmation that they have followed the relevant principle(s) and achieved the sought-after result.[3] This complex relationship – among knower, knowing, knowable, known, guiding principle, and confirmation – is always inhabited in a spiritual direction, fundamentally in orientation either toward or away from the God who loves creation and who calls human beings to love in return. Knowledge as a whole, like the entirety of human life, always has a direction with respect to the call to love.[4]

At the same time, knowledge as a whole has different specific components in different social domains, such that one can specify different types of knowledge. My main hypothesis, then, is that the structure of knowledge as a whole – involving the complex relationship already stated – shows up in different domain-specific ways. Further, the structure of knowledge in each social domain, while distinct, is isomorphic both with the structure of knowledge in every other social domain and with the structure of knowledge as a whole. In other words, there are different *types* of knowledge, linked to different social domains, yet all of them are types of *knowledge*: all of them have the structure of knowledge, and all of them contribute to knowledge as a whole.[5]

Although, so far as I can tell, no other reformational thinker has spelled out the structure of knowledge in exactly this fashion, one can find all of these relata – knower, knowing, knowable, known, principle(s), confirmation – in the extended discussion of the structure of the analytic provided by Vollenhoven's 1948 *Hoofdlijnen der Logica* as well as in his shorter treatment of human knowing in *Isagôgè Philosophiae*. Vollenhoven, however, distinguishes two stages (*stadia*) in what I call knowing, namely (analytic) coming to know (*het leren kennen*) and actual (analytic) knowing (*het kennen*),[6] and he does not treat confirmation as a separate element but rather lumps it together with other results (such as concepts and judgments) under the headings of proof (*het bewijzen*) and demonstration (*het betogen*).[7] Moreover, although *Isagôgè Philosophiae* suggests that "coming to know differs modally according to the law spheres within which it takes place,"[8] it concentrates on analytic knowing and says little about types of knowing that are qualified in nonanalytic ways.

Standard epistemologies that define knowledge as *justified true belief* reflect some of the complex relationship I have described.[9] *Justified* indicates a certain sort of confirmation for a certain sort of result. *True* points to the principle relevant for seeking this result. And *belief* specifies the sort of result being sought. The standard definition does not capture all sides to the knowledge relationship, however: it omits or downplays the knower, the knowing, and the knowable. Further, as I hope to show, the standard definition pertains to only one sort of knowledge, and the definition treats this sort of knowledge not as a relationship to inhabit but as a thing to possess: either one has a justified true belief about something or one does not.

If "justified true belief" captures only part of just one sort of knowledge, then that poses a double challenge for a holistic and pluralist epistemology. First, one needs to spell out a sufficiently comprehensive conception of knowledge, in order to include what the standard definition captures but not reduce knowledge to justified true belief. Second, one must show how the standard definition, suitably revised and expanded, does indeed single out an important sort of knowledge within the entire knowledge relationship.[10] In what follows, I take initial steps toward addressing both challenges. First I try to characterize knowledge in general in such a way that one can regard different types of knowledge as indeed types of knowledge. Then I explore two types – technical and religious – at greater length.

2. KNOWLEDGE AND INSIGHT

The first challenge immediately poses a problem. It is extremely difficult to find sufficiently broad terms to encompass a wide diversity of types of knowledge, including scientific knowledge, artistic knowledge, and religious knowledge. K.J. Popma, for example, who has no difficulty distinguishing among various types of knowledge, seems to throw up his hands in defeat when asked about the nature of knowledge in general.[11] If beliefs are not the sought-after results for *all* of these types, then what are, and how can we discuss all of them in relation to the same term? After considerable reflection on this issue, I have settled on the term *insight*, which Blomberg's dissertation also often uses, as being sufficiently expansive to indicate what we seek to attain within different types of knowledge and in the knowledge relationship as a whole. The attainment of insight can occur in conjunction with different sorts of practices and results. Whether conducting a scientific experiment, making or interpreting an artwork, or participating in worship, for example, what knowers seek within these practices is insight into that which can be known, into the knowable.[12]

Must the insight a knower seeks be accompanied by a belief in order to be known? No, not necessarily. My performance of a piece of vocal music may yield an insight into how best to sing it on a particular occasion without yielding any beliefs in this regard. Such insights regularly occur during musical performance, and they rarely receive linguistic articulation. It makes sense to say one knows such performance-connected insights, even when they are not accompanied by beliefs and are not propositional. Conversely, beliefs, which typically either receive or can receive linguistic articulation and can have propositional content, also convey insights. To come to the belief that it is seventy degrees Fahrenheit outside is to come to an insight into weather conditions today. The fact that one can arrive at such a belief very quickly, without much discussion or thought, is not a reason to deny its status as a known insight, no more than the speed with which singers adjust their voices to handle difficult passages in performance is a reason to deny that their prelingual awareness of the adjustment required is a known insight, closer perhaps to knowing-how than to knowing-that.

It would be a mistake, however, to think that knowledge as a whole is reducible to known results, whether propositional or not. For, as I claimed earlier, knowledge is a complex relationship in which the result – the known – is only one ingredient. Equally important are the knower, the knowing, the knowable, the guiding principle(s), and the confirmation. Moreover, attending to these other ingredients is crucial for establishing both the sort of insight sought and the type of knowledge involved.

Especially important are the practices whereby the knowers (come to) know and the principles that guide these practices. It makes a fundamental difference, for example, whether, within the social institution of the arts, a filmmaker seeks to imaginatively disclose the fraught atmosphere of an approaching hurricane, with all its foreboding threats to human life and the built environment, or, within the social institution of academic work, a scientist tries to discursively disclose the conditions and consequences of such a "weather event." The artist's insight will stem from artistic practices guided by the principle of imaginative cogency; the scientist's insight will stem from scientific practices guided by the principle of logical validity. The artist and the scientist might seek to know the same hurricane, but they seek two different types of knowledge: imaginative and discursive, respectively. Further, this affects what can count as confirmation in each case. Confirmation in the artistic case occurs when an audience or a public experiences the film as a cogent imaginative disclosure. In the scientific case, it occurs when the research findings are discursively justified as valid in either expert or public forums.

Note, however, that the distinction between these two sorts of practices and principles does not render them incomparable, such that only one and not the other could count as practices and principles of knowledge. Just as what both artistic and scientific knowing attain can be called insights, so too their distinctive practices can be called disclosive, and both sorts are guided by principles of validity, a principle of aesthetic validity in art and a principle of logical validity in science. Moreover, as I have suggested elsewhere, the confirmation in each case can be considered a form of authentication[13] – a form of testimony to the validity or soundness of the insight attained.

To the extent that art and science (in a broad sense that includes the humanities) provide distinct social-institutional frameworks for distinct types of knowledge, we should also be able to detect differences in how the knowable shows up in each. This is indeed the case. As I have argued elsewhere, the objects of scientific knowledge show up as virtualized entities "under a single aspect or within a scientifically interpreted domain," in a process of "predicative self-dis/closure."[14] In the arts, by contrast, the knowable offers itself primarily in the manner of aesthetic signs that present nuances of meaning via intrinsically nuanceful artistic practices and products.[15] Hence the difference between scientific and artistic knowledge is not simply one in a type of distancing on the part of the knower – between a theoretical Gegenstand relation (Dooyeweerd)[16] and an imaginative *Hineinlebenshaltung*,[17] for example. It is also a difference in how the knowable shows up in each case, whether in predicative self-dis/closure or in nuanceful self-presentation.

Following on this brief comparison between art and science, and assuming my thesis about knowledge as a complex relationship, we can propose that knowledge occurs when human beings (the knowers) engage in disclosive practices (the knowing) whereby they attain insight into themselves, others, and the world (the knowable). They attain such insight via various results, guided by principles of validity, and expecting this insight to be authenticated (confirmation). Moreover, this description applies to knowledge not only as a whole but also in its diverse types. Knowledge is a complex relationship involving the six relata I have mentioned.

But what indications do we have that there are types of knowledge beyond art and science? Do distinct types like what Blomberg's dissertation calls "ways of distantial knowing" occur within the framework of other social institutions? On a social ontology indebted to Dooyeweerd and Vollenhoven but informed by Seerveld's re-ordering of the modal scale,[18] one can expect up to seven distinct types of knowledge to surface in other social domains of knowledge, in addition to the arts and sciences, two of them qualified by pre-analytic functions (i.e., in technology and language), and five of them qualified by postanalytic functions (i.e., in civil-societal, economic, political, familial, and religious institutions).[19]

Of these, technology and religion have received the most attention from other philosophers as possible sites for distinct types of knowledge, in reflections on technical know-how as a form of knowing, for example, and in disputes about the cognitive status of religious beliefs. Although contemporary philosophical discussions of these topics often assume the (disputed) understanding of knowledge as justified true belief, it makes sense, when one tries to distinguish multiple types of knowledge, to start with technology and religion.

WORK AND TECHNOLOGY

Debates about the cognitive status of *technê* and its relation to *epistêmê* have a long history, beginning in ancient Greek and Hellenistic philosophy.[20] In a contemporary setting, however, we immediately face a prior question. Is technology (1) a social institution or is it (2) simply a region in society that crisscrosses all social institutions and provides their basis? In favour of the first hypothesis, for example, would be the fact that engineering is a very large professional field, and it is distinct from other professions and occupations. In favour of the second hypothesis would be the fact that tools, machinery, techniques, and other "forces of production" (and reproduction) are so pervasive in society, and this makes it hard to imagine a type of organization or pattern of interaction that would be simply technological and not already subsumed into other types of organization or interaction. Tools that fashion other tools (e.g., robotics) and programs that govern vast networks of information (e.g., artificial intelligence) are not exceptions, because they too are subsumed into nontechnological frameworks, primarily into economic ones. Perhaps not much turns on settling this question here. In any case, when I write of technology as a *social institution*, I do so with reservations about whether this label actually applies.

The term *technology* raises other questions as well. On one common understanding, it would refer to the *study* of know-how (*technê*), regardless of whether that study is scientific. On another understanding, *technology* would refer to the tools, machinery, and procedures used to make things or solve problems. Yet neither such study nor such instruments would count as a distinct type of knowledge: studying something amounts to a sort of analytic knowing, and instruments are not capable of primary knowing.[21] For reasons like these, *technology* can be a misleading term for know-how as a type of knowledge. I use it sparingly, preferring to use terms related to human work and labour instead.

Human work involves a complex relationship among more or less capable agents (the workers) who make or repair something (the product) from more or less suitable resources (the materials) in order to meet some need in a more or less satisfactory manner. This complex relationship has all the ingredients one would expect in a type of knowledge: knowers (workers) knowing (making/repairing) the known result (product) from the knowable (materials), under the guidance of a specific principle (serviceability to meet a need) and subject to confirmation (when the work and product indeed satisfy the need). Moreover, it is not difficult to see how working up materials in order to fashion a product or make a repair involves insight into the materials and their potentials, insight acquired through trial and error, imitation, or apprenticeship, that is of a different sort from both (artistic) imaginative disclosure and (scientific) discursive disclosure. It is hard to find the right term for such insight: "technical" sounds too specialized, and "artisanal," too precious. Perhaps we can call it *worked disclosure*, on the understanding that the disclosure occurs in the very process of working up materials to satisfy a need. Moreover, the materials lend themselves to this process as objects having "technical" potentials to become products that have "technical" qualifying functions.[22]

Here, however, it is important to distinguish insight gained *within* the process of working from insight gained *about* this process. When people use the term *technology* to refer to the study of *technê*, they usually have *insight about* in view. One acquires insight about working when one engages in analytic knowing and comes to reflective awareness of what working involves, how it is done, how to improve it, etc. But such insight is not the same as the insight one gains as an actual worker, when one acquires or exercises the requisite skills to work up the materials in order to satisfy some need. The insight one gains as a worker comes with *knowing how* to do something. The insight one gains as someone who studies work, by contrast, comes with *knowing that* something is what it is, in distinction from and in relation to other matters. Even though knowing how and knowing that are closely linked, and they rarely occur in complete isolation from each other, they belong to two distinct types of knowledge, the one technical and the other analytic.[23]

This implies, in turn, that these two sorts of insight also involve distinct sorts of normativity, namely, need-oriented serviceability and identity-oriented logical validity, respectively. Too many philosophical discussions of work and technology approach them as if they were "simply" instrumental and hence not subject to normative evaluation and critique. This approach lends support to the cynical position that all human interactions and relations come down to struggles for power and nothing more. Cynicism finds support in the purported value-neutrality of work and technology because human power is rooted in the ability to make and repair, to shape and reshape. It would be better to recognize that human power is just as normatively laden as work and technology are. If work does not satisfy the needs it is intended to meet, and if the exercise of power does not contribute to human flourishing and the interlinked flourishing of other creatures, then they are normatively deficient and deserve to be challenged and changed.

4. RELIGION AND BELIEF

In contrast with how many philosophers understand technology, they seldom view religion as normatively neutral. Rather, they tend to regard it as normatively overwrought, in a way that endangers rationality and human autonomy. One can trace this attitude back to Greek philosophy, as illustrated in the critique of the gods and their "morality" offered by Plato's *Republic*. As a result, philosophical debates about the cognitive status of religion often revolve around the rationality or irrationality of religious beliefs. By making this issue of rationality central, the debates already assume that a capacity to embody or yield justified or warranted true beliefs would be the key to religion as a type of knowledge.

Rejecting this assumption, and understanding knowledge as a complex relationship, I would ask instead whether religion offers its own sort of insight and, if so, what sort of insight it offers. By *religion* I mean a distinct social institution characterized by organized worship and faith.[24] As I explain elsewhere, the dominant practices within this institution include telling or retelling the stories of faith and enacting or reenacting the rituals of worship.[25] Although propositional beliefs and discursive arguments are part of religion, as they are part of political, economic, and other social institutions, they are not the keys to religion as a social domain of knowledge. Instead, their meaning and role within religion depends on a different type of knowledge.

Religious knowing occurs within and via the practices of faith and worship, especially story-telling and ritual enactment. Faith-oriented worshippers[26] undertake these practices with respect to what ultimately sustains them, which many worshippers name "God."[27] In this process, "God" is disclosed as the ultimate source of their sustenance, disclosed in the very stories of faith and rituals of worship. As a result of such disclosure, their lives and the world they inhabit can have ultimate meaning or can receive this anew. Such meaning belongs to the insight that religion embodies and offers, under the guidance of faith as hopeful trust, an insight confirmed as valid when worshippers live it out as they interact with others amid the practices and institutions of their society.

In other words, religious knowledge is a complex relationship involving religious knowers (faith-oriented worshippers) who come to know (faithfully worship) the knowable ("God"), with a known result (ultimate meaning) that emerges under the guidance of the principle of hopeful trust and receives confirmation in lives of faith. Admittedly, calling "God" the knowable object of such knowledge seems peculiar. "God" is no ordinary object, and "God" certainly seems dramatically different from such knowable objects as the materials of worked disclosure, the doubled aesthetic signs of artistic disclosure, and the virtualized entities of scientific disclosure. It is precisely this peculiarity that renders problematic any attempt to reduce religious knowledge to religious beliefs, instead of subsuming religious beliefs into worshipful disclosure.

To get at this, let me take up a pathbreaking discussion of the relation between faith and reason in Hendrik Hart's 1983 essay "The Articulation of Belief." Published in the volume from a 1981 conference held at the Institute for Christian Studies in Toronto, this essay crystallizes the holistic epistemology in Hart's *Draft Syllabus*[28] and points it toward the integral ontology proposed in his *Understanding Our World*.[29] Hart argues that both faith ("commitment," in his vocabulary) and reason ("rationality") are dimensions of knowledge as a whole. Both dimensions are rooted in spirituality ("religion," in Hart's vocabulary), and they are interdependent in such a way that reason (rationality) can never be ultimate, but faith (commitment) can: "I will argue that rationality must be rooted in commitment and directed by a commitment outside of rationality. Faith gives reason the ultimate word on what is ultimately true."[30]

Although I have objected on various occasions to the implications of this argument,[31] many of the moves Hart makes in "The Articulation of Belief" have inspired my own account of religious knowledge. Like Hart, I distinguish analytic knowledge from other types of knowledge, and I regard this type as conceptual, propositional, inferential, and discursive. I agree that what Hart means by *rationality* – i.e., analytic knowing or knowing *that* – "is a dimension of all knowing, but not all knowing is rationally dominated."[32] I would put this somewhat differently, however, both because I focus on practices and institutions within social domains of knowledge (and not on modal functions), and because I think there are types of knowledge (e.g., technical knowledge and artistic knowledge) whose qualifying functions are pre-analytic, such that the role of analytic knowing in these types is different from the role it plays in types of knowledge whose qualifying functions are postanalytic. To say that not all knowing is rationally dominated is simply to say that knowledge as a whole encompasses more than analytic knowledge, and it includes types of knowledge qualified by nonanalytic functions.

So too, I agree that religious knowing – "fiduciary knowing," in Hart's terms – belongs to a distinct type of knowledge that is characterized, for example, by "trusting ... accepting, and relying." It, too, is a dimension of all knowing.[33] Again, I would state this point a bit differently, since for me religious knowledge, although led by the practices of faithful worship, is a multi-dimensional type rather than a modal function. So I would say religious knowledge is a distinct and legitimate sort of knowledge that belongs to and contributes to knowledge as a whole.

Despite these areas of agreement, however, Hart and I part ways over the objects of these distinct types of knowledge (i.e., the knowable), the nature of the interrelation between both types, and the role of beliefs in each. Let me discuss the objects first.

4.1 Objects of Religious Knowledge

For Hart, the objects of analytic knowing – of what he characterizes as conceptual and propositional understanding – are general or universal matters that have the status of structure or order. "Rational knowing is our *understanding* of structures, our grasp of general patterns, our insight into laws, kinds and properties," he writes. It is how "we grasp the order or structure of reality (nature of things) either in terms of that order (mostly in theory) or in relation to our ordinary world of concrete things, events and relations (mostly in everyday affairs)."[34] Because this purported connection between analytic knowing and universal structure or order is a hard link, Hart appears to preclude rational grasps of either individual matters as such or the origin of order (i.e., God, in his account).[35]

Correlatively, the objects of religious knowledge – of "fiduciary knowing" or faith as "commitment-dominated knowing"[36] – seem underdetermined in Hart's account. For example, taking *belief* as an element of faith and not an element of reason (i.e., as not inherently propositional), Hart is happy to include propositions among the objects of faith – as what one can believe – but he refuses to include nonpropositional objects of faith among the objects of analytic knowing: "I distinguish sharply between understanding a proposition (primarily a rational matter) and believing a proposition (primarily a fiduciary matter) ... A belief need not be a believed proposition, whereas a proposition must always be understood. A proposition *is* no more than an understanding, i.e., a conceptual or intellectual grasping."[37] And a little later he writes that "because commitment is itself not a function of rationality, the content [of commitment] can never be fully stated in a proposition, nor can it be adequately defined propositionally."[38]

When Hart does specify the objects of faith, he usually does so in terms of that which is *ultimate* – the "ultimate basis" for even the most basic of propositions, for example, or "the ultimate" that belief "grasps," or the "ultimate foundation" that we need to grasp in faith – something "outside of reason and propositions, on which we can ground our rationality and our propositions."[39] This leads Hart to describe faith as an ultimate grasp of the ultimate that provides the ultimate ground for rationality: "What we need [for rationality] is an ultimate grasp of an ultimate ground or foundation. The human function in which we reach out ultimately to what is ultimate is the trusting function of faith or commitment. Faith grasps the foundation of ultimate certitude."[40] Moreover, the statements in which we articulate this grasp are not propositional, according to Hart. They are confessions of "what has become known in faith and consequently stated in creedal beliefs"[41] – and, as we saw, Hart regards creedal beliefs as not inherently propositional.[42]

Strangely, however, all this talk of "grasping" the ultimate and of having an "ultimate grasp" sounds very conceptual and propositional. I say "strangely" because Hart does not think God can be an object of analysis (whereas I do think this), yet I do not think *grasping* is the right way to characterize our religious knowing. On the one hand, if, as I have suggested, the "object" of faith is what ultimately sustains us, and if religious knowing consists in faithfully worshipping this "object" and thereby having the ultimate meaning of our lives disclosed, then this "object" cannot be one we "grasp" in our religious knowing. On the other hand, if God and ultimate meaning are indeed disclosed in faithful worship, it would seem very odd for what worship discloses to lie beyond our analytic knowing. How could the knowable object and the known insight of religious knowledge address us in the fullness of our knowledge if they did not address us in the analytic dimension? By characterizing the object of "fiduciary knowing" as something ultimate to be grasped in faith, while declaring this object beyond the reach of conceptual/propositional understanding, Hart turns it into an inscrutable mystery: "Faith statements point to mysteries beyond our finite knowledge."[43] This suggests either that fiduciary knowing, as he describes it, is not really part of human knowledge as a whole or that God does not get disclosed to any type of knowledge other than faith – and certainly not to reason.

4.2 Interrelation of Analytic and Religious Knowledge

Hart tries to avoid the horns of this dilemma, however. Rather than concede either that fiduciary knowing is not knowledge or that God's self-revelation is limited to fiduciary knowing, he argues that faith and reason are linked in the articulation of belief. The argument proceeds by distinguishing two different senses in which faith or reason can have priority in relation to the other: either one can be "founded on" (or "based on") the other, or it can be "rooted in" the other.

In the background to this distinction lies Dooyeweerd's distinguishing between the foundational (retrocipatory) and the transcendental (anticipatory) directions of time and of the intermodal order in *A New Critique of Theoretical Thought*.[44] Hart's *Draft Syllabus* discusses this under the heading "Foundational Structure and Transcendental Direction as Dimensions of Time."[45] In *Understanding Our World*, he considers it under the heading "Temporal Direction" and says: "Time has an anticipatory qualifying direction as well as a retrocipatory founding direction," such that one can distinguish between "the founding and directing orders of time."[46] So the phrase *founded/based on* in "The Articulation of Belief" appears to mean something like "presupposing x in the ontological order of functions." *Rooted in* appears to mean "receiving its ultimate meaning from." Because faith or commitment is ontologically "later" than reason or rationality – indeed, because it is the terminal mode of functioning in the transcendental or anticipatory direction of time, according to Dooyeweerd and Hart – faith can never be *rooted in* reason (i.e., faith cannot receive its ultimate meaning from reason), but faith is always *based on* reason (i.e., fiduciary functioning ontologically presupposes analytic functioning, and many other modes of functioning, of course). Likewise, because reason or rationality is ontologically "earlier" than faith or commitment, and because faith is always latest in the order of functioning, reason can never be *based on* faith, but it is always *rooted in* faith.[47]

Accordingly, Hart explains the relationship "between the confessed content of faith (creedal beliefs) and the conceived content of rationality (propositions)" as one in which creedal beliefs are based on propositions but are not propositional, and propositions are rooted in creedal beliefs but are not beliefs, strictly speaking: "*all* beliefs, whether propositional (of conceived order) or creedal (of the grasped ultimate) are still beliefs, and as such matters of trust and not matters of rationality. Functionally speaking, all beliefs as beliefs have an ultimate foundation in commitment to the ultimate." At the same time, however, "all our beliefs do have a basis in propositions, i.e., in our understanding of the nature of things ... For this reason, we can say propositional beliefs are basic to our faith."[48] Hence the articulation of belief involves a two-way process: rooting propositional "beliefs" in creedal or confessional beliefs, on the one hand, and basing creedal or confessional beliefs on believed propositions, on the other. We can articulate our confessional beliefs in true statements, but as "confessed statements" these are "not genuine propositions." And we can genuinely believe the propositions we assert, but such believing "is not itself an act of rationality such as inference would be."[49]

If I were to translate Hart's explanation into my own vocabulary, it would go something like this. Analytic knowing and religious knowing give priority to different sorts of practices: predication and argument, in the case of analytic knowing, and faith-story-telling and liturgy, in the case of religious knowing.[50] Correlatively, the results gained in each also have a distinctive character: propositional claims in the one, and ultimate meaning in the other. Moreover, for those who practice a religion, the ultimate meaning disclosed in their faithful worship certainly will encompass the propositional claims they make throughout their lives, just as propositional claims will support their practices of worship.

Yet I see no reason to treat the beliefs of religion as nonpropositional, no more than I think that "God" or any other "ultimate" must somehow lie beyond the reach of analytic knowing. It suffices, in my view, to insist that analytic knowledge is only one sort of knowledge, with its own characteristic practices and its own sort of insight, and to recognize that analytic knowledge never occurs in complete isolation from religious knowing. Yet the same holds in the other direction as well: religious knowledge, too, is only one sort, and it is never completely detached from analytic knowing.

In fact, I find many discussions of the relation between faith and reason (or commitment and rationality, in Hart's preferred terms) somewhat contrived. The diverse practices of knowing do not occur in airtight compartments. Nor do the knowable objects about which we seek various types of insight come with neat labels classifying them as "religiously knowable but not analytically knowable," for example, or "object of imaginative disclosure – off limits to scientific discourse." Although the fact that distinct social institutions help organize knowledge might create illusions of such compartmentalization, careful study of any social institution should suffice to dispel these illusions. So, for example, the predominance of practices of faithful worship in religion as a social institution does not mean that practices of work, imagination, and discourse do not also have rightful roles in a religious context or that the social institutions of technology, art, and science do not or ought not contribute to the practices of faithful worship. In contemporary society, worship unavoidably draws upon the latest technologies, incorporates various forms of art making and art interpretation, and both responds to and relies upon the academic enterprise – most notably, but by no means exclusively, in the areas of theology and religious studies. It would be nonsense to picture worshippers as unskilled or unimaginative or discursively inarticulate simply because the weight of religion as a social institution falls on the practices of faithful worship. Indeed, worship itself involves its own aptitudes, imagination, and discourse, such that the practices of worship can be better or worse in each of these regards.

Specifically, it is crucial not to pit worship against discourse or religion against science, as if they were somehow intrinsically at odds. Unavoidably, albeit inadvertently, Hart's account of the relationship between commitment and rationality, specifically between creedal beliefs and believed propositions, does exactly that. He tries to create a proposition-free space within religion (i.e., creedal beliefs) where something like analytic knowing can occur (*grasping* the ultimate) but without incurring the justificatory expectations and obligations that normally attach to our making propositional claims.[51] At the same time, by assigning ultimacy to both the object and the insight of fiduciary knowing, Hart puts religion (faith or commitment, in his terms) in the position of always already trumping the deliverances of reason (rationality). That is how he ends up with (creedal) beliefs that are not propositional and (believed) propositions that are neither justified nor justifiable.

4.3 Beliefs

Contra Hart, I would say that creedal beliefs are no less propositional than any other beliefs. Beliefs arise in the ordinary course of life as articulable insights we rely on in practice. Often we do not need to spell them out in language, but when pressed by others, or when problems arise, we usually can and often do give them linguistic articulation. As soon as they are linguistically articulated, their content becomes available in our speech acts and can acquire propositional form.[52] So, although unarticulated beliefs need not be propositional, in principle, articulated beliefs are propositional – i.e., they can be asserted, challenged, and linguistically revised in ways that involve both reference and predication and that can yield propositions of the form *x is y*. Hence, for example, there is no structural difference between the linguistically articulated belief "God is love" and the linguistically articulated belief "The water is warm (enough)" – and both could occur, and be articulated, in exactly the same Christian worship setting, say, when preparing the water to baptize an infant and then baptizing the child. Both beliefs can be relied on, asserted, challenged, restated, or denied. The first belief might have greater overall significance in a worship setting, for it summarizes something crucial about the primary object of worship, but it is no less propositional than the belief about the water, which has its own importance, especially for the primary celebrants.

Moreover, the practices of religion are just as dependent on propositional beliefs as are the practices in many other social institutions, it seems to me. In a scriptural religion, for example, where certain sacred writings are canonical, telling and retelling the stories of faith will depend on a vast array of articulable beliefs about what the scriptural texts say, how they are interrelated, and how they are best interpreted. Although many of these beliefs might be more implicit than explicit among ordinary worshippers, that does not mean the beliefs are somehow nonpropositional, nor does it lessen the importance of their supportive role.

Yet it is crucial – and this is one of Hart's main concerns – that we neither reduce religious knowledge to propositional beliefs or to other results of analytic knowing nor make them the key to religious knowledge, even though they are part of religious knowledge. There are three reasons for saying this. First, analytic knowledge involves much more than its results (beliefs, assertions, propositions, and the like). It also involves those who know analytically ("thinkers"), their practices of knowing (predication and argument), whatever is analytically knowable, the principle of logical validity, and the process of justifying beliefs and the like. Hence, to provide a fuller picture of how analytic knowledge interrelates with religious knowledge, one would need to discuss much more than beliefs and propositions.

Second, religious knowledge, although it finds support in propositional beliefs, is not itself primarily propositional. It primarily involves, as I have said, a process of faithfully worshipping "God" and finding ultimate meaning in this process. The linguistic articulations and propositional claims that occur during this process can help it along, but they cannot set the tone for the process as such. If they did, it would quickly become "academic" rather than "worshipful." In Hartian language, religious knowledge is fiducially, not analytically, qualified.

Third, religious knowledge gives an unusual twist to analytic results, for what is religiously knowable stretches the limits of what is analytically knowable. As I have argued elsewhere,[53] that which is analytically knowable must present itself in the manner of predicative self-disclosure, such that how it is available for reference and predication aligns with other ways in which it is available for human practice. But the primary "object" of religious knowing – "God" – as all-sustaining, always exceeds the manner of predicative self-disclosure and thereby stretches what can be predicated and what can be analytically known. Hence garden-variety beliefs formed in everyday experience seem never fully to satisfy as supports for religious knowledge. The reason for this, however, is not that "God" cannot be known analytically but that the "God" to be known religiously stretches the limits of what analytic practices can accomplish. If "God" is a mystery, it is not because "God" is analytically unknowable but because "God" overflows the limits of distinct types of knowledge, in an abundance of self-disclosure that pushes thought, and not only thought, beyond its comfort zones.

5. CONCLUSION

The upshot to my argument about religious knowledge is this: Although both the object and the characteristic practices of religious knowledge serve to distinguish it from analytic knowledge, "God" does not lie beyond what we can analytically know, nor do the practices of worship float free from analytic practices. Rather, religious and analytic practices are interlinked, as are the religious meaning and propositional beliefs in which they result. Hence it would be better to describe religious knowledge not as nonpropositional but as post-propositional: it goes beyond analytic knowing by going through it.

Technology and art, by contrast, involve pre-propositional types of knowledge. In principle, the insights that technology and art offer, being attained via worked and imaginative disclosure, respectively, do not require linguistic articulation and propositional claims in order to become available and to play a role in human life. Saying this does not diminish the importance of (linguistic) "art talk"[54] or of (analytic) study, but it does indicate an order of priority: all the talk in the world about art cannot substitute for the imaginative insights art offers, and no amount of studying will attain the know-how that comes with actually working up materials into products.

Because I emphasize practices and institutions and employ a Seerveldian modal order, my account of knowledge poses new puzzles in areas either settled or ignored by Dooyeweerd, Vollenhoven, and their colleagues. Some of these puzzles pertain to the status of sensory, felt, and "bodily" knowledge.[55] Although, according to van Woudenberg, Dooyeweerd and Vollenhoven allow for sensory and felt knowledge, they do not think there is any knowledge qualified biotically or pre-biotically.[56] If, however, one recognizes sensory and felt knowledge, which is pre-analytic and thereby pre-propositional, why should one not also allow for "bodily" knowledge?

Another puzzle concerns the relation between linguistic knowledge and propositional knowledge. This was not a puzzle for Dooyeweerd and Vollenhoven: they regarded lingual functions as postanalytic and thereby post-propositional. If, however, one considers the primary practices of language to be pre-analytic and regards analytic knowing (thought) as significantly dependent on linguistic knowing, then one needs to account for linguistic knowledge as being significantly pre-propositional, with all of the complications this implies for both epistemology and logic. Like the topic of "bodily" knowledge, pre-propositional linguistic knowledge poses issues not addressed by the founders of reformational epistemology. These puzzles await later discussions.[57]

For now, I hope to have indicated how my opening thesis can be borne out by further reflection. Knowledge is a complex relationship to inhabit, and it takes on distinct contours within different social domains. In addition to the domains I have discussed – technology and religion in some detail and, more briefly, art and science – one can project language as another social domain of pre-propositional knowledge, alongside technology and art. One can also project civil-societal, economic, political, and familial domains that, like religion, would be social domains of post-propositional knowledge. If one could show that each of these domains involves distinctive practices, objects, results, principles, and confirmations of knowledge, or if one could show why one or another cannot count as a social domain of knowledge, then the reformational promise of a holistic and pluralist epistemology would indeed be fulfilled.[58]

5

Transformational Social Critique and a Politics of Hope

Holistic pluralism concerning knowledge, as proposed in the previous two chapters, has both sociopolitical implications and metaphilosophical underpinnings. It not only implies a critique of contemporary society, where knowledge is often limited to science and rational discourse, but also relies on a specific vision of how philosophy should contribute to social transformation. The current chapter and the next, which stem from an online book symposium about *Religion, Truth, and Social Transformation*,[1] explore such sociopolitical implications (chapter 5) and articulate my underlying vision of philosophy in society (chapter 6).

The current chapter has two sections. The first addresses questions about social critique raised by Jonathan Chaplin's comments on chapters 12 and 13 in *Religion, Truth, and Social Transformation*. The second section takes up the primarily political questions raised by Clinton Stockwell, Ruthanne Crapo, Ben Fulman, Michael DeMoor, and Farshid Baghai on chapters 11, 12, 13, 15, and the book's epilogue, respectively.

I. TRANSFORMATIONAL SOCIAL CRITIQUE

Jonathan Chaplin is the world's top expert on Herman Dooyeweerd's social philosophy.[2] He is also a former colleague at ICS and a leading social theorist in the reformational tradition. To have him comment on not just one but two of the chapters in *Religion, Truth, and Social Transformation* is both an honour and a stimulus to further reflection. Consequently, I devote this entire section to his astute readings.

1.1 Public Justice and Prophetic Religion

Chaplin's commentary on the essay "Religion in Public" (chapter 12) raises two sets of illuminating questions, the first about the relation between religion and the state, and the second about religion and the public sphere.[3] His questions about the religion/state relation have to do with the kind of authority religious spokespersons can legitimately claim when they address the state in public. Chaplin asks how religion's political utopian dimension should be publicly expressed, and whether such expression would be anything more than a critique of the state's current operations.

For me, this utopian dimension amounts to a future-oriented vision of society as a whole. Certainly it has a direct bearing on religiously motivated critiques of current state operations, but it goes beyond such critiques. The Rev Dr Martin Luther King Jr's "I Have a Dream" speech in 1963 is a good example. Calling for constitutionally anchored and legislatively secured civil rights for all African Americans, Dr King envisions a day of freedom, justice, and reconciliation that goes far beyond what can be accomplished by the state, thereby providing a larger rationale and deeper motivation for the civil rights struggle.

Clearly, to utter a clarion call in public, as Dr King did, religious spokespersons need to have firm personal convictions and the strong support of their religious communities. Yet I do not think such prophetic utterances to the state need to claim absolute truth or dogmatic certainty, nor should they. One reason for this, as Chaplin rightly indicates, is that, like all other claims made in public, these are fallible claims made by fallible human beings. At the same time, however, because religious claims have to do with what ultimately sustains us, their scope can make them seem absolute in a very specific sense: they seem to relativize every human attempt to provide sustenance, including those tied to the state and its operations. This scope is, if you will, a negative absolute: a continual reminder that what the state provides is not enough, and it will never be enough.

I do not think this dynamic between religion and political institutions is limited to modern religions. One can find it in the Jewish prophetic literature, which chapter 12 mentions, as well as in medieval and Reformation Christianity, as Chaplin points out. Nevertheless, I do think the development of the modern state, especially the modern constitutional democratic state, together with the concomitant pluralization and institutional specification of religion, has given contemporary religions "a new degree" of "critical freedom" toward the state.[4] This is a new *degree*, not a new *quality*: certain degrees of critical freedom pre-exist modernity. Unfortunately, contemporary religious communities often ignore or squander this new degree of critical freedom, and it readily degenerates into either indifference or abuse.

Chaplin also raises several issues about how religion should relate to the public sphere. Perhaps I can capture his concerns in two questions. First, if the state must adhere to a "nonreligious" conception of public justice, what does this imply for both religionists and secularists in the public sphere? I would allow religionists considerable leeway in both informal (e.g., media) and formal (e.g., parliaments) political public spheres, more or less along the lines Chaplin suggests in his example of a Christian Democratic party. Yet his example presupposes a sense of political propriety and constitutional self-restraint that I find sadly lacking, for example, among political parties in the United States. So I am not sure whether one can devise a prescription that suits all constitutional democracies. Similarly, I am wary about the implied juxtaposition between "religious" and "secularist" conceptions of public justice. Secularism is not a religion, in the sense that I define religion. An official invocation of a "secular worldview" would not do an injustice to religious communities unless it specifically tried to ban all religious discourse from the political public sphere. No doubt there are examples of such attempted injustice, but I'm not sure whether they are what Chaplin has in mind.

Second, what does it mean to say that the state's official conception of justice must be "publicly accessible"? As Chaplin notes, there are many rocky waters to navigate if one wants to address this question, and I cannot do that adequately here. Let me agree, however, that if one means by public accessibility both intelligibility and recognizability, then the public accessibility of religiously grounded claims is an empirical matter, as Chaplin's examples show. I also think that, in principle, religious claims need not be publicly unintelligible, and that Paul's proclamation at the Areopagus (Acts 17:16–34) does exemplify an effort at democratic communication (at least on the universal respect side; I'm not sure about the egalitarian reciprocity of Paul's speech). Yet, when it comes to *the state's* official conception of justice, we need something more robust. We need accessibility that is not just empirically determinable and is not reducible to intelligibility and recognizability. The conception of public justice enshrined in the state's constitution, for example, should be such that in principle everyone who lives within the state's jurisdiction can accept it.[5] Such acceptability is not simply an empirical matter. There is a matter of principle here. Contemporary attempts to enshrine religious conceptions of justice in the constitution or in constitutional decisions violate this principle.[6]

The wider background to Chaplin's questions about "Religion in Public" emerges in his commentary on chapter 13 ("Macrostructures and Societal Principles"),[7] which itself fills in the social-philosophical background to my account of religion in public. Chaplin raises many important questions about my proposed architectonic critique of contemporary Western society. Permit me to group them under three headings: the relation between macrostructures and differentiated social spheres, the historical character of societal principles, and the relation between divine calling and human response. In terms of the Kuyperian tradition of social thought, these headings pertain to sphere sovereignty, creational ordinances, and God's will for human life, respectively.

1.2 Differential Transformation

Under the first heading, Chaplin asks whether my account of macrostructural systems is overly deterministic and whether I pay too little attention to "highly variable 'differentiated spheres'" in contemporary society. Also, in a response to Chaplin's commentary, Bob Sweetman asks whether I regard the macrostructural organization of contemporary society as "normative," or whether I find the predominance of a proprietary economy and administrative state problematic.

Chaplin's response to Sweetman's question is exactly right: my concept of macrostructures is "primarily diagnostic and critical," aimed at identifying "large-scale societal distortions" of what in principle could have been – and could still become – a worthwhile historical achievement, namely, a properly differentiated and integrated society where principles of solidarity, resourcefulness, and justice are honoured and interconnected flourishing is promoted. I have tried to uncover structural distortions internal to each macrostructure and in their relations to each other. I have also argued that each macrostructure is normatively deficient, and that to address the normative deficiencies of one we need to address those of the others. What is required, then, is a large-scale change in society as a whole, a process I call *differential transformation*. So, no, I do not think the predominance of the proprietary economy and administrative state in contemporary Western society is normative. Yet I do consider it unavoidable, given the way history has unfolded. I also recognize that with such predominance come many developments that are worth maintaining, strengthening, or redirecting. Differential transformation is not the same as either resignation or revolt.

It is difficult to describe the predominance of economic and political systems without sounding like a determinist of some sort. For these systems are indeed massive, self-reinforcing, and tight knit. Yet it would make no sense to subject them to internal normative critique, as I do, if one did not think they can be normatively redirected by human beings who act in concert via protest movements, enlightened government regulations, and new ways of doing business, for example. Also, there would be little point in seeking out hidden potentials for normative redirection inside these systems (e.g., elements of a social economy and a social polity) if one thinks the proprietary economy and administrative state are completely closed systems. Perhaps the language I have borrowed, via Habermas, from systems theory has a misleadingly deterministic ring to it. In any case, I agree with Chaplin that "democratic mobilizations can indeed effect structural changes." Yet I would still want to ask about the long-term trajectory of such changes: do they contribute, or can they contribute, for example, to the democratization of state structures, to a heightened pursuit of public justice, and to turning the dominant economy from turbo-capitalist exploitation toward postcapitalist resourcefulness and solidarity? Not all structural changes are equally effective or appropriate for the differential transformation we need.

This is the context within which I would want to pay more attention to what Chaplin calls "highly variable 'differentiated spheres.'" Here much work remains to be done, and I have barely begun to scratch the surface. The closest I have come to this work is in trying to think about the differences and interconnections among art, science, and religion as differentiated social domains of knowledge and truth. I have many unaddressed puzzles about relations between what I call civil society and what Dooyeweerd and Vollenhoven might have called ethical institutions of friendship, marriage, and family.[8] In addition, there are crucial sociological phenomena and categories of gender, race, class, and sexual orientation that barely register in traditional reformational social thought. I also wonder about the impact on all social institutions of an anti-institutional ethos among younger generations, reinforced, it seems, by their immersion in new social media. Any serious attempts to theorize the potential for what I have called "a democratic politics of global transformation"[9] would need to take these variegated and variable societal matters into account. Perhaps, however, my triaxial model of society, which distinguishes levels of social interaction (i.e., institutions, practices, and interpersonal relations) from both societal macrostructures and societal principles, can help organize such theoretical efforts and keep them honed toward questions of differential transformation.

1.3 Societal Principles

Chaplin's second group of questions about chapter 13 concerns my account of societal principles. He wonders how my challenging the ontological and unhistorical givenness of creational ordinances relates to Dooyeweerd's account of structural principles. He asks why I question Chaplin's own concept of "the created structure of human personhood." And he suggests that perhaps, despite my own claims to the contrary, insisting on the historical character of societal principles makes their content arbitrary after all. Chaplin is right to call attention to these issues: replacing creational ordinances with societal principles, and treating societal principles as both historical and eschatological, mark significant departures from the first generation of reformational social philosophy. Just how dramatic is this departure? Although (in addition to chapter 13) chapter 14 and the epilogue in *Religion, Truth, and Social Transformation* aim to indicate what the departure comes to, let me give this another try.

First, Dooyeweerd's "structural principles" are not what I have in mind with "societal principles." Whereas Dooyeweerd's "structural principles" are the principles of social structures such as the state and church, "societal principles" are more like what Dooyeweerd calls modal laws or the law-side of (logical and postlogical) modalities. Whereas Dooyeweerd regards modal laws as temporal but not historical, however, I regard societal principles as both historical and eschatological. Moreover, in the case of Dooyeweerd's structural principles, I am not convinced that he thinks these change via historical formation. Rather, what changes historically, for Dooyeweerd, is how these (invariant) structural principles "come to expression."

Second, whereas Dooyeweerd's philosophical anthropology is strongly anti-evolutionary, my own is not. I really do think that humankind evolved from nonhuman and prehuman forms of life, and that, increasingly, in the process of hominization, the creatures undergoing this process began to shape their own forms of social and cultural existence. We can say, as Chaplin suggests, that it has become characteristic of the creatures who became human that they "have the capacity of formative human agency." Yet I would add that they were themselves involved in the formation of that capacity. The concept of a "created structure of human personhood" seems to downplay or ignore this process of self-formation. If there is such a structure, it is one the creatures who became human created – or co-created – in the very process of becoming human.

Further, the development of personhood is a later stage in this process. As I suggest in chapter 13, it involves the development of legal frameworks within which people can be recognized as persons as well as ethical frameworks within which they can have and can exercise responsibility for their actions. Obviously, my approach raises unsettling questions about what humanness and personhood might mean in the future, as Chaplin indicates. Yet I do not think we can give adequate answers to such questions by simply postulating a created structure of human personhood.

Similarly unsettling questions arise because of my insistence on the historical character of societal principles. Chaplin asks, for example, how what solidarity means and requires today could have been unintelligible in a premodern world, and why, in my view, we do not know now what solidarity will mean and require in a hundred years. These are good questions, and I should clarify.

I think solidarity has become a prominent societal principle in the modern world, in conjunction with the development of a market economy, more democratic forms of government, and the emergence of a more fully fledged civil society. There are obvious precursors to this principle in the premodern world, and one can trace its emergence to prominence out of that world.[10] Yet I think premoderns would have had a hard time understanding the dramatically pluralistic tone and global reach that solidarity has now, and they would not have given it the prominence it has acquired. In that sense, what solidarity means and requires today would have been "unavailable and incomprehensible in a premodern world."[11]

So too, given current trends in economic globalization, environmental change, and (forced) immigration, I think we are just beginning to understand what societal principles such as solidarity, resourcefulness, and justice might mean and require in a hundred years. Can we really foresee what the world will be like then, and what it will mean then to show mutual recognition, to steward the earth's resources, and to pursue public justice? By "mean" in this context I do not intend a simple verbal definition but rather the socially textured implications of such principles for social life. We of course have some idea of what these principles will mean in one hundred years, but there is much we do not know, and much we are not in a sociohistorical position to know.

Accordingly, although there is continuity between contemporary societal principles and their historical precursors and their future meaning, this continuity unfolds historically: it involves change just as much as it involves continuity. This might be deeply unsatisfying for philosophers who wish to give real definitions, specifying necessary and sufficient conditions for what counts as, say, justice. Nonetheless, I believe it is the very character of historically mediated societal principles that they resist real definitions.

1.4 Call and Response

That brings me to the third group of questions, which concern the relation between divine call and human response. I have posited, with respect to justice, that God calls us to justice and gifts us with justice. Human beings respond to this gift and call as they work out what it means to flourish in a social context, and their responses become constitutive of what justice means and requires. Chaplin asks what content human beings respond to, and he suggests that it cannot simply be whatever content they pour in. I agree: it cannot be *simply* that. But it also cannot be devoid of what human beings contribute.

My point is that the content of societal principles such as justice and solidarity, which are societal and historical outworkings of God's call to love, *emerges in the ongoing dialogue between God and humankind*. God intends for human beings and all creation to flourish, and God calls us to live in this way. But God also responds to the responses we make to God's call, sometimes sounding the call in a new way, in a new incarnation. And human beings, in responding, also re-issue God's call, which re-sounds in their response. Their first posture may be one of "respondents," as Chaplin says, but that is not their only posture.

On this approach, human beings are responsible not only for how they respond to God's call but also for how that call re-sounds in their responses, responsible not only for their fidelity to societal principles but also, to a significant extent, for the content of the societal principles they try to honour. The upshot, I think, is not an arbitrariness of content but the urgency of a faithful response. That is why, as Chaplin notes, I characterize the pursuit of society-wide transformation in terms of "faithful disclosure." For, in the end, this pursuit is caught up in more or less faithful responses to a call to love that comes from God's own future, carrying, as it does, the promise of a new Earth.

2. TOWARD A NEW POLITICS

Whereas Chaplin's discussion of chapters 12 and 13 in *Religion, Truth, and Social Transformation* raises crucial conceptual issues in social critique, many of the other commentaries on Part Three and the epilogue pose important questions about political possibilities and implications, from Fulman's concerns about civil society to Stockwell and Crapo's reflections on cultural pluralism, Baghai's reservations about the politics of "patient hope," and DeMoor's issues concerning the politics of science. Let me take up each of these in turn.

2.1 Civil Society

Approaching chapter 13 from a different intellectual tradition than Jonathan Chaplin's, Ben Fulman sees here "the blueprints for the future of Critical Theory."[12] What he especially appreciates, in relation to the successive generations of Critical Theory (from Theodor Adorno through Rainer Forst, one could say), is my combining an emphasis on the transformative potential of civil society with a call for normative critique and redirection of economic and political systems. In this combination he sees the potential for both emancipatory theory and emancipatory praxis. Fulman wonders, however, how agencies in civil society (he mentions art in particular) can stand up to new "nationalistic spirits" that "suffocate any opposing voices," and how civil society can "withstand attacks" from the administrative state, or from the proprietary economy, for that matter.

I have tried to identify "systemic pressures" on the arts (and, more broadly, on civil society) in my book *Art in Public*, where I also tell the story of one arts organization – the Urban Institute for Contemporary Arts in Grand Rapids, Michigan – that has negotiated these pressures while promoting a social economy and democratic communication.[13] The story I tell there presupposes a setting where civil-societal organizations are relatively robust, where there is a mixed economy (i.e., the economy is not simply proprietary and not simply governmental and also not simply a combination of these two), and where, in at least a modest fashion, the state supports and protects agencies in civil society (e.g., through tax policies and copyright laws). Typically, countries driven by a nationalist spirit or under a dictatorial regime are not like that. Nevertheless, efforts in such countries to counter nationalism or dictatorship require proto-civil-societal agencies, for example, in the arts, education, and the media, where political resistance and new social visions can take shape. One could see this take place during the so-called Arab Spring, despite the repression that has followed within many countries in North Africa and the Middle East.

Perhaps the larger worry in Western countries is that too many agencies in civil society buy into the "objectives" of economic and political systems – on which, of course, they depend – and too many economic and political leaders fail to understand the normative roles of the civic sector and the public sphere in a life-giving society. That provides a larger background to the current Western "crisis in the humanities" and the degeneration of public debate into a bizarre brew of ideological attacks and celebrity politics. And yet; and yet ... I remain convinced that such tendencies are not irreversible; that people and institutions can change; and that educators, artists, and public figures – including religious leaders – can make a difference in how society is organized and in the direction society heads. Indeed, as Fulman demonstrates, and as Sweetman notes in his response to Fulman's commentary, the architectonic critique sketched in chapter 13 and painted more fully in other writings is not a merely theoretical exercise: it is praxis oriented. Further, because the critique is praxis oriented, ongoing work in social psychology is required – as Fulman indicates, and as Adorno and the Frankfurt School also understood.

2.2 Pluralism and Praxis

The commentaries by Clinton Stockwell and Ruthanne Crapo on chapters 11 ("Good Cities or Cities of the Good?") and 12 ("Religion in Public"), respectively, share this orientation toward praxis. Both of them emphasize the challenges of pursuing justice and solidarity in the context of radical religious and cultural pluralism. Compared with the time and setting in which reformational philosophy first emerged, these are new challenges – or newly visible challenges – and they call for significant revisions in social-philosophical categories and research programs.

I am not convinced, however, that, as Stockwell suggests, an interconnected and holistic "shalom vision for the world" means we should lessen our concern to protect institutional differentiation and to maintain "vestiges of modernism."[14] Interconnection presupposes differentiation, and holism needs to come to expression via differentiated integration. I retain this social-philosophical understanding from Dooyeweerd and Vollenhoven, and I am quite wary of any creeping eco-communitarian holism-bolism where, like Hegel's famous night when all cows are black,[15] all (people, institutions, creatures) become one.

Quite concretely, in modern differentiated societies and complex urban environments such as many readers of this book likely inhabit, efforts at institutional de-differentiation would have two results that no shalom vision could want: one kind of institution (whether religious, political, or economic – most likely economic, and most likely proprietary) would come to dominate the others, and one sociopolitical grouping would secure or reinforce its own hegemony. In other words, both institutional and cultural pluralism would suffer, at the price of both public injustice and a lack of intercultural solidarity. For me, then, the question to ask is not whether we should set aside or downplay modern differentiation. Rather, given modern differentiation, what would be the normatively appropriate way to transform it for the sake of interconnected flourishing – for the sake of shalom? As is obvious by now, my answer is what I call differential transformation.

Commenting eloquently on the experiences of her own highly diverse students, Ruthanne Crapo raises several questions about the intersections among spirituality, religion, and cultural pluralism.[16] She also suggests that cooperative efforts within the social economy of civil society might be the best way for her millennial students to either learn religious practices or work out the social and political implications of such practices. I suspect one reason why civil society feels like a safe space for younger people, even a "religious space," is that it is less highly structured and more informal than either traditional social institutions such as religion, family, and marriage or contemporary economic and political systems. Civil society is attractive to people who share an anti-institutional ethos. This ethos poses a challenge not only for traditional religions but also for established educational, political, and familial institutions.[17]

Here it is crucial, however, to sort out the differences and connections between genuine cultural pluralism and good ol'-fashioned individualism and consumerism. It is one thing for a student to say, for example, I am a Muslim immigrant woman protesting "gender injustice, Islamophobia, and institutionalized racism," and quite another to say, I think I'll try out some practices of mindfulness, yoga, and Ramadan fasting – they might give me more grit, align my chakras, and help out some poor people to boot. Without wishing to cast aspersions, I'd say the first of these probably involves a struggle over cultural identity; the second could very well be simply another consumerist pursuit of individual self-fulfillment.

If my hasty diagnosis is on the right track, then the challenge for the first student will be to find a sufficiently flexible sense of cultural identity. The challenge for the second student will be to find any sense of cultural identity at all. And the challenge for both students will be to reflect on the spiritual orientation that comes to expression in their searches for cultural identity, recognizing, for example, that even individualistic consumerism is a spiritually directed way of life.[18] If religious adherents support young people in such quests, then traditional religions will contribute to the development of genuine cultural pluralism and intercultural solidarity, and their houses of worship might, just might, become safe spaces, houses of refuge and renewal, where disenchanted young people experience, as Crapo says, "the joys, intimacy, and justice that religious communities ... ought to offer."

2.3 *Politics of Hope*

Farshid Baghai's commentary on the epilogue "Earth's Lament" raises two other sets of questions concerning the orientation of a transformational philosophy toward praxis.[19] One has to do with whether what I call "patient hope" for "God's future" compromises "our openness to the *singular* character of suffering." If I understand Baghai's concern correctly, it seems as if having an assurance that God will usher in a new Earth would make us complacent toward real suffering and toward those who really suffer. If everything will work out fine in the end, why bother with lending a voice to suffering and resisting the sources of suffering? Don't we need some sense of hopelessness to take suffering seriously?

These are profound questions, and I do not have ready answers. But let me make two comments. First, whatever the brief epilogue suggests, I would not equate having hope with having assurance. If you make a promise, I might hope you will keep it. I might even trust you to keep it. Yet I might not be assured you will keep it. Even though fellow religionists might disagree, that is how I understand and experience the promise of a new Earth. I hope this promise will be kept and, on my less desperate days, I even trust that it will be kept. But I do not have assurance about this, and, on my more desperate days, I do wonder whether we are fooling ourselves, whether, as Baghai worries, we simply block our philosophical ears with false consolations. Perhaps this unsettled mixture of hope and doubt helps explain why, in chapter 12, the book describes faith as "hopeful trust"[20] and not as assurance, confidence, or belief. God's future is promised; it is not assured.

My second comment concerns how this future would arrive. A new Earth, in which, as the psalmist says, justice and peace embrace, would not arrive *without* human effort. Yet it also would not arrive *because of* human effort. Perhaps this is where Baghai's "primary hopelessness" comes in. For, try as we might, human beings cannot rid the world of all sources of suffering, and yet we are called to keep trying. The patience of hope is to keep trying even though the object of hope – a new Earth – seems unachievable.

Baghai's other set of questions has to do with the relation between patient hope and politics. He is right that the epilogue says little about politics, although I would not agree that a concept of the political is completely absent. I mentioned earlier my call in *Social Philosophy after Adorno* for "a democratic politics of global transformation." Such a politics would aim at the long-term structural transformation and normative redirection of the three societal macrostructures that organize much of social life in Western countries and, arguably, in many other countries as well. What the epilogue calls "societal evil" largely nests in the mutually reinforcing dynamics within and across these macrostructures, as sustained by patterns of exploitation, domination, and boundless consumption. I think this calls for a new form of politics, one aimed at wresting economic control from the "one per cent" while building a global civil society and strengthening or establishing democratic forms of suprastate legislation and governance. Such a politics would not preclude or supersede existing forms of environmental activism, struggles for recognition, and fights for economic equality, to mention a few examples. It would, however, provide a larger context and rationale for such local, regional, and national political efforts. I do not spell any of this out in the epilogue, which began as a brief public address, but I think it is compatible with the social vision the epilogue sets forth.

Would this new form of politics be revolutionary? In one sense, yes: it would aim at the thorough transformation of society as a whole. In another sense, however, the proposed politics would not be revolutionary, for it would not pretend that overthrowing one class or institution or systemic complex would suffice. I do not deny that political revolutions might be required in countries controlled by dictatorial regimes or ruthless corporations – provided the conditions for revolution are in fact in place. Yet I do not think political revolutions are enough in our highly globalized world. To put this as a paradox: by themselves, political revolutions might not be sufficiently revolutionary.

2.4 *Science and Politics*

Michael DeMoor also asks about the politics implied by a transformational philosophy, specifically about the politics of science.[21] His questions arise in response to the essay "Science, Society, and Culture" (chapter 15) where, after criticizing Joseph Rouse's pragmatic and deflationary approach, I propose a robust conception of scientific truth as one social domain within a more comprehensive and multidimensional process of truth. What prompts DeMoor's questions is my call for the "*normative* rather than systemic" integration of science with society.[22] This leads to two sorts of questions. First, what would such normative integration look like, and would it lead to an overburdening of civil society? Second, how exactly should scientific knowledge and expertise "be integrated into the working of our various social institutions and practices," especially in the field of public policy? These are pertinent and perceptive questions, and I'd like to take a shot at addressing them.

When I first gave various versions of the lecture (in 2004–07) from which chapter 15 stems, I had not yet worked out the architectonic critique sketched in chapter 13. Nor had I written the long study on Dooyeweerd's conception of truth[23] that resulted in the essays reproduced as chapters 3 and 14 in *Religion, Truth, and Social Transformation*. The architectonic critique took shape in my subsequent work on the book *Art in Public*, which appeared in 2011. With the benefit of hindsight, I can say that the formulation in chapter 15 concerning the normative integration of science is incomplete. For there are two different but interlinked issues of integration here. One is the relation between normative and structural integration. The other is the relation between civil-societal and systemic integration.

In chapter 15 I did not intend to suggest that systemic integration is completely illegitimate and to be avoided. Rather, given the high degree of systemic integration that is already in effect, contemporary attempts "to open science for public discussion" must aim at normative integration, and for this "a proper conception of scientific truth is crucial."[24] My background understanding was that many of the sciences are already deeply embedded in our economic and political systems, and that public discussion of the sciences currently tends not to ask broadly normative questions but rather narrower questions about systemic integration – roughly, how can we better insure that the sciences "pay off" economically and advance the agenda of administrative states? Public discussion about the sciences, and about university-level research and education, needs to break out of this straitjacket.

What chapter 15 fails to say is that *systemic integration should also be normative*. In other words, how scientific research and applications feed into economic and political systems should help redirect these systems toward genuine resourcefulness and justice; they should not simply grease "the flywheels of turbocapitalism."[25] Conversely, the economic support and administrative regulation of science provided by these systems should encourage science's own normative redirection, toward a robust and life-giving pursuit of scientific truth. So the choice at this level does not lie between either normative or systemic integration, but rather between normatively deficient or normatively redirected systemic integration.

Similarly, with respect to civil society, it would be a mistake to think that a stronger integration of science with civil society would, in and of itself, lead to a genuine "democratization" of science. The simple reason for this is that civil society itself suffers from internal normative deficits, especially with respect to robust solidarity. So any attempt to strengthen the structural integration of science with civil society – for example, through new forms of education that raise public literacy in science or through not-for-profit centres of public deliberation about science – would also need to pursue a normative redirection of both science and civil society.

I am not sure what all of this means in practice, although I have tried elsewhere to offer a general vision of what I call social-ethical scholarship for the common good.[26] I definitely do not intend to "unduly burden civil-society institutions" or to "prevent political and economic actors and agencies from doing necessary work that only they can do," as DeMoor puts it. Yet I do think civil society should have a greater role in shaping the scientific enterprise than universities and governments have been ready to acknowledge, especially when it comes to the priorities of government-funded research and the social-ethical assumptions and implications of the latest scientific discoveries.

Conversely, I also think scientific expertise, when properly oriented toward the common good and not simply toward maintaining science for its own sake, needs to inform public deliberation to a greater extent than populist politicians of various stripes seem willing to allow. That would be my initial response to DeMoor's second question, about the integration of science into how various social institutions and practices work. I would be the last to affirm that only scientific experts have the authority to make assertoric truth claims in a public setting. This is the responsibility of all communicative actors in a society and especially all citizens in a democratic polity. Yet I also would want to affirm that, because of the gifts, training, and professional standing scientists have received, they have a special responsibility, and thereby a specific authority, to pursue, uphold, and disseminate scientific truth. So I would describe the relation between scientific expertise and public deliberation as one of "directed coresponsibility," a phrase I first developed to describe the relation between artists and their publics.[27]

At the same time, as I claimed in my "Living at the Crossroads" address, scientists have "an obligation to be trustworthy, accountable, and responsive in their work: trustworthy with respect to the tasks of learning, inquiry, and exploration, accountable for the significance and worth of their contributions, and responsive to the opportunities, issues, and contexts that deserve their attention. Although nonacademic institutions cannot prescribe what this means for any individual or group, socially responsible scholars will acknowledge the obligation to be trustworthy, accountable, and responsive, and they will constantly ask whether they are meeting it in their work."[28]

Accordingly, when there is public deliberation about, say, climate change or the causes of poverty or the long-range impact of genetically modifying plants and animals, we need to take seriously the theories and findings of scientific experts and not dismiss them as simply one set of opinions among others or as ideologically motivated from the get-go. But we also should not immunize them against serious public deliberation. I am not sure whether the current political climate in North America and the operations of our legislative assemblies permit such a nuanced weighing of matters, but they should. Perhaps livelier engagements between scientists and citizens in the informal spaces of civil society would encourage this. Our colleges and universities, to the extent that they remain "centres within civil society for dialogical learning, critical inquiry, and creative exploration,"[29] should take the lead in promoting such engagements.

In both of the ways this chapter details – both by calling for an architectonic critique of contemporary society and by supporting a democratic politics of global transformation – reformational philosophy itself aims to practice social-ethical scholarship for the common good. This means, in turn, that schools and research centres such as ICS and CPRSE where reformational philosophy is practiced also need to maintain or create proper spaces for public dialogue and debate between scholars and citizens. Such sector-crossing deliberation is vital for both social critique and a politics of hope.

6

Reformational Philosophy Revisited

If, as the previous chapter argues, contemporary reformational philosophy implies an architectonic critique of society and supports a politics of global transformation, then that raises questions about the nature and tasks of philosophy itself. Such metaphilosophical questions are the topic of the current chapter. Whereas the previous chapter focuses on Part Three (Social Transformation) in *Religion, Truth, and Social Transformation*, the current chapter responds primarily to commentaries on essays in Parts One and Two.[1] The first section, titled "Philosophy Art, and Religion," reflects on the essays about second-generation reformational philosophy in Part Two (Reforming Reason). The second section, titled "Dooyeweerd, Truth, and Faithful Criticism," takes up the remaining symposium contributions, ranging over the book's introduction, four chapters in Part One (Critical Retrieval), chapter 10 in Part Two, chapter 14 in Part Three, and the epilogue.

I. PHILOSOPHY, ART, AND RELIGION

The pioneering contributions of Hendrik Hart and Calvin Seerveld when I studied at ICS in the 1970s have shaped all of my work since then. I hold them in the highest esteem, both as scholars and as persons. That has not stopped me from sometimes disagreeing with them, however, or from taking their contributions in directions they might not have gone. So the essays on second-generation reformational philosophy in Part Two of *Religion, Truth, and Social Transformation* have particular significance, especially for my ongoing work in truth theory. At stake, for me, are the character and contemporary tasks of philosophy.

1.1 *Totality and Mystery*

My colleague Ron Kuipers raises questions concerning the philosophical character of discussions about "ultimate beliefs and conceptions of divinity."[2] Specifically, he wonders about my "seeming insistence that critical intellectual discussion" of such matters "must be or is always 'philosophical' in nature" – why couldn't it be theological or sociological, for example? I can quickly set readers at ease on this score. I do not think such discussions *must* be philosophical. My point in "God, Law, and Cosmos" (chapter 6) is more delimited. It has to do with what one can expect of such discussions *when they occur in a philosophical book written by a philosopher and when they do significant philosophical work*.

Perhaps Kuipers does not think one should have such expectations – he describes philosophical writing as "just another kind of writing, with its own virtues and vices." But if it is a kind of writing, and if it has its own virtues and vices, then one can at least ask how philosophical writing differs from other kinds of writing, and what its virtues and vices are. If one takes a position on such questions, one will have definite expectations about the sorts of discussions that occur in a philosophical book written by a philosopher and that do significant philosophical work.

Kuipers himself calls attention to the "totalitarian pretensions of philosophical discourse," and he shares Henk Hart's suspicions about them. Kuipers also shares Hart's desire to leave room for mystery, although he says we can experience mystery in language. But to describe philosophical discourse as having "totalitarian pretensions" is to conflate two different issues, it seems to me. One issue has to do with the scope and methods of philosophical inquiry. On this issue I agree with Dooyeweerd, Vollenhoven, and much of the Western philosophical tradition: philosophy properly studies all of creation, and it does so in a comprehensive and theoretically vigorous way. It should do so, I think, with a view both to inquiries and findings in other disciplines and to issues and challenges in society and daily life. In this sense, philosophy is what one could call a "totality discipline." There is nothing improper or dangerous about that. Indeed, Hart's

Understanding Our World takes a similar stance on the tasks of philosophy in general and of ontology in particular.[3]

The second issue raised by calling philosophical discourse "totalitarian" pertains to the finality and power philosophers have assigned to their work – which, to be sure, can be both ideologically loaded and idolatrous in spirit. Like Kuipers and Hart, I have little patience for illegitimate pretensions to absolute knowledge in philosophy. Yet I do think exposing such pretensions and offering an alternative, one that embraces philosophy's traditional aspirations to be a totality discipline, are crucial contributions for reformational philosophers to make. For this, playing Wittgensteinian language games or engaging in Rortian edification will not suffice.

But what about mystery? What about that which exceeds the grasp of philosophical knowledge? What about that which does not belong to "all of creation"? What about God? To begin, one must acknowledge that mystery is not external to philosophy – philosophy itself begins in wonder at much that resists human understanding. I see no reason why philosophy should stop before it starts, why it should not try to meet wonder with attempts to understand, even when the mystery pertains to what exceeds philosophy's grasp or is not within creation or is considered divine.

Simply to speak of what exists as "creation" is to assume a divinity belief of some sort; any attempt to provide a full-scale ontology for "all of creation" will require some elaboration of such a divinity belief. In my own work, for example, when I describe societal principles as "love-callings," I rely upon an understanding of God as not only creator and redeemer but also as a creation-partnering God of love. Even though many contemporary philosophers would frown upon including such openly "theological" language within philosophical writing, here too I see no reason why philosophy should stop before it starts. God-talk is intrinsic to good reformational philosophy. I see no reason either to relegate it to the margins of a "prescientific" appendix or to restrict it to overtly religious or poetic endeavours.

1.2 Normativity and Differentiation

Saying this raises issues about how I view the relations between religion, art, and philosophy. It also points to questions about my account of rationality. These matters come up in the commentaries by Adrian Atanasescu and Hendrik Hart on chapters 7 and 8, respectively.

Atanasescu raises two sets of questions vis-à-vis chapter 7 ("Artistic Truth, Linguistically Turned").[4] The first set pertains to the nexus of modern differentiation and "Habermas's idea of rationality as the discursive redemption of the three validity claims" of truth, rightness, and sincerity or authenticity.

Because I have addressed such questions in other writings, and because adequate answers would require a much longer essay, let me make a few incomplete remarks. I regard modern differentiation as a relatively good process that nevertheless is deeply problematic. My historiographic story is not one of "rationalization" but rather of a "dialectic between structural differentiation and normative distortion," within the horizon of "interconnected flourishing," as I put it in chapter 13.[5] For me, normativity has primarily to do with socially embedded fidelity to societal principles. Moreover, the Hegelian distinction between "morality" and "ethics" applies to every social domain, including not only polity, economy, and civil society but also art, religion, and science. A specific societal principle sets the tone in each of these domains, such that the relevant practices within a domain involve an ongoing tension between more parochial and more universal pursuits of fidelity to, say, justice or resourcefulness or solidarity. In this sense, if by "morality" one means a distinct social domain devoted to the making and vindicating of rightness claims, then, contra Habermas, there is no moral domain.[6] There is, however, a heightened awareness in modern Western societies of the tensions between more parochial and more universal attempts to be faithful to societal principles.

This stance on normativity implies, in turn, that, as a social institution, art has its own "normativity" whose relation to the normativity of other social domains is not simply external to art. Elsewhere I try to explain such intrinsic normativity in terms of art's "relational autonomy."[7] I argue that art is (or should be) autonomous, but art's autonomy is both anchored in what I call "artistic truth" and tied up with what I call "social ethics." In other words, the modern differentiation of art from science, "morality," and religion need not be – indeed, should not be – regarded as a separation. Rather it is a (potentially) life-enriching complexification, despite the powerful systemic, cultural, and technological countervailing forces that the modern process of differentiation unleashes.[8]

The second set of issues raised by Atanasescu pertains to the "secularist premise" built into Habermas's linguistic turn and how that premise affects my understanding of disclosure in art and religion. Although Habermas's discourse principle (D) holds important insights into the presuppositions and parameters of rational discourse, I do not think discourse ethics "can replace the authority of the sacred," as Habermas claims in *The Theory of Communicative Action*.[9] Rational discourse can "redeem" (i.e., vindicate) validity claims, but it cannot redeem us or the societies and cultures we inhabit. Nor does the discursive redemption of validity claims provide the key to either artistic or religious truth.

Artistic truth and religious truth do give rise to validity claims, and participants in art and religion do need to enter discourse about such claims when these are challenged. Yet validity claims and discourse about them are not the key to such truth. Rather, as I explain at greater length elsewhere,[10] a dynamic correlation between imaginative cogency (i.e., the societal principle of aesthetic validity) and imaginative disclosure makes up artistic truth. The related claims *about* authenticity, integrity, and significance that arise in art talk are rooted in this dynamic correlation. If authenticity, integrity, and significance were never achieved in art itself, no art talk about them would be valid, no matter how sophisticated the discursive attempts to vindicate such claims.

A similar pattern holds for religious truth. As chapter 12 in *Religion, Truth, and Social Transformation* argues, organized religion is a distinct social institution. As such it also is a distinct social domain of truth, distinct not only from art but also from science. The distinctness of religious truth lies in the specific correlation of fidelity and disclosure that occurs in organized religion. It does not take place between imaginative cogency and imaginative disclosure, as it does in artistic truth. Nor does it occur between logical validity and propositional disclosure, as it does, in a heightened form, within scientific truth. Rather, religious truth consists in a dynamic correlation between the societal principle of hopeful trust and the sort of disclosure that occurs in worship. Or, to say this a little more carefully and completely, I characterize religious truth as a process of worshipful disclosure in dynamic correlation with human fidelity to the societal principle of hopeful trust.

This characterization does not mean that imagination and propositional insight play no role in religious practices. Nor does it mean that the search for religious truth can ignore the societal principles of imaginative cogency and logical validity. Like art, and like science too, religion is multidimensional, and the truth it promotes is connected with truth in other social domains. Yet my approach does suggest that, within religion as a distinct social institution, neither imaginative nor propositional truth properly predominates. It is a mistake to reduce religious insight to nothing more than either the work of imagination or a topic for argumentation. Hence, with respect to the imaginative dimension of religious practices, it is probably better to say that imagination serves the pursuit of worshipful disclosure in hopeful trust than to say, as I misleadingly said in chapter 7, that "faith talk and beliefs of faith function as means of imaginative disclosure" within religion.[11] Similarly, with respect to the propositional and logical dimension of religious practices, which is indeed propositional and logical, one can say that this dimension should serve the pursuit of religious truth.

1.3 Faith and Reason

Perhaps this last point sheds light on the running debate about rationality that I have had with my mentor Hendrik Hart since the early 1980s: where I hear him giving up the rationality of faith, he hears me placing my faith in rationality. Both descriptions are caricatures, of course, but there's something to them. Hart's commentary on chapter 8 ("The Inner Reformation of Reason") raises several questions about my attempt to reframe the notion of rationality from one that emphasizes propositions and order to one that emphasizes linguistic communication and intersubjective validity claims.[12] First, does this attempt actually avoid realism? Second, does it give reason a privileged or exclusive relation to validity? Third, does it make reason the source of legitimacy for practices of faith? Fourth, do I subscribe to an "ontic realism of the Trinity"? Let me respond briefly, without pretending to address these questions adequately.

First, it is hard to see how a focus on communicative validity would commit one to a realist account of the relation between reason and what reason is about. On the account I recommend, reason has to do with primarily linguistic practices in which people raise and vindicate validity claims. When they make an assertion, for example, they simultaneously raise a claim to the correctness of this assertion. When they make a promise, they simultaneously raise a claim to the appropriateness or legitimacy of making this promise. So the focus of my account lies on the claims people make and on how they make and vindicate them, not on some "mind-independent" reality.

It is so, of course, that when we discursively sort out such validity claims, we do appeal, for example, to "how things are" or "what is the right thing to do." Yet one can account for such matters without positing a mind-independent reality, whether that reality be Order or Validity or Law. At least one can do this if one begins with the intersubjective character of linguistic communication and the interdependence of "subject" and "object," as I have tried to show in an essay on Habermas's truth theory,[13] and as I aim to demonstrate at greater length in two monographs on truth.[14]

Nevertheless, one might wonder, as Hart does, whether what I call a "post-anti/realist" approach gives reason a privileged or exclusive relation to validity. At one level, it does. For I argue that detecting and testing the validity of our claims is precisely the specific task of rational practices. Yet there is much that rational practices cannot do with respect to validity, and at these levels reason does not have a privileged or exclusive relation to validity. For example, rational practices cannot make an artwork authentic when it is inauthentic, nor can they make our religious practices true when they are false. Nor can rational practices ensure that we do justice, love kindness, and walk humbly with our God (Micah 6:8).

Still, rational practices can and do help us sort out whether our linguistically articulated claims are valid, and in which respects. If I say an artwork is authentic, you can challenge this assertion and I can try to back it up. If I claim to do something out of love for God and you doubt this, you can ask me to demonstrate religious sincerity. Given the grandiose claims made about reason in the past, such sorting of validity claims may not seem like much. It is not to be sneezed at, however, especially in a society where religious fundamentalism, celebrity politics, and xenophobic hatred run rampant. At the same time, of course, my account gives reason a limited role: I do not trust in reason to save us.

Does my approach nonetheless make reason the source of legitimacy for practices of faith? I would say no, no more than this approach makes rational practices the source of legitimacy for artistic practices. What makes religious practices and artistic practices legitimate is whether they are true, and what makes them true is the extent to which, within their own distinctive social domains, they manifest fidelity to societal principles and contribute to interconnected flourishing.[15] Hence the legitimacy of religious practices neither stems from rational practices nor requires a final stamp of approval from reason.

Nevertheless, the truth of religious practices needs to be borne out, in a multidimensional process I call authentication, and part of authenticating truth is to offer justification for claims made in the name of religion when these claims are challenged. The fact, for example, that assertions about God's will for human life function as means of faithful and worshipful disclosure in a religious context does not exempt these assertions from rational scrutiny and contestation, whether among the members of a religious community or within a wider public. If one does not see such discursive justification as part and parcel of what it means to practice religion in the contemporary world, one throws the doors wide open for the worst sorts of religious dogmatism and fundamentalism, which are not only politically problematic but also, and most importantly, religiously false. Perhaps most religious adherents do not worship and trust as they do *because* they have rational justification for doing so. This, however, does not – and should not – exempt them from attempting such justification when their religious claims are challenged. In this very specific sense, I cannot accept Hart's assertion that "whatever the faithful are confessionally committed to in their life of faith will be held as non-negotiable." Worship and trust need not be – and should not be – dogmatic.

Yet, somewhat surprisingly, I seem to have a more tolerant view of classical Christian theology than Hart has. From my passing reference to "the Trinitarian complexity of God's relationships to creation,"[16] he launches into a diatribe against "the rational theology of early Christianity," detecting there "a gateway to onto-theology," and suggesting that I subscribe to "the ontic realism of the Trinity." Where does one begin to respond to such a broadside blast?

Like Hart, I regard doctrinal accounts of the Trinity as having narrative and liturgical sources – sources in inscripturated stories of faith and in rituals of Jewish and Christian worship. As I say in the essay "Religion in Public" (chapter 12), doctrines are "attempts to render explicit the significant meaning of a [religious] community's stories of faith and rituals of worship." I also hold that the propositional truth of doctrines such as those that pertain to the Trinity is "indexed to such significant meaning."[17] So if classical Trinitarian theology fails to render well the meaning of our inscripturated stories and worshipful rituals, then it needs to be criticized and revised.

Notice, however, that doctrinal criticism and doctrinal revision rely heavily on rational practices, and these are intrinsic to the practice of a religion that, like Christianity, includes not only teachings and doctrines but also theological explications of teachings and doctrines. If classical Christian theology messed up on "the Trinity," then this must be demonstrated, and alternative formulations need to be offered. One "Trinitarian" formulation I have found helpful is to say that God calls, guides, and inspires us "in the very stuff of creation and human life."[18] So far as I can tell, this formulation carries not a whiff of ontic realism with respect to the Trinity. Yet I would want to remain open to correction from those who are better versed in Christian theology than I am. Moreover, if I were a theologian, I would want to show, through immanent criticism, how classical formulations fail and how, when elaborated, a formulation like the one just suggested is better suited to render explicit the significant meaning of Christianity's inscripturated stories and rituals of worship. Instead of broadsides aimed at classical Christian theology, I would recommend immanent criticism with metacritical intent.

1.4 Immanent Criticism with Metacritical Intent

That, essentially, is what I recommend for contemporary reformational philosophers too, whether they address their own immediate tradition or take up topics and texts in the wider philosophical tradition. Not all of my readers will endorse this recommendation, however, and questions about it have arisen in two commentaries. Bob Sweetman's discussion of the essay "Reformational Philosophy after Dooyeweerd and Vollenhoven" (chapter 2) asks whether, with its emphasis on immanent criticism, my critical retrieval of earlier generations of reformational philosophy errs on the side of philosophical solidarity at the expense of religious difference. Ben Hampshire's commentary on the essay "Metacritique" (chapter 9) wonders whether my emphasis on historiography's making a creative contribution would impede the transmission of an intellectual tradition to subsequent generations.

Sweetman rightly highlights the appeal to solidarity that underlies my emphasis on immanent criticism. He describes this as "solidarity with philosophy [as] a cultural form," and he raises two questions about it.[19] First, does such solidarity let one maintain the central reformational task of "witnessing to the religious root of all human endeavours." Second, have the conditions that prompted Dooyeweerd and Vollenhoven's "dichotomizing edginess" toward other philosophical traditions really changed so much that now reformational philosophers can afford "greater solidarity with the religiously heterogeneous ethos of current philosophy"?

Permit me two clarifying remarks before I address these excellent questions. First, the solidarity that motivates my emphasis on immanent critique is not in the first instance solidarity with philosophy as a cultural form but rather solidarity with fellow human beings who, among other activities, try to make sense of their lives and society and sometimes do this in the vigorously disciplined manner of academic philosophy. I start from the assumption that "we are all in this together" – i.e., we are all created, fallen, and redeemable, to use traditional reformational language. Further, we all owe each other solidarity – mutual recognition – in a social setting, no matter how difficult on occasion this may be to muster. Solidarity is not mere tolerance, however, and it is not incompatible with critique and transformation.

Second, and in line with what I have just said, I do not emphasize immanent criticism *tout court*. As becomes more obvious in the book's chapters 9 and 14, I emphasize immanent criticism *with metacritical intent*. I begin with the assumption that I can learn from another philosopher's contributions – why else would one bother to study them? – and I do not begin with the assumption that these are either fundamentally right or fundamentally wrong. Whether they are right or wrong, and in which respects, needs to be discovered through careful scrutiny, paying close attention to the texts, arguments, rhetoric, and hidden assumptions in which potential contributions are wrapped up. Yet, in the end, the goal of immanent criticism is neither immanence nor criticism but to attain transformative insight. This is a laborious process. I see it as a labour of love, love not simply for philosophy but for fellow human beings and for all of creation.

Accordingly, in response to Sweetman's first question, I do not see the exercise of philosophical solidarity as either impeding or neglecting the challenge to bear witness to the heartedness of all human efforts. I do, however, believe that such witness is better borne, at least in contemporary circumstances, by showing rather than telling, by demonstrating in the very manner of doing philosophy that the entire enterprise, like the rest of society and culture, hinges on the spiritual direction in which it proceeds. Moreover, matters of spiritual direction do not line up neatly with one tradition or another in either philosophy or religion. Reformational philosophy, too, must remain open to spiritual redirection.

Do I say this because I think there has been a dramatic shift in the conditions that prompted the reformational "edginess" of an earlier generation? On one hand, my answer is yes. We live in an economically and technologically globalizing society where religious adherents often exacerbate political conflicts rather than develop the global ethic that would be required not only to redirect economic and technological systems but also to fashion suitable transnational frameworks of law and governance. At the same time, by now the ancient, medieval, and modern philosophies that Dooyeweerd and Vollenhoven challenged have been thoroughly problematized both within and outside philosophy. Indeed, philosophy itself, both as a tradition and as an academic discipline, is under severe threat from powerful bureaucratic, economic, and cultural forces. How should reformational philosophers address such a world? To begin with an emphasis on religious difference and antithesis seems both parochial and outdated.

On the other hand, the spiritual conflicts that Dooyeweerd and Vollenhoven noted and articulated have not gone away, and the "ethos" of professional philosophy is even less hospitable to wide-ranging, religiously informed, and spiritually motivated thought than it was in their day. It would be naïve to write and speak as if reformational philosophers are simply "part of the (professional) club." Nevertheless, I think it is incumbent on reformational philosophers today to let the opposition come to them, as it surely will and surely does, rather than to begin in an oppositional stance.

Reformational solidarity, then, does not ignore deep-going differences, but it looks for life-giving insights both within and beyond these differences. That is one reason why, when I discuss the role of metacritique in the historiography of philosophy, I say philosophical historians must not only move beyond the positions they immanently criticize but also participate creatively in the history they report. They should not simply report on this history. They should also make a contribution with regard to the problems and solutions they locate via immanent criticism. Philosophical historiography, too, should be a redemptive enterprise.

This approach makes Ben Hampshire wonder whether it precludes efforts simply to pass on the philosophical tradition, an urgent task, he says, "because most people have little or no knowledge, familiarity, or experience with philosophy and its perennial questions."[20] Having taught philosophy to undergraduates for more than twenty years, I recognize his worry as legitimate. Yet I do not think creative participation and faithful transmission are at odds. When I taught undergraduate aesthetics at Calvin College, my course touched down in historically significant figures and texts, from Plato and Aristotle to Hume and Kant to Adorno and Benjamin, for example. I framed our historical inquiry around the emergence, articulation, and contestation of two issues: aesthetic normativity and artistic autonomy. The students and I also examined how feminist, postmodernist, and other critiques of the Western philosophical tradition do or do not help address these issues. Both issues are important in my own work as a systematic philosopher, and they have salience in the tradition of reformational aesthetics.

I like to think my aesthetics students simultaneously received a solid grounding in the history of Western philosophical aesthetics and became proto-participants in creatively addressing its issues, not only in the classroom but also in their own lives. I also believe that historically grounded, problem-posing pedagogy like this does more to keep the philosophical tradition and its questions alive than a more "impartial" and "comprehensive" survey of the history of aesthetics would at the undergraduate level. So, although I recognize the tension Hampshire mentions, I do not think creative participation and faithful transmission must be at odds in a pedagogical context – nor in scholarly research and writing either.[21]

2. DOOYEWEERD, TRUTH, AND FAITHFUL CRITICISM

Religion, Truth, and Social Transformation begins and ends with attempts at critically retrieving crucial insights from the first generation of reformational philosophy. In this section I respond primarily to commentaries on such attempts in the book's introduction, Part One, and epilogue. Because of topical relationships, however, I also take up commentaries on chapters 10 and 14, having already discussed Bob Sweetman's commentary on chapter 2 in the previous section.

2.1 *Temporality and Spirituality*

In response to the introduction, Neal DeRoo asks reformational philosophers to pay greater attention to "Dooyeweerd's unique account of the inherent temporality of the created order," with its emphasis on the "supra-temporal heart" of human existence.[22] If we do not, DeRoo says, we will "ignore the *spiritual* critique that forms the ultimate basis of Dooyeweerd's work" and will construe his work in a "deistic direction" that makes us, not Christ, the redeemer(s) of creation. I am not sure whether DeRoo sees such debilitating tendencies in my own work, but I do want to take up the provocative challenge he has posed.

Let me be blunt: I regard Dooyeweerd's notion of supra-temporality as a non-starter. Although I agree that his account of creation's temporality, with its two distinct directions (i.e., expressive and concentric), merits close attention, especially at the intersection of normativity and eschatology, his notion of a supra-temporal heart is not internally coherent. Nor is it required in order to do the work DeRoo thinks it does. Although I retain an emphasis on the "heartedness" of human existence, which Dooyeweerd and Vollenhoven share, I see no need to construe this in terms of supra-temporality, nor do I see any advantage in so construing it.

Human beings are creatures through and through, and creatures are temporal through and through. Why, then, would we want to say about human creatures that, at their very core, they are supra-temporal? Perhaps DeRoo's central claim in response would be that the idea of supra-temporality enables Dooyeweerd "to maintain a constant, direct engagement between the eternal and the temporal (and so avoid deism)." But is this the only way to avoid deism? And why would one want to maintain such an eternal/temporal engagement, which presupposes that "eternality" best captures that which is not creaturely? Why not, for example, simply talk about the continual and direct engagement (i.e., covenant) between God and creation and the ever-emerging dialogue between God and humankind?

DeRoo worries that, if one gives up the notion of supra-temporality, then one will no longer see structural problems in society as "first and foremost problems of spiritual expression," to be fixed by "a spiritual and not merely a social transformation." This formulation, however, poses a false dilemma: either structural or spiritual. Of course, structural problems are not merely structural. They are directional too. Yet that does not mean that they are *primarily* spiritual problems.

The peculiarity of spirituality is that it cannot be juxtaposed in this way to some domain or institution or structure in society. In fact, one could say that all problems in society, whether structural or not, are spiritual problems, but that would not get us very far in understanding and addressing them.

DeRoo, however, has something more specific in mind. To diagnose social problems properly, he says, we must discern "the spiritual forces" that "particular communities" express, for it is the "attunement between a particular community and the spirit of God" that determines truth. Here my deepest reservations about Dooyeweerd's supra-temporality set in. For his notion of supra-temporality comes paired with an emphasis on the spiritual antithesis (the conflict between ground motives and between "religious" – i.e., spiritual – communities). This emphasis tends both to reduce the scope of divine revelation and to place certain communities among the sheep – and the rest among the goats.[23]

So, while I agree with DeRoo that the struggle with societal evil is a spiritual struggle – see the book's epilogue – and while I agree that reformational philosophers must strive to discern the spiritual forces at work in society and culture, I resist the Dooyeweerdian move to link such forces directly with "particular communities." That move surrenders too easily to the temptation among faith-oriented thinkers "to place their own account of spiritual struggle on the right side of this battle."[24]

I hope these comments suffice to indicate why I regard Dooyeweerd's notion of supra-temporality as a non-starter. I have not shown how this notion is internally incoherent, although Michael DeMoor's responses to DeRoo's commentary call attention to some of the incoherence. In any case, it is not so much the notion's internal incoherence as its problematic implications that lead me, while retaining the emphasis on heartedness, to jettison the notion of supratemporality. I do not believe this puts me on a slippery slope to deism.

2.2 Anthropocentrism and Transcendence

Some of these issues return, albeit indirectly, in the discussions that respond to Peter Lok's commentary on "Defining Humankind" (chapter 10).[25] Lok claims that reformational anthropology, as articulated by Hendrik Hart and briefly sketched in this chapter, "overcomes some of the theoretical problems brought on by contemporary posthumanism." Two problems in particular draw Lok's attention. One is a failure to see qualitative differences in the bodily functions that humans and animals share. The other is a failure to account for the distinctive humanness of being human. An approach along Hartian lines can address these two problems, he says, by emphasizing the reciprocity between animals and human beings in various functional dimensions while insisting that, in their heartedness, human beings are uniquely responsive and responsible creatures.

Lok's commentary has prompted an extensive discussion, from which I'd like to single out two issues. One, raised by Dean Dettloff, is whether the ontology that underlies reformational anthropology is latently anthropocentric. The other, raised by Peter Lok, is what a reformational concept of transcendence should look like. Both issues are linked to Dooyeweerd's notion of a supra-temporal heart, and they remain important issues for philosophers who retain the heartedness of human existence but jettison its supra-temporality.

Without going into the details of Dettloff and Lok's debate about posthumanism, let me make a few comments on these issues. First, if by anthropocentrism one means a philosophical position that puts human existence (or, more narrowly, human perception) at the centre of the universe, such that all other creatures are both inferior and subservient to human beings, then in principle reformational philosophy need not be – indeed, should not be – anthropocentric. From the very beginning the reformational tradition has emphasized the cosmic scope of divine creation, redemption, and fulfillment, as well as the brokenness of all creation. It has struggled to do justice to this "biblical ground motive" (Dooyeweerd) in its ontology, epistemology, and social philosophy. Having said that, however, I consider some formulations less successful than others in this regard. For example, by suggesting that cosmic time refracts through the human supra-temporal heart, Dooyeweerd does tend toward a type of anthropocentrism, it seems to me. That's another reason why I believe we should abandon his notion of supra-temporality.

The theory of a modal scale does not need to be conceived in a hierarchical fashion, however. In fact, the genius of reformational modal theory is to break with all the hierarchical orderings of functional dimensions that one finds in the history of Western philosophy, right through the humanist philosophical anthropologies of Max Scheler and Ernst Cassirer. Further, whether the dimension of worship and faith (the so-called "pistic" mode) lies at one end of the modal scale, whether "higher" or "later" or simply "terminal," is a matter for functional analysis and debate. To complicate matters even more, if one has an evolutionary and historical understanding of how functional capacities emerge, this question is also a matter for empirical study (e.g., in evolutionary biology, cultural anthropology, and religious studies).

When one gets around to characterizing the distinctiveness of multidimensional human existence, however, and accounting for its "place in the cosmos," to use Scheler's phrase, reformational philosophy can easily slip into a form of anthropocentrism. Precisely for this reason, along with reservations I have about certain divinity beliefs, I would urge caution around the concept of transcendence. If by "transcendence" one means that human beings, in their uniqueness, are inextricably caught up in "multiple relations that carry us beyond merely human existence,"[26] as I put it in chapter 10, then I would not object. Or if one means that human existence "is always already oriented with respect to its origin and destiny,"[27] again, I would have no problem. Historically, however, the notion of transcendence often has implied an ability to go beyond our humanness, our temporality, our creatureliness, our earthliness. That implication strikes me as not only intrinsically problematic but also dangerously anthropocentric. My own recommendation, then, is to give up the vocabulary of transcendence, along with the notion of supra-temporality.

2.3 Incoherence and Antithesis

If, by contrast, one hangs on to Dooyeweerd's supra-temporality and older notions of transcendence, the problems in Dooyeweerd's transcendental critique that I identify in "The Great Turning Point" (chapter 1) will become nearly unavoidable. For pressure will mount to make theoretical claims about what one declares supra-theoretical (because it is "transcendent" and "supra-temporal"), and conflict will arise between regarding spirituality (i.e., religion, in Dooyeweerd's terms) as a temporal phenomenon (and historical, cultural, and social), on the one hand, and maintaining it as a supra-temporal noumenon, on the other.

Without discussing the notions of supra-temporality and transcendence, Jazz Feyer Salo's commentary on chapter 1 finds a potential solution to one of Dooyeweerd's transcendental problems in the writings of Jacob Klapwijk.[28] Although I, too, find Klapwijk's emphases on historical situatedness and creation's dynamic highly congenial, I'm not sure exactly how they help address the problem of self-referential incoherence in Dooyeweerd's transcendental critique. Perhaps Feyer Salo means to say that the limits to what theoretical thought can grasp are temporal or historical limits, and eventually they will give way as creation and history unfold (and perhaps as new limits emerge?). This would be one way to understand his suggestion that "Klapwijk's extended articulation of dynamicity" may reconceive Dooyeweerd's "neo-Kantian understanding of the limit of theoretical thought ... as a dialectical pilgrimage to the kingdom of God."

Yet this approach, reminiscent of Hegel's dialectical *Aufhebung* of Kant's antinomies, does not tell us much about the peculiar structure and dynamics of theoretical thought. Unless one takes up this topic, one does not really address the issues that give rise to Dooyeweerd's self-referential incoherence. Chapter 1 does not do this. That's why it does not claim to have offered adequate repairs to Dooyeweerd's transcendental critique. Although the book begins to clear a site for this in chapters 3, 4, 14, and 15, adequate repairs will require additional work on a comprehensive conception of truth – my current research project.

As I have hinted already, one of my objections to Dooyeweerd's notion of supra-temporality is that it comes paired with a problematic emphasis on the spiritual antithesis. Joshua Harris, in his discussion of "Dooyeweerd's Conception of Truth" (chapter 3), rightly calls attention to my discomfort with this emphasis: it wreaks havoc on Dooyeweerd's general conception of truth, undermines his account of theoretical truth, and does not do justice to either spirituality (what Dooyeweerd calls religion) or religion (what Dooyeweerd calls faith).[29] Yet Harris wants to push me a bit farther. He asks, in effect, whether my criticisms of Dooyeweerd's idea of religious truth imply an embrace of theological universalism – which, of course, would be incompatible with Dooyeweerd's theological self-understanding and with most of the Calvinist tradition from which his philosophy arises.

Not being a theologian, I am unsure how to respond to Harris's insightful provocation. On the one hand, the traditional debate about theological universalism employs such outdated and, I suspect, problematic concepts of salvation, damnation, and eternal life that it seems pointless to take a stance on this debate. On the other hand, I do see how my criticisms of Dooyeweerd reject even the glimmer of "a vicious dualism between faithful and apostate," as Harris puts it, and in this sense, they seem more compatible with theological universalism than with its opposite.

I want to be careful here. God's calling everyone, without exception, into the truth does not mean that everyone, without exception, lives in the truth. Some of us live the Lie, and all of us struggle to know and do what is true, amid what I call societal evil. My objection to Dooyeweerd is not that he distinguishes spiritual truth from spiritual falsehood. Rather, my objection is that he tends to let this distinction collapse into an antithesis between spiritual communities and sometimes even between religious (i.e., confessional) communities. In my view, we are none of us – we human beings – wholly in the truth or wholly outside it. To hope for a new Earth, however, is to work and wait for a day when everyone lives wholly in the truth. To borrow from the title of a great book on this topic by my colleague Nik Ansell, it is to have hope for the annihilation of hell.[30]

2.4 Intuitionism and Essentialism

Another side to my criticisms of Dooyeweerd's conception of truth concerns his problematic appeal to what he calls theoretical intuition. This issue also arises in "Dooyeweerd's Modal Theory" (chapter 4), which examines Dooyeweerd's ontology of science. Commenting on this chapter, Dan Rudisill raises questions about the relation between ontology and epistemology in Dooyeweerd's modal theory.[31] Rudisill also wonders whether an apparent "essentialism" in Dooyeweerd's account of the structures of individuality also infects his modal theory.

Concerning the first topic, I would say Dooyeweerd definitely intends his modal theory to be an ontological account, and he sees it as the basis for any adequate epistemology. Yet his preferred route for discovering and testing modal insights is via the basic concepts of the academic disciplines (what he calls special sciences). In a sense, then, Dooyeweerd's ontological modal theory emerges from a phenomenology – not a phenomenology of the "lifeworld" (later Husserl) or of "naïve experience" (Dooyeweerd), but a phenomenology of the sciences. In this respect, his approach is somewhat reminiscent of the early Husserl's *Logical Investigations* (1900–01). Moreover, Dooyeweerd's appeal to theoretical intuition as the final court of appeal for grasping modal nuclei has more than a little resemblance to middle Husserl's appeal to eidetic intuition (*Wesensschau*), which itself stems from the account of categorial intuition (*kategoriale Anschauung*) in the *Logical Investigations*.[32] Significantly, Dooyeweerd appeals to *theoretical* intuition, not to, say, lifeworldly intuition. As is nicely illustrated by the 1922 quotation from Dooyeweerd that Peter Enneson provides in his comment,[33] Dooyeweerd's attempt to move from neo-Kantian methodology to a full-blown modal ontology lands midway between Husserlian phenomenology and Heideggerian ontology.

Dooyeweerd's emphasis on the theoretical intuition of modal nuclei need not entail essentialism. I agree with Bob Sweetman's comment in this regard. Nevertheless, because Dooyeweerd specifies structures of individuality in terms of modally delimited qualifying and founding functions, any essentialism with respect to actual creatures and kinds of creatures would have retrospective ramifications for his modal theory. And, with respect to individuality structures and especially type laws, I agree with Klapwijk that Dooyeweerd was an essentialist, in the following sense: he reduced variable type structures to invariant laws, a topic *Religion, Truth, and Social Transformation* takes up in chapter 5.

If one gives up such essentialism in order to allow for emergent evolution, as Klapwijk does, then one can also begin to open the door for a more processual understanding of how functional capacities emerge. This, in turn, could encourage a more processual understanding of the how these capacities interrelate and how one should systematize their interrelations in a modal theory – a "genealogy of modes," to use a phrase introduced in the comments. I have considerable sympathy with such a project. Certainly, my dialectical "partial phenomenology" of imagination, as the historically emergent aesthetic aspect of life and society, points in this direction,[34] as does my historical/eschatological understanding of societal principles. Perhaps such a more processual approach to modal theory is a challenge for the fourth generation of reformational philosophy to take up: to put it enigmatically, perhaps we need a greater temporalization of modal temporality.

2.5 Structure and Change

As Tricia Van Dyk indicates in her commentary on chapter 5 ("Fantastic Things"), an emphasis on the specifically social and historical temporality of art underlies my critique of Dooyeweerd's underdeveloped philosophy of art.[35] I applaud her insisting on lived experience as a touchstone for reformational philosophy. Yet I'm not sure the problematic "reductions" in Dooyeweerd's philosophy of art stem from a lack of lived experience. He was, after all, a relatively cosmopolitan person and an accomplished pianist. Rather, spiritually rooted and socio-politically motivated anxieties about historicism and evolutionism, combined with a structuralist understanding of social and cultural phenomena, led him to squeeze such experience into an essentialist mold.

Dooyeweerd, however, was not unaware of problematic essentialist tendencies in his account of individuality structures. Perhaps that is why he insists so vigorously on the *temporal* character of "constant structural laws" in the 1936 essay cited in Peter Enneson's comment.[36] Yet such passages illustrate precisely the problems I have tried to demonstrate in his philosophy of art. First, structures become laws: "structural laws." Second, they become invariant: "constant." Third, they become constituents of the very horizon of cosmic time, not, however, as structures that emerge, change, and possibly disappear, but rather as structures that make possible any changes in time. In principle, then, Dooyeweerdian structures, whether modal or individual and typical, can never change. To posit their changeability would be to place them on the subject-side rather than the law-side of creation. Dooyeweerd might say, contra Plato, that they are not timeless ideas or forms, but this does not make them temporal, not to mention historical. They are the constant, unchanging order of creation, including human culture and society. Both in my accounts of social institutions such as art and religion and in my conceptions of truth and societal principles, I have tried to retrieve Dooyeweerd's ontological insights without embracing his fixation on unchanging order. In these ways, despite our disagreements about rationality, I am highly indebted to Hendrik Hart.

2.6 Faithful Criticism

All of the issues discussed already come to the surface in chapter 14 ("Unfinished Business: Toward a Reformational Conception of Truth"), itself a companion essay to chapter 3 ("Dooyeweerd's Conception of Truth"). As Allyson Carr perceptively notes, chapter 14 tries to make explicit the reformational ground from which my ongoing work on truth grows. But the chapter also offers an argument "for inclusion" and addresses this argument "to the reformational community."[37]

Carr rightly understands that, in my view, an emphasis on the spiritual antithesis has taken a drastic toll on the reformational community: it has either prompted or underwritten attempts to reject rather than embrace those who would make a creative contribution to reformational philosophy. At the same time, perhaps despite Dooyeweerd's intentions, an emphasis on the spiritual antithesis has impeded or prevented fruitful dialogues between reformational philosophers and their closest "relatives," such as Reformed epistemologists, not to mention schools of thought that lie farther afield from the Kuyperian tradition. Hence my argument for inclusion in chapter 14 is a double argument. Not only do I want my own work to be perceived as "fruit from the reformational 'tree,'" as Carr puts it, but also I wish that tree to be more welcoming toward the many birds of a different feather who, from time to time, and with a taste for one fruit or another, could flock together.

This wish may or may not be true to some of Dooyeweerd's specific formulations. In fact, I think there is an ongoing tension in his work between inclusion and exclusion, between a call for open-hearted dialogue and an insistence on the spiritual antithesis. Yet I hope my wish is true, as Carr says, "to the animating spirit of the reformational tradition." That spirit, as I have tried to give it voice, grounds every spiritual struggle for the truth in the generosity, the inclusiveness, the original blessing of God's love for all of creation.

Amid my criticisms of Dooyeweerd's notions of supra-temporality, spiritual antithesis, theoretical intuition, and invariant structures, then, I have tried to remain faithful to the reformational tradition. As Doug Blomberg points out in the two commentaries that bookend our symposium – one on the book's introduction and the other on the epilogue – such fidelity has several sides.[38] One is to try to do scholarship that is "accountable to everyday people in their everyday lives," as Blomberg puts it. Another side is to approach one's tradition in the spirit of "ongoing reformation – *semper reformanda*." A third is to play close attention to both differences and fundamental agreements among the tradition's founding figures and texts. Fourth, and most important, is to approach all of this in love and out of love, love not simply for one's tradition but for the creation this tradition seeks to serve, and in response to the love with which all people are gifted and to which they are called.

When my critique of Dooyeweerd and other reformational thinkers becomes pointed, this is not because I think they are hopelessly wrong. Rather, it is because I want the insights they have gained to become available once more in fresh ways, in ways that help and that heal and that hear Earth's lament. Adorno rightly says, in a passage the epilogue quotes, "The need to let suffering speak is a condition of all truth."[39] As a reformational philosopher, let me simply add: to help those who suffer is the point of all truth. I see no better reason than this to remain faithful, amid criticism, to the reformational tradition.

7

The Tree of Life:
Hegel, Malick, and the Postsecular Sublime

Poor sublime: relic of other centuries, perennially misused as an attractive way to express the power of art, kept afloat by academics interested in other people's ideas, used – ineffectually – as a covertly religious term, to permit academics to speak about religion while remaining appropriately secular.

James Elkins[1]

A philosophy that refuses to compartmentalize knowledge, politics, and social critique calls for an expansive approach to interpreting and evaluating the arts. Like philosophy and religion, the arts, too, are a social domain of knowledge, and they are neither apolitical nor incapable of social criticism. A properly expansive approach to the arts would not divorce questions of aesthetic quality from concerns about meaning or truth. Nor would it isolate issues of technical expertise from the economic underpinnings and political impact of artistic activities. For dance, film, music, and the like belong to a differentiated social institution, and this institution – art – is both multidimensional and interconnected with other social institutions.

Accordingly, the best way to comment on specific products and events in the arts is to engage in what I call *redemptive art criticism*. Redemptive art criticism tries to interpret the meaning of an artwork in light of its artifactual and aesthetic character, with a view to its import and reception, and with reference to its roles in society. Although the emerging import of an artwork guides such interpretation, the work's artifactual, aesthetic, and societal features, all of which mediate this import, also receive careful attention. Moreover, the approach is critical: it raises normative questions about technical achievement, aesthetic validity, interpretive needs, and social ethics. Redemptive criticism regards the meaning of an artwork not as a neutral fact but as a more or less worthwhile contribution to human flourishing in society. In this it recalls the wide-ranging aesthetics of G.W.F. Hegel, sharpened by the Critical Theory of Theodor W. Adorno.

To illustrate what redemptive art criticism involves, and also to uncover its Hegelian sources, the current chapter explores whether an expansive account of "the sublime" can shed light on contemporary film, in particular Terrence Malick's *The Tree of Life*.[2] Ever since Hegel purportedly declared "the death of art," scholars have periodically announced the end of the cultural forms with which he most closely associated the arts: the demise of beauty, the deflation of truth, the withering of religion, even the end of philosophy. The sublime is yet another entry in the recent annals of academic necrology, with James Elkins as the leading signatory to its death warrant. Not without protest however, as expressed by Timothy Costelloe in the introduction to his anthology on the sublime: "The sublime can no more disappear than the experiences to which it refers; for that we should be grateful and wish it in return a long and healthy life."[3] Yet, of the fifteen essays in Costelloe's collection, only one, by Paul Guyer, discusses Hegel's contribution. Guyer claims that Hegel "diminishes the importance of the sublime compared to the place it held for eighteenth-century thinkers" and thereby contributes significantly to "the virtual disappearance of the category from aesthetics" in the century that followed.[4] Guyer links this diminishment of the sublime with a strong form of Hegel's purported "death of art" thesis.[5]

Clearly, if Hegel did not regard the sublime as important, and if he contributed to its demise as a philosophical category, then there would be good reasons not to take his conception seriously in debates about the contemporary viability and significance of the sublime. What these debates often overlook, however, is the interrelatedness of the cultural forms that are tightly interlinked in Hegel's conception. Moreover, when an author such as Guyer does note this interlinkage, its contemporary significance gets ignored. As a result, Hegel's conception of the sublime appears to have no contemporary significance and, not surprisingly, it is ignored.

This chapter takes issue with such readings and nonreadings of Hegel. It argues that Hegel's conception can help establish the contemporary significance of the sublime, especially in the world of film. I develop this argument in four stages. First I summarize the conception of the sublime in Hegel's *Aesthetics*. Next I explore the potential significance of Hegel's conception today. Then I discuss Terrence Malick's *The Tree of Life* as postsecular art of the sublime, arguing that this Hegelian category illuminates Malick's body of work as well as the film's sociohistorical setting and film-critical context. I suggest in conclusion that postsecular art of the sublime such as *The Tree of Life* provides an important reason why we need to reconceive the contemporary status of religion, art, and philosophy and their interrelations.

1. THE HEGELIAN SUBLIME

For Immanuel Kant, the experience of the sublime involves the exercise of reflective or reflecting judgment (*reflektierende Urteilskraft*), which seeks the universal for a given particular. To judge something as "sublime" is to raise a claim to universal validity without employing any specific beliefs. The claim gets raised with reference to reason as the faculty of ideas that governs our moral life, and it presupposes that all human beings possess what Kant calls "moral feeling."[6] Hegel's *Aesthetics*,[7] by contrast, locates the sublime at the intersection between art and religion. For Hegel, the sublime is not primarily a matter of individual, reflective, and felt experience. Instead, it is communal, historical, and substantial. His concept of the sublime is both a historiographic and a systematic category: it indicates a historical stage in the emergence of art proper, and it indicates a tendency that recurs in later historical stages and has a stronger presence in some art-forms than in others. For Hegel, the sublime cannot be reduced to a type of reflective/reflecting judgment à la Kant.

1.1 Symbolic Art-Form

As a Hegelian historiographic category, the sublime indicates a phase within the first stage of art's development. Hegel distinguishes three such stages – the symbolic, the classical, and the romantic "art-form" (*Kunstform*) – and these stages roughly correlate with the pre-Hellenic, Greco-Roman, and Christian eras of civilization. Each stage represents a further unfolding of "the beauty of art" (*das Kunstschöne*), which Hegel also calls "the Ideal" (*das Ideal*). The Ideal that drives art's development across three stages or forms of art is for the truth of what exists to be presented in such a way that the form of this presentation completely suits the content presented. In Hegel's own words, "art has the function of grasping and displaying existence, in its appearance, as *true*, i.e., in its suitability to the content which is adequate to itself, the content which is both implicit and explicit *[(zu) dem an und für sich seienden Inhalt]*."[8] For Hegel, such artistic presentation of the truth is at bottom a disclosure of the divine: "art has above all to make the Divine the centre of its representations *[Darstellungen]*."[9] Because, in principle, the divine is a unity and universal, and can receive complete conceptual understanding as such only in abstract thinking, whereas art is sensuous, the challenge for art is to present such unity and universality in concrete appearance. Hegel's philosophical historiography traces art's development in response to this challenge. The progression from symbolic through classical to romantic forms of art is a process in which the divine becomes individualized, humanized, and internalized.

Hegel traces three phases within the development of the symbolic art-form, each of which has two or three subphases.[10] Only in the second or middle phase, itself divided into pantheistic and monotheistic subphases, is symbolic art fully sublime. Within this middle phase, the monotheistic subphase unfolded in Hebrew poetry represents both the pinnacle and the undoing of sublime symbolism. Hegel calls this middle phase "Symbolism of the Sublime" (*Die Symbolik der Erhabenheit*).

1.2 Symbolism of the Sublime

If, as a whole, symbolic art is "a continuing struggle for compatibility of meaning [*Bedeutung*] and shape [*Gestalt*]"[11] – a struggle in which religiously inflected ideas of the divine cannot find adequate sensuous presentation – then sublime art, properly so called, brings this struggle to a head by showing the inherent deficiency of any symbolic attempt to present the divine: "Here the meaning, as spiritual explicit universality, is separated for the first time from the concrete existent, and makes that existent known as its negative, external to it, and its servant. In order to express *itself* therein, the meaning … must posit [this existent] as the inherently deficient, something to be superseded – although it has for its expression nothing other than precisely this existent which is external to it and null."[12]

Hegel says this positing of inherent deficiency takes two forms: in the positive relation between the divine and finite appearances that occurs in "the art of sublime pantheism" (i.e., some Hindu art, the mystical art of Islam, and Christian mysticism), and in the negative relation that occurs in the "poetry of sublimity" (i.e., Hebrew poetry).[13] Common to both forms is the fact that such art does not obscure its fundamental meaning in multiple and diverse sensuous presentations of the divine. Rather this meaning "has at last wrung its way to freedom and so comes explicitly into consciousness in its clarity." In sublime art, both positive and negative, "the absolute meaning is grasped as the universal all-pervading *substance* of the entire phenomenal world" – not the noumenal substrate to which Kant said judgments of the sublime refer us, but the divine in all its unity and universality, indeed, in its infinity.[14]

Accordingly, when discussing Kant's account, Hegel gives the following general definition of the sublime (*das Erhabene*): It is "the attempt to express the infinite, without finding in the sphere of phenomena [*Erscheinungen*] an object which proves adequate for this representation [*Darstellung*]. Precisely because the infinite is set apart from the entire complex of objectivity as explicitly an invisible meaning devoid of shape and is made inner, it remains, in accordance with its infinity, unutterable and sublime above any expression through the finite."[15] Contra Kant, for whom nature rather than art is the primary occasion for judgments of the sublime, sublime art does not in the first instance point us toward human reason and moral feeling. Rather it points us toward "the one absolute substance *qua* the content which is to be represented," and it does so by simultaneously revealing its content and superseding this revelation in being annihilated by what it reveals.[16]

The "pantheistic art" of Hindu poetry (e.g., *Bhagavad Gita*), Islamic poetry (e.g., Rumi), and Christian mysticism (e.g., Angelus Silesius) posits an affirmative relation of substance to the phenomenal world. It envisages substance – the divine in its infinity – "as immanent in all its created accidents, which thus are ... preserved affirmatively through the substance dwelling in them, although in every single thing it is only the One and the Divine which is to be imaged and exalted." This allows the poet to "preserve a positive relation to the substance to which [the poet] links everything."[17]

In view of art's historical vocation to individualize, humanize, and internalize the divine, however, the limitation of pantheism is as follows. While affirming divine substance and its appearance in everything, pantheistic art neither fully individualizes substance nor substantiates individual things: "since the substance in everything particular is this One, the substance becomes *implicitly* something particular and accidental; yet, conversely, this individual thing changes all the same, and imagination does not restrict the substance to a specific existent but advances over each determinacy, abandoning it in order to proceed to another, and thus the individual existent becomes for its part something accidental, away [from] and above which the one substance rises and therefore is sublime."[18]

1.3 Art of the Sublime

Perhaps it is because pantheistic art fails to individualize substance, rendering both the divine and the individual existent insubstantial ("accidental"), that Hegel reserves the title "The Art of the Sublime" (*Die Kunst der Erhabenheit*) for his treatment of Judaism's sacred poetry.[19] Indeed, compared with the entire range of symbolic art, the "art of the sublime" – Hebrew poetry – is, according to Hegel, "*the* sacred art as such" because "it gives honour to God alone."[20] If we had any doubt before, now we cannot avoid Hegel's fundamental intuition about the sublime: it is where the distinction between art and religion breaks down. But it is also where art and religion break apart, such that in the next phase of symbolic art – "Conscious Symbolism" – little divine content remains. On the one hand, art of the sublime takes to its outer limit the effort to use sensuous configuration to present the divine substance. On the other hand, such art makes apparent why and how this effort must fail. Now, in the historical unfolding of artforms, the only pathway toward relating "shape and meaning" lies in the subjective consciousness of the artist or art interpreter, as becomes apparent in what Hegel calls "Conscious Symbolism of the Comparative Art-Form."[21] In fables, allegories, metaphors, and the like, "the Absolute, the one Lord, can no longer be taken as the meaning."[22] Either such conscious symbolism lacks significant religious content or, when it expresses religious content, it does so in a capricious way. Only in the subsequent classical art-form, according to Hegel, is the divergence between religion and art (temporarily) overcome.

This double movement in art of the sublime – the simultaneous fusion and differentiation of art and religion – stems from the negative relation between meaning and configuration, between divine substance and the phenomenal world. Whereas the pantheist poet finds God in everything, for the Hebrew psalmist God is above it all. On the one hand, divine substance has become supremely self-related, "brought back into itself, as pure inwardness and substantial might," from its sojourn amid the phenomena. Hence it is "made *independent* ... over against finitude." That allows God to be a "purely spiritual" being, and nothing in the phenomenal world can attain this height. On the other hand, the entire world, including humanity, takes on an "inherently negative" relation to its substantial meaning: it is nothing in itself but fully *dependent* on God. The world may reveal God, but God alone is what allows the world to exist and thrive. Hence the finite that reveals the infinite God is itself "without substance."[23]

Hegel elaborates this characterization of the art of the sublime by discussing God as creator and lord of the world, the finite world as bereft of God, and the human being as newly individualized in recognizing "the nullity of things," exalting God, and learning, with respect to God's law, to pursue either good or evil. Although the latter pursuit puts human beings into an "*affirmative* relation to God," this rests in turn upon the negative relation between creation and God:[24] "Sublimity presupposes the meaning in an independence in comparison with which the external must appear as merely subordinate, because the inner does not appear in it but so transcends it that nothing comes into the representation [*Darstellung*] except as this transcendence and superiority."[25] Hence, more than any other symbolic art, Hebrew poetry is sublime because it presents nothing more than a supreme transcendence that refuses sensuous presentation.

Clearly Hegel offers a selective reading of the Psalms and has a one-sided understanding of the Jewish religion. Whereas, for example, he quotes passages from Psalms 90 and 104 that highlight God's majesty and creation's "nullity,"[26] he ignores passages that celebrate divine compassion (e.g., Psalms 111:4 and 145:8–9) and human dignity (e.g., Psalm 8:4–9).[27] Similarly, although Hegel emphasizes the sublime spirituality of the Genesis account of God's creating the universe – God verbally commands things into existence[28] – he says nothing in *Aesthetics* about the same book's portrayal of companionship between God and humanity from the very beginning – "They heard the sound of God walking in the garden at the time of the evening breeze" (Genesis 3:8, NRSV). So too, Hegel says nothing about how the Hebrew scriptures picture God as being immanent as well as transcendent to creation or as having covenantal relations with Israel and, more broadly, with humankind. While it is so that Hebrew sacred poetry portrays God as one supreme creator and ruler, and all creation as finite and dependent on God, the relations it presents between God and creation and between God and humankind are more complicated and nuanced than the stark sublimity Hegel finds there.

Be that as it may, the point I wish to pursue pertains to the kind of concept Hegel takes the sublime to be. It is not the concept of a reflective judgment that raises a subjective claim to universal validity, à la Kant. Nor is it merely a descriptive label that properly applies only to "romantic art and belated romantic art," à la Elkins.[29] Rather, the sublime is an art-historiographic concept that enables us to interpret ancient religiously inflected poetry arising from a communal way of life. This has implications for how we understand art, religion, and their relation. It also raises questions about whether and how we can use the concept of sublimity to interpret contemporary phenomena, whether artistic or otherwise. Let me next discuss relations between art and religion and then consider the contemporary applicability of "the sublime."

2. TRUTH AND THE SUBLIME

2.1 Forms of Absolute Spirit

For Hegel, art of the sublime marks a crucial step toward the fulfillment of art's historical vocation, namely, a step toward *individualization*. In sublime art, the divine is individualized as one God, and human beings become individually responsible agents of God's will. Nevertheless, the *humanization* of the divine awaits the stage of classical art, especially the art of classical Greece, and the *internalization* of the divine awaits the emergence of romantic art in the Christian era. Only in the Christian era, when God becomes recognized as a spirit, to be worshipped in spirit and in truth, does the divine become fully internalized within human consciousness and self-consciousness. That is when art comes completely into its own as a form of absolute spirit – a realm of culture, alongside religion and philosophy, where the divine comes to articulation within the individual products of art making and art interpretation. Despite Hegel's strong appreciation for the art of classical Greece, which he shared with other German intellectuals of his generation, the art of his own time represents the temporary telos of art's historical trajectory – temporary because, on my reading of Hegel, he neither predicts nor precludes future historical development.

What unites art, religion, and philosophy on Hegel's account is that they all have comprehensive truth as their preoccupation. This comprehensive truth is the divine meaning of existence as individualized, humanized, and internalized via the historical process he traces. Hegel's term for such meaning is "absolute truth." Art, religion, and philosophy are for him three complementary forms of "absolute spirit" that differ in their modes of presentation. We would not stray too far from Hegel if we said that in absolute spirit the divine recognizes itself in human consciousness and the human recognizes itself in God and, with the human, the entire world. Hegel puts it like this: "The spirit in its truth is absolute [*Der Geist als wahrer Geist ist an und für sich*]. Therefore it is not an essence lying in abstraction beyond the objective world. On the contrary, it is present within objectivity in the finite spirit's recollection or inwardization [*Erinnerung*] of the essence of all things – i.e., the finite apprehends itself in its own essence and so itself becomes essential and absolute."[30]

Art accomplishes such self-recognition in the mode of "*sensuous knowing* [*sinnliches Wissen*]." The task of art is to apprehend comprehensive truth via sensuous configuration and thereby to present it for perceptual interpretation (*Anschauung und Empfindung*).[31] Religion accomplishes the finite's self-recognition as infinite in the mode of "pictorial thinking" (*Vorstellung*), whereby the meaning that art presents in external products can be inwardly embraced by heart and soul (*Herz und Gemüt*) via the practices of worship (*Andacht*).[32] Philosophy, by contrast, unites the productive objectivity of art and the subjective pictorial thinking of religion in an untrammeled conceptual comprehension of the truth. The content of philosophy as "divine service" or "liturgy" (*Gottesdienst*) would not be available to it if truth were not apprehended in art and religion. Yet, on their own, art and religion cannot provide the true thought of truth: "true thought, the Idea, is at the same time the most real and most objective [*sachlichste*] universality which only in thinking can apprehend itself in the form of its own self."[33]

Like the entire discussion of art in Hegel's *Aesthetics*, his concept of the sublime both assumes and embodies his conception of art, religion, and philosophy as complementary realms of absolute spirit. But what are we to make of such Hegelian reflections on absolute spirit today, in a society where the dominant philosophies aim to be postmetaphysical, and where much of what Hegel calls "fine art" (*schöne Kunst*) has become anti-art? In particular, what are we to make of his art-historiographic concept of sublime art, which presupposes his understanding of art as absolute spirit?

2.2 Contemporary Art of the Sublime

In the essay cited earlier, James Elkins argues against using the concept of the sublime to discuss contemporary art: it is too vague, he claims, and it lets writers "smuggle covert religious meaning into texts that are putatively secular."[34] At one level Hegel would agree with Elkins. If the art being interpreted is indeed thoroughly secular, then it is highly unlikely to bear much resemblance to the ancient sacred poetry that epitomizes the sublime in Hegel's account. At another level, however, Hegel might think a vast portion of contemporary art historiography, not to mention philosophy, casts its sublimity-seeking net too short, largely because it employs too sketchy a map of art, religion, and philosophy. If, at bottom, art, religion, and philosophy are complementary attempts to apprehend and present comprehensive truth, and if the nexus of divinity and humanity is at the centre of truth, then it would be odd indeed if no post-symbolic art, including contemporary art, carries traces of the sublime. It would also be strange if historically informed scholars could not find such traces.

Hegel acknowledged as much in his own day when he said we can find the form of symbolic art "recurring in the classical and romantic art-forms"[35] and, when discussing "the new gods of Greek art," he suggested that their shapes require "the expression of loftiness, of classical *beautiful* sublimity."[36] Moreover, William Desmond rightly says that Hegel's account of romantic art "points us to an inward sublime, the abyss of infinite interiority of (for Hegel) Christian and modern [humanity],"[37] and Donald Burke has argued that, insofar as art as a whole fails to achieve the absolute in its conceptual purity, "Hegel's entire project in the *Aesthetics* depends on the category of the sublime," such that it is "a quasi-sublime text."[38] Even Theodor Adorno, no fan of either Kant's subjectivism or Hegel's absolute spirit, suggests at one point that "in a subtle way, after the [historical] fall of formal beauty, the sublime was the only aesthetic idea left to modernism [*die Moderne*]."[39]

Finding traces of the sublime would not be the same as simply applying Hegel's concept of the sublime to contemporary phenomena, thereby distorting his conception and ignoring his insistence on the historical character of various art-forms. Rather, it would be an attempt to discover significant historical continuity between the artistic practices and products he labeled sublime and elements of art production and interpretation today. Such continuity could reside in traditions of art making and art interpretation. It also could lie in a social-institutional complex of problems taken up from one generation to the next. Without pretending to establish the relevant lines of continuity, which would require a much longer discussion, let me at least indicate why this would be worth doing.

One way to trace the sublime in contemporary art is to ask whether a poem or film or art installation or musical performance simultaneously points toward transcendence, thematizes its own nontranscendence, and acknowledges its dependence on that toward which it points. Because, for various reasons, I am uncomfortable with the language of "transcendence" and "nontranscendence," let me rephrase this as follows. Does a specific art product or art event simultaneously point toward something radically other than itself, thematize its own difference from what is radically other, and acknowledge its dependence on the other toward which it points? It seems to me entirely plausible that many contemporary art products or events could display such a tendency toward the sublime.

Prominent among them would be ones that struggle with deep loss or suffering but refuse to let societal evil have the last word.[40] Although one should not equate such refusal with what Hegel describes as ancient Hebrew poetry's sublime attempt and unavoidable failure to present the Lord, the two are not unconnected. According to Hegel, in relation to God as supreme creator and ruler of the universe, Hebrew poetry portrays the creature as "perishing and powerless," the world as "bereft of God" (*entgötterte*), and the human individual as finite, perishable, unworthy before God, aware of one's own wickedness, and yet responsible for both good and evil.[41] Contemporary art that struggles with societal evil has a similar sense of human finitude and failure. Often it also resonates with the Hebrew sublime's insistence on the difference between good and evil, its recognition that evil is both our responsibility and beyond our own power to undo, and its sense that evil cannot have the last word. Unlike the ancient Hebrew sublime as described by Hegel, however, the contemporary sublime might point to a different basis for hope in the face of societal evil – not a dependence on God as supreme creator and ruler, but something else, yet something radically other than the societal world we currently inhabit.[42] Terrence Malick's film *The Tree of Life* (2011) provides an especially striking and telling example.

3. THE TREE OF LIFE

Critics both celebrated and denounced *The Tree of Life* when it premiered in 2011. By all accounts, it is an ambitious and extraordinary film. One issue that has divided the film's critics concerns its use of fragmented non-linear narrative. The key to understanding this usage, it seems to me, is to view the film as art of the sublime. Writing in the *New York Times*, A.O. Scott gets at this when he says: "The sheer beauty of this film is almost overwhelming, but ... its aesthetic glories are tethered to a humble and exalted purpose, which is to shine the light of the sacred on secular reality."[43] No coherent and linear narrative would suffice to convey the grandeur of life and its mysterious origins and destiny – whether the life of the film's "protagonist" Jack O'Brien or the life of creation as a whole. In the divine words from the book of Job that open the film:

Where were you when I laid the foundations of the earth? ...
When the morning stars sang together
And all the [children] of God shouted for joy? (Job 38:4, 7)

By opening with these words, the film signals that a struggle with suffering is central to the fragmented narrative to follow, as does a sermon midway through the film on Job and the suffering of the innocent.

3.1 Fragmented Narrative

The first words Jack O'Brien (Sean Penn) speaks in voiceover give us the perspective from which this struggle is told: "Brother. Mother. It was they who led me to your door." The film unfolds Jack's adult quest to reconnect both with his younger brother R.L. (Laramie Eppler), whose death at age nineteen had shattered Jack's mother, and with his mother, whose voice soon tells of two paths through life – grace, which loves and accepts, and nature, which dominates and only wants to please itself. Late in the film Jack's quest will bring him to a desert threshold. Crossing this threshold, he enters an otherworldly place where his family can embrace and where his mother, opening her hands into the light, finally can say in voiceover, "I give him to you. I give you my son." The intricate structure of the film assigns this voiceover a triple meaning: Jack's mother, played by Jessica Chastain, accepts the anguish and mystery of her middle son's death; she points Jack to the light of grace; and she echoes a Christian narrative of divine redemption through the gift of God's child. The images and sounds from nature and an urban landscape that follow affirm the peacefulness of this release.

From Jack's perspective, the struggle with suffering also has a triple meaning. First, it is a struggle to reconcile the deep division within himself between his mother's way of grace and his father's way of nature. A recognized architect, Jack clearly has succeeded where his father failed. He has become the accomplished artist and businessperson that his father strove unsuccessfully to be. Yet Jack cannot accept the grimly competitive motivation his father has repeatedly urged upon him. Similarly, Jack has retained his mother's open spirit and her love of creation. In a voiceover about thirty-six minutes into the film he says, "You spoke to me through her. You spoke to me from the sky. The trees. Before I knew I loved you, believed in you. When did you first touch my heart?" Although "you" is left open-ended, it clearly refers to something beyond human striving and accomplishment. (In a vignette several minutes later, Mrs O'Brien, holding one of her toddlers and pointing to the sky, says, "That's where God lives.") Yet, as an adult, Jack cannot embrace his mother's seeming naïveté.

Nevertheless, neither parent is as one-dimensional as this brief description suggests. In fact, it is in recognizing their complexity that Jack finally comes to accept both sides of his divided self. Late in the film, for example, Jack's father, played by Brad Bitt, loses his job, and confesses in voiceover, "I wanted to be loved because I was great." Then, surprisingly, he says, "Look ... at the glory around us. Trees and birds. I lived in shame. I dishonored it all and didn't notice the glory. I'm a foolish man." Right after this remarkable confession, the young Jack (Hunter McCracken) in voiceover says, "Father. Mother. Always you wrestle inside me. Always you will." Then he admits to Mr O'Brien, "I'm as bad as you are. I'm more like you than her," and his father, embracing him, murmurs, "My sweet boy." The father and mother wrestling inside Jack are more nuanced than the father whom Jack in voiceover had asked God to kill and more than the mother toward whom the young Jack had showed an erotic attraction, in two separate scenes not long before his father's confession.

The second arena of struggle lies in Jack's responses to death and disease as a boy. When a childhood friend drowns, the young Jack wonders in voiceover, "Was he bad?" This quickly turns into accusations: "Where were you? You let a boy die. You'll let anything happen. Why should I be good ... if you aren't?"

The third arena, closely related to these responses, is more immediate and intimate, namely, his mother's response to the death of her second son. In the film's first dramatic action, right after Mrs O'Brien says in voiceover "I will be true to you. Whatever comes," she receives a telegram announcing the nineteen-year-old R.L.'s death. She is devastated, crying out "Oh God!" Then, "My son." And, "I just want to die ... to be with him." The condolences uttered by Jack's grandmother ring hollow. Jack's father, more stoical in his response, seems to experience remorse rather than grief: "I made him feel shame. My shame. That poor boy. That poor boy." At this point the flickering flame from the film's opening returns, and Jack in voiceover asks, "How did you come to me? In what shape? What disguise?" Soon we see Jack as an adult lighting a candle, presumably in his brother's memory, and reflecting: "I see the child that I was. I see my brother. True. Kind. He died when he was nineteen."

This is the crisis from which the film unfolds, as Jack, now in his sterile office amid glass-and-steel skyscrapers, says, "I just feel like I'm bumping into walls. My world's gone to the dogs." Amid sounds of the waves and wind and images of the desert and sea, we hear in voiceover a son's "How did I lose you? Wandered? Forgot you?," a young boy's "Find me," the son's "How did she bear it? Mother," and the mother's "Was I false to you?" Mrs O'Brien's gaze into the treetops suggests she is not simply asking another human being. Jack's struggle is to come to terms with his own youthful jealousy and cruelty toward the brother he has lost, to accept his mother's special attachment to R.L., and to move past her refusal to accept R.L.'s death.

All of this reaches a resolution near the end of the film, in the otherworldly scene already mentioned. This scene unfolds to the sound of the "Agnus Dei" from Hector Berlioz's *Requiem*, *Opus 5*. Jack embraces his mother and places a hand on his father's shoulder. We see a tree, then the hand of Jack's brother R.L. cupping a candle. Now Jack and then his dad carry his brother. Mom tenderly holds R.L. and kisses an elderly hand. The sun sets over the sea. A lone seagull calls. Darkness falls. A blue candle burns. Sunlight returns. Mother and R.L. are together once more. A theatrical mask floats down in the water. Jack and his mother look to the horizon as R.L. walks away. Then Jack's mother walks calmly toward the sunlight. Her eyes close as in death, to be tended by angelic friends, and we hear her voiceover, "I give him to you. I give you my son." In accepting her son's death, Mrs O'Brien has also released Jack from his own guilt and anguish.

3.2 Hermeneutic Sublimation

Like the main characters – Jack and his parents – this film is multilayered. My summary of the narrative only begins to unpeel some layers, and I have said very little about the film's rich visual imagery and powerful soundtrack. Nevertheless, I have uncovered enough to suggest three reasons why it makes sense to interpret *The Tree of Life* as art of the sublime. They have to do with the body of Malick's work, the film's sociohistorical setting, and its film-critical context.

First, such an interpretation helps establish the film's continuity with Malick's earlier work. As Steven Rybin notes, the characters in Malick's previous films are open ended, and they require the viewer to accompany them "as they creatively imagine and shape meaning and identity."[44] The resulting search for meaning, both within the film and on the viewer's part, points beyond the film and the film experience to what makes them possible. Malick's films do not so much give us "perceptions of a world transcending history" as they give us "perceptions of worlds existing within the materiality of history." They posit "the desire for transcendence ... as just one aspect of, and potential response to, existential life."[45] This implies, on the one hand, that human experience never fully encompasses the mysteries of nature in Malick's films and, on the other hand, that human experience is never self-enclosed.

Yet *The Tree of Life* does add something new to Malick's filmic quest for meaning, Rybin says. The characters in this film "are not so much concerned with voicing meaning but are rather on a spiritual quest for the very origins that 'spark' their voice and cause their search for narratives to happen." In lighting a candle for R.L., for example, Jack O'Brien simultaneously signals the question "why the human being is driven to light the candle ... in the first place,"[46] and this opens Jack's story potentially to be the viewer's own story. In *The Tree of Life*, Malick's decades-long quest for filmic transcendence from within everyday experience culminates in questions about the spiritual origin and destiny of that very quest.

Second, to interpret *The Tree of Life* as art of the sublime allows one to acknowledge the specifically American lineage of Malick's filmmaking. Citing John Orr's *Contemporary Cinema*, for example, Hannah Patterson identifies Malick's first three feature-length films – *Badlands* (1973), *Days of Heaven* (1978), and *The Thin Red Line* (1998) – as an emphatically American "cinema of poetry," alongside the work of David Lynch, Robert Altman, and Martin Scorsese. Such cinema thematizes the myths of the American Dream, exploring what these myths both promise and preclude.[47] One sees this, for example, in an Emersonian emphasis on the "spiritual, transcendental nature of war" in Malick's *The Thin Red Line*, which dramatizes "the opposition between nature as paradise and modern human society as paradise lost."[48]

More broadly, one can plausibly view Malick's films, especially *The Tree of Life*, as belonging to the literary and visual-artistic tradition that Mary Arensberg and others call "the American sublime."[49] Centrally identified with Ralph Waldo Emerson and Walt Whitman in the nineteenth century and with Wallace Stevens in the twentieth, the American sublime, according to Rob Wilson, is a "poetic genre" and an "imaginal ideology" that has roots in seventeenth-century Puritanism (e.g., Anne Bradstreet) and eighteenth-century liberalism (e.g., William Livingston) and that persists to the present.[50] What distinguishes the American sublime from European versions is a close attachment between the vastness of nature and the grandeur of American national ambitions. The self both interrogated and celebrated in the American sublime is not the rational and moral self of the Kantian sublime.[51] Nor is it the imaginative and intuitive self of the Romantic sublime (e.g., William Wordsworth and J.M.W. Turner).[52] Rather, the American sublime foregrounds the self-reliant and self-affirming selves of Emerson and Whitman, respectively – selves whose identity is wrapped up in a national narrative of technological invention, reinvention, domination, destruction, and loss.[53]

When viewed within the historically rooted "imaginal ideology" of the American sublime, *The Tree of Life* appears both to enact and to challenge a powerful national narrative at the moment of its apparent collapse, namely, the American story of competitive greatness predestined by nature to conquer the world. The film turns the vastness of nature into a reminder of all that has been lost, and it lets the skyscrapered achievements of a can-do nation fade into the memory of a mysterious origin that overreaches all human efforts. As played out in the spiritual quest of Jack O'Brien, the confident self of the American sublime becomes a shattered and divided self, one whose only hope for healing and wholeness lies in love: love of nature, love of others, and love of the silent call, a flickering flame, from which everything comes and to which all return.

A third reason for interpreting this film as art of the sublime is to challenge a dominant paradigm in literary and cultural studies. The publication of Thomas Weiskel's brilliant book *The Romantic Sublime* in 1976, just a few years after Malick released his first feature film, set the stage for repeated poststructuralist readings of "the sublime." What has since become known as "the postmodern sublime" is not so much a literary and artistic tradition as it is a theoretical construct that strips away the religious and spiritual aura of the Romantic tradition and replaces it with a poststructuralist penumbra. In a game-changing move, Weiskel reformulates the Kantian sublime along semiotic and psychoanalytic lines. On his reading of "the structure of Romantic transcendence," the representational unattainability of nature and reason's superiority in the Kantian sublime become a disruption due to excess on the part of either signifier or signified.[54] The explanation for such disruption and excess lies in the role repression plays within the "subject's" libidinal economy, specifically in either superego anxiety or narcissistic fear of deprivation.[55]

By taking this approach, Weiskel aims to do justice to "what separates our era" from the age of nineteenth-century Romanticism, namely, our "general assumption" that we can do without "god-terms."[56] Yet he runs the risk, as Wilson pointedly puts it, of so oedipalizing the sublime as to dehistoricize it altogether and thereby "to subject the agents and contexts of the sublime to the eternal return of the same Western plot: Daddy, Mommy, and Me in poetic disguise."[57]

Obviously, one *could* easily use this oedipal plot as a hermeneutical lens through which to view *The Tree of Life*. Jack O'Brien seems to suffer from both superego anxiety and narcissistic fear, and this suggests, in Weiskel's terms, that, surprisingly, both the "negative" and the "positive" sublime are the objects of Jack's quest and perhaps of the film as a whole. Yet to take such a poststructuralist approach would be either to ignore the obvious "god-terms" in Malick's film or to so "detranscendentalize" or "desublimate" them that the film's spiritual meaning gets lost. To resist this despiritualizing paradigm, as well as to understand *The Tree of Life* within Malick's oeuvre and sociohistorical setting, it makes sense to interpret his film as art of the sublime.

4. THE POSTSECULAR SUBLIME

Indeed, to my way of interpretation, Malick's *The Tree of Life* very movingly presents a *postsecular* sublime. Far from sharing "our era's" assumption that we can dispense with "god-terms," the film asks how we might experience divine love anew. It also raises the question whether, after all, we do not live in the secular society presupposed by Weiskel's poststructuralist paradigm, whether, instead, we live in a postsecular society.

Here I use the term *postsecular* to refer to a society that has undergone secularization, only to find that dominant tendencies in a secularized society are not as obvious as they once appeared. Let me call attention to three secularizing tendencies: institutional differentiation, religious privatization, and the dominance of social institutions, such as an administrative state and a turbocapitalist economy, that are not religious in character. In a postsecular society it becomes apparent that institutional differentiation need not make religious institutions and practices irrelevant to public life; that religion itself is not a private matter but plays important roles in society; and that the dominance of so-called "secular" institutions might be neither as secure nor as salutary as it once seemed. In such a society, there would be room for what I am calling "the postsecular sublime."

The postsecular sublime would be a nexus of artistic practices and genres in which the supposed secularity of contemporary society is both acknowledged and challenged. Such art would acknowledge institutional differentiation, religious privatization, and the dominance of nonreligious institutions but refuse to let these tendencies be decisive for the meaning this art seeks. Instead, postsecularly sublime art would point beyond secular tendencies toward something that supersedes them. As a film of the postsecular sublime, for example, *The Tree of Life* points us toward something incomparably greater than ourselves; something with which we long to connect but cannot reach; something on which our very lives depend. Is it nature? Is it grace? Or is it an ongoing tension between the two? The film also points toward transformations that range from the intimately personal to family dynamics, the artworld (specifically film, music, and architecture), society as a whole, and perhaps the entire cosmos.

The Tree of Life is art of the postsecular sublime – sublime not only in its content but also in its structure and effects. Meditative voiceovers, chronological displacements of the family narrative, unexpected transitions from intimate scenes to the swirling cosmos – all these nonlinear techniques crack open the film's structure toward the enigmatic flickering flame that begins and ends the film. They have the effect of placing the viewer in a suspended state of perpetual wonder. *The Tree of Life* is not simply *about* the sublime. It aims to *be* what it is about.

Perhaps it is no accident that the artistic vision from which this film arises is informed by a spiritual or religious sensibility, as seen in Jewish and Christian scriptural imagery of the "tree of life." It is an open question whether the contemporary sublime *must* draw on such sensibilities. I certainly would not want to limit its historical roots to ones that are overtly or covertly religious. Yet commentary and criticism on works such as *The Tree of Life* will not do justice to their sublime character if the interpretation rigorously ignores or suppresses the spiritual or religious sensibilities at work in their creation.

These contexts are more than what Elkins calls "crypto-religious." They involve, for example, both a Christian heritage and religious schooling on Terrence Malick's part. Moreover, Malick received training in philosophy, having studied with Stanley Cavell at Harvard University, published a translation of Martin Heidegger's *Vom Wesen des Grundes*,[58] and taught philosophy at MIT. To ignore these contexts and the larger connections they imply would be to remove the film from historical traditions and social-institutional problems that can help us make sense of its sublime character.

That, in turn, points to the larger concern of my discussion, namely, the contemporary status of art, religion, and philosophy, and the relations among them. Let me conclude with a controversial proposal: to have adequate interpretations for postsecular art, scholars and critics would do well to reclaim a Hegelian understanding of art, religion, and philosophy as complementary pursuits of comprehensive truth. This is not to say that every single artwork or religious practice or philosophical theory must pursue comprehensive truth. Rather, the vocations of these cultural fields as a whole, and their contributions as cultural fields to society and human life, are circumscribed by their complementary pursuit of comprehensive truth.

I do not have space here to make an extended argument for this proposal. Suffice it to say that my proposal requires and implies a conception of truth that, like Hegel's, does not restrict it to propositional truth. Moreover, the proposal regards both art and religion as primarily, although not exclusively, *non*propositional modes of seeking, knowing, and telling the truth. As I have argued elsewhere, the arts are truth-related as modes of imaginative disclosure. The hallmarks of their capacity for truth are authenticity, integrity, and significance.[59] So too, religious traditions and practices are truth-related as modes of worshipful disclosure. Religious communities seek through their stories and rituals of faith to remember and celebrate what they take and trust to be the ultimate source of sustenance, and thereby to disclose the meaning of their lives and of the societies they inhabit.[60] Neither imaginative nor worshipful disclosure is primarily propositional, even though what I call "art talk" is necessarily propositional, as are the teachings and doctrines that figure prominently in theologically informed religions. Rather, as I have suggested in chapter 4, artistic truth is pre-propositional, and religious truth is post-propositional. Although not exactly in line with Hegel's understanding of art and religion as complementary forms of absolute spirit, to regard them as modes of primarily nonpropositional disclosure allows one to retain his sense of their historical vocation, now in a contemporary context.

Philosophical truth, by contrast, *is* propositional, but in a way that disturbs standard philosophical models of propositional truth. Hegel speaks in this connection of the "speculative proposition" (*spekulativer Satz*).[61] The claims that are central to philosophy, while they take propositional form, are not straightforwardly empirical or logical truth claims. Instead, they address the ontological and epistemological and sociohistorical conditions or, better, processes within which empirical and logical truth claims get made. Perhaps there is no better indication of this than the claims philosophers make about the nature and role of truth itself. If one does not allow for truth to be more comprehensive than propositional truth, philosophical propositions about truth will turn out not to fit the criteria identified in a theory of truth. To what facts, for example, do the propositions about truth within a correspondence theory of truth correspond?

Yet there is more to Hegel's understanding of philosophical truth than this metalogical point. For he thinks art and religion offer the comprehensive truth content to which philosophy gives propositional articulation. Hence a philosophy that holds art and religion at arm's length – for the sake of conceptual purity or postmetaphysical respectability, for example – empties itself of crucial content. Alternatively, a philosophy that makes art and religion central to its own self-reflection is in a position to live up to the vocation of philosophy. This vocation, in contemporary language, is to pursue the dialectical disclosure of life and society, faithful to the principle of logical validity, with a view to other societal principles such as solidarity and justice, and in step with what art and religion disclose.

Contemporary art of the sublime is one important reason why such a philosophy is both needed and required. For if we want to interpret the larger meaning of artworks such as *The Tree of Life*, we need to go beyond debates about technical merits, aesthetic qualities, and the culture industry. We must consider how such works are positioned within sociohistorical traditions and institutions that have deep roots in spiritual orientations and religious practices. We also need to ask how they contribute to our understanding and addressing apparently intractable issues of societal evil.

A philosophy that regards its task as the dialectical disclosure of life and society, in tandem with artistic and religious disclosure, can help us find the requisite interpretative language and categories. It can help us see that "the sublime" is not, contra Elkins, a mere "relic of other centuries" best abandoned in favour of more precise terminology. It is a historically rich and relevant concept for imaginative disclosures of the meaning people seek amid societally shaped disasters for which we have no ready answers.

Adorno once described (modern) art as a language of suffering.[62] We can debate whether this description applies to all art. But it certainly captures the import of many significant artworks today. Postsecular art of the sublime gives voice to suffering amid societal evil. Philosophers need to help historians, critics, and theorists of the arts find ways to interpret what such art offers. For, in Adorno's words, "The need to let suffering speak is a condition of all truth."[63]

8

Toronto to Berlin and Back Again

Note: This chapter and the next two are the lightly revised transcripts of three interviews conducted by Dean Dettloff between March 2017 and July 2018. For more details, see "Publication Information" at the end of this book. Three ellipsis dots in brackets [...] indicate where passages from the original transcripts are omitted.

1. RETHINKING TRUTH

Dettloff: I want to get to some of the work you've done over the years, but I'd like to start off with some questions related to your current theoretical work. For several years now, you have been researching the topic of truth across a variety of philosophical traditions, including the broad umbrellas of so-called "analytic" and "continental" philosophy, along with subspecies therein. What made you want to take on a topic so perennial and complex as truth?

Zuidervaart: Well, this topic has been on the horizon for me from the beginning of my graduate studies. When I arrived at ICS in 1972, one of my first courses, alongside the courses I was taking with Cal Seerveld, was with Henk Hart. Henk Hart was engaged in a project of rethinking knowledge and truth. The work he was doing involved talking about the significance of the spirit and the movement of truth; talking about the importance of pragmatism as a way of helping us understand truth beyond what is simply propositional; talking about the Gospel of John, and the entire Hebrew tradition behind it, how that gives you a completely different notion of what truth is all about. He said it's much more about faithfulness, fidelity, dependability, reliability, walking in the right ways. That was all very exciting for me. It opened up a variety of avenues for thinking anew about the whole project of truth.

At the same time, I became interested in the question of how in the arts we acquire knowledge, test that knowledge, learn from that knowledge. As soon as you ask those questions about knowledge and art you get into the question of whether there can be truth in art, and what that comes to. So these two things were happening simultaneously. I was working primarily in aesthetics and on topics having to do with philosophy of art, but also working with Henk Hart and getting excited about systematic questions concerning the nature of knowledge and the nature of truth.

From the very beginning of my graduate studies, forty-five years ago, these topics interested me. If you look at the Master's thesis that I wrote on Kant's aesthetics, you'll see that there's a very long last chapter.[1] That last chapter was an addition to the actual Master's thesis, which I was not satisfied with. I took six months after finishing my Master's thesis to write a new last chapter, and it's all about whether there can be truth in aesthetic experience and aesthetic judgments. I'm sorting it out in Kant, who basically divorces these topics. Truth goes over here, beauty, or at least taste, goes over there, and they don't intersect anymore. For me that wasn't satisfactory. And some of my formulations in the Master's thesis, the language of the formulations, actually come from Henk Hart.

In 1977, Cal Seerveld organized a summer seminar in aesthetics, which attracted graduate students and faculty from many different campuses. He invited me to present a paper as part of that. The paper I presented was "Musical and Musicological Knowledge." At the beginning of that paper, I lay out a short synopsis of a view of knowledge, analysis, and theory that comes directly from the work of Henk Hart. On the basis of that, I go on to say you have to understand theoretical knowledge in order to understand *musicological* knowledge, but you have to understand some other kinds of knowledge in order to understand *musical* knowledge. The question is: how does musical knowledge – the knowledge you have as a practicing musician or as an audience member – how does that relate to one's musicological knowledge as a scholar, when you study the structure and history of music? And then I illustrate how those two things go together. That was all part of my graduate studies before I got into Adorno.

When I got into Adorno, the topic of truth and art was central, because it's central to his work. It comes out of Hegel and Marx. So yes, this topic has been on my horizon for forty-five years. Then, of course, in pursuing it, I needed first to work out to my own satisfaction an idea of artistic truth, which I did.[2] But I knew that the only way to make this idea actually stick would be to have a broad enough notion of truth that could incorporate artistic truth, but not fall into the trap of saying artistic truth is the only type of truth that matters, or the only type of truth that's really true. This meant I needed a broader conception of truth that could also make sense of scientific truth and propositional truth. So by taking on the topic of artistic truth, I was committing myself to this bigger project, which I've been working on since.

Dettloff: So it's not so much taking on the topic of truth at the end of your career as it is the culminating or apex point of where you started.

Zuidervaart: Exactly. And in a sense the topic took me on. Somehow, the issue grabbed me, because it seemed like it was so central to the project of reformational philosophy, but it was not addressed well. I was never satisfied with the stuff in Dooyeweerd's *New Critique* on the topic of theoretical truth. I always found it incomplete or inadequate. And Vollenhoven was always so cryptic, he hardly says anything about it, even though in the background, you think, there's got to be a different notion of truth going on here. I read some of his early work where he was still more of a Platonist, and he did have a stronger view of truth, a "*logos* speculation." The "Word" (*logos*) kind of means the structure of being, but that stuff is really weird.

Trying to propose a new understanding of philosophy and its role in society, a new understanding of society, a new understanding of human life in society, and rooting these understandings in the inspiration of Scripture, the reformational tradition really has owed an account of these big topics in philosophy, and it hasn't given it. Henk was working on it, and I still go back to his stuff. Within the last three months I reread his entire draft syllabus for systematic philosophy, which is in two volumes.[3] [...] I read the whole thing again, because I had to remind myself, what were some of the key ideas and key moves that attracted me?

2. PHILOSOPHY OF MUSIC: BACKING INTO ADORNO

Dettloff: You moved from Kant to Adorno, and, as you're talking now, to the problem of truth. From there you continued to work on other figures in Critical Theory like Honneth and Habermas, and sort of inculcated a particular Marxist tradition. But this work on musicality seems to undergird a lot of your motivations. Could you say more about that?

Zuidervaart: When I finished my Master's thesis, I wanted to write my own philosophy of music, so my dissertation was going to be a systematic philosophy of music.[4] Cal Seerveld, who is very wise, said, well maybe that would be too ambitious for a dissertation, and maybe it would be better to work on somebody else's philosophy of music. I understood the wisdom of his advice, and I always intended to write my own philosophy of music later, which I haven't done. [...]

Back then, the question [...] was which philosopher would be worth working on? Because that's what we did – take on major figures, study them, work out a response to their work. We came down to two options. One was Susanne K. Langer, whose *Philosophy in a New Key* has quite a lot to say about music, and then she went on to write a book called *Feeling and Form*. It's very good stuff, really trying to propose a way of thinking about art that gives it some knowledge character and doesn't reduce it to somehow conveying propositional knowledge. So I was interested in that.

But Cal also wanted me to spend time in Germany, because he thought that would be an important formation for me as a scholar, similar to his formation. He had studied at the Free University of Amsterdam, but then he had a *Wanderjahr*, a wandering year, where he set off to Basel and studied with Karl Jaspers, and ended up in Italy to study with Carlo Antoni, who was *the* Croce expert (Cal wrote his dissertation on Benedetto Croce).[5] He had this European experience and thought that's what I needed. This tipped the scales in the direction of working on somebody in the German tradition, to justify my going to Germany, and that was Adorno. Theodor Adorno was clearly the figure I needed to take on.

So I backed my way into Adorno, into the Critical Theory tradition, because of philosophy of music. And the first things by Adorno that I read were in the philosophy of music, in what was at the time translated as *Philosophy of Modern Music* (now it's translated better as

Philosophy of New Music). I also read some of his articles about Schoenberg and so on. It was exciting stuff; I was extremely fascinated. I was trained in composition and conducting and the history of music and had a strong musical background, and I was really interested in contemporary concert music [...] Well here's a philosopher – Adorno – who's making sense of contemporary music in a philosophically rich way.

Then, of course, once I started reading more widely, I thought, I really need to work my way into his sources. One of the things about Adorno is that he doesn't really *cite* his sources, he *uses* his sources. He's using Hegel, he's using Nietzsche, he's using Marx, he's using Lukács, he's using Freud, using Kierkegaard – it's just *rich*. But it's not spelled out, so you have to find out where it's all coming from.

I went to Berlin in 1977 because there was a musicologist and music philosopher in Berlin, the leading philosopher of music in Germany, probably in the world at the time, Carl Dahlhaus. He was at the Technical University of Berlin, and he had a one-man show, his own institute there, actually as part of the communications department. He was holding forth on music, musicology, and he ended up doing an entire seminar on Adorno's *Aesthetic Theory* while I was there.[6] I contacted him ahead of time and said I'd like to work with him.

When I first arrived there, I spent some time getting to know Professor Dahlhaus. He was a quiet, reticent man who didn't say much. I asked him, in German, as I was still struggling to articulate things in German, "What have you learned from Adorno?" He threw up his hands very starkly and said, "Oh mein Gott!" Adorno was a huge figure in German culture, especially in music and the arts. He was the leading intellectual figure in contemporary music; he had always been at the big contemporary music festivals where Karlheinz Stockhausen, Pierre Boulez, and all these younger composers were doing their stuff. He was writing program notes for the opera and was on the radio a lot, so he was a very big figure in Germany.

That's why I went to Berlin, because Dahlhaus was there. But once I arrived there, I thought, shoot, I've got to understand Hegel and Marx and all these others, so I went to seminars at the Free University of Berlin, which was also a popular spot for Marxists. I was taking three or four seminars, just sitting in on them, every semester. Hegel's *Phenomenology of Spirit* – I went to two seminars on that. I sat in on an entire lecture series about Nietzsche by Wolfgang Müller-Lauter, one of the editors of the critical edition of Nietzsche's works. He gave a survey of Nietzsche's work and life in a semester lecture course. I also sat in on the last seminar that Helmut Gollwitzer gave. He was one of the leading theologians, the intended successor to Karl Barth, and his last seminar was on liberation theology.

3. BERLINER LUFT

Dettloff: Wow, what was the full time period you were in Germany?

Zuidervaart: From 1977 to 1980.

Dettloff: With Gollwitzer and people like Rudi Dutschke around, that must have been an interesting environment to be a Christian scholar in.

Zuidervaart: Yes. Gollwitzer was a big figure, that seminar was packed. Everybody knew who he was, and that this was going to be the last seminar he ever gave.

Dettloff: Did you study other figures in the Frankfurt School?

Zuidervaart: Walter Benjamin was such an important figure in Adorno's work. He was actually respected more highly by people on the left than Adorno was. Benjamin was where it was at, as if Benjamin was the real Marxist and Adorno was sort of a suburban Marxist. Of course, Benjamin didn't write much that had anything to do with Marxist theory or sociology or psychology or any of the stuff that Adorno got into; by his not having written much it was easier to make him out to be the real Marxist. There were a lot of seminars on Benjamin, too, that I sat in on.

One was led by Jacob Taubes, who was also a big figure. He was at the Philosophical Institute at the Free University of Berlin. He made sure they assigned him the smallest room, because he wanted to have an intimate seminar. There was room for about twelve people to sit around the table. He didn't want to have a big crowd. But of course, because Walter Benjamin was such an important figure, all the people on the left were there, and there was no restriction on attending seminars, you could attend no matter who you are; the room was overflowing into the hallway. There were probably sixty people who wanted to be at this seminar.

So Taubes comes in, he sits down. There's no room for anybody. He looks around the room, and he says, "I will not begin this seminar until all of you but twelve leave." Nobody budged. And that was it, that was the end of the first three-hour seminar session. We all went home. Next week, same thing. The room was packed, overflowing into the hallway, people standing, sitting on the floor, like a zoo. He looks around the room and says, "I'm sorry, this room can accommodate twelve people, and I'm not going to start until all but twelve of you leave." Nothing happened, nobody budged. Third week, same thing happened. He looks around the room and says, "Wir beginnen," we start.

Dettloff: What was that Taubes seminar like?

Zuidervaart: Oh, Taubes was full of himself. He was a prima donna: a lot of it was about him, not just about Benjamin. But he was like a rabbinical scholar, committed to working out the details of the text. We spent almost the entire semester on just a couple of essays. One was "Theses on the Philosophy of History," one of the last essays that Benjamin wrote; we spent a long time on the image of the puppet at the very beginning of the essay. We covered two essays the entire semester, because Professor Taubes would worry his way around these sentences, what they meant, what the images were about.

Anyway, that's how I got into studying Marxism: in order to understand Adorno. And I read Georg Lukács, I read Karl Korsch, really key figures at the time that Adorno was a young scholar finding his way. They shaped the discourse of Western Marxism, especially Lukács. Lukács's big essay on the reification of consciousness[7] probably was the single most important essay in the formation of Adorno's version of Marxism, although Adorno never thought that the proletariat would be like the commodity that would achieve consciousness of itself, and thereby become revolutionary. Nevertheless, all the themes in that essay, and the subject-object dialectic and how it has to be reconciled, are throughout Adorno's work. In 2001, I went back to Germany, to Frankfurt this time, for a research visit, and spent most of my time at the Adorno Archive reading his lectures on aesthetics, which hadn't been published yet.[8] I was in the archive, and they had all his books around on the shelves. His piano was there too. But you couldn't actually look at the books on the shelves. Finally I got permission to look at a couple of things, and one was the Lukács book *History and Class Consciousness*. It was falling apart. Adorno had obviously beat this thing up over the years.

The other one I wanted to look at was his copy of *Sein und Zeit*, Heidegger's *Being and Time*. What's always bothered me about Adorno and Heidegger is that Adorno is such an aggressive reader that I'm not sure he actually understood what Heidegger was on about.[9] I just wanted to see what notations were in his copy, how carefully he had read it. So finally I got permission to look at it. Michael Schwartz, who was supervising things, went to the shelf to pull it off – and it's not there! He had no idea it had wandered off. He said, "Oh, Herr Tiedemann must have it!" – to edit the lectures Adorno gave on Heidegger's ontology![10]

4. RETHINKING REFORMATIONAL THOUGHT

Dettloff: I should tell you this story. A friend of mine was working on an MA in philosophy in England, and we were catching up. He had been reading about Critical Theory and art, and he said, "You must have heard of this Christian person writing on Critical Theory and art, I'm really impressed actually that a Christian understands and is doing something creative with Critical Theory." I asked him who it was, and he said it was Lambert Zuidervaart, and asked if I had ever heard of him. At the time I was taking a course with you on theories of interpretation. That interaction was really interesting to me, because what I find so compelling about your work and about ICS in general is that Christianity doesn't preclude but demands creative and unintimidated work with people of other traditions. How does your faith and participation in the reformational tradition relate to the Frankfurt School?

Zuidervaart: Well, I had to struggle with this a lot when I was in Berlin on my own. When Joyce and I arrived there, we knew nobody, absolutely nobody. This was the first time in my life that I had been outside my comfort zone. I grew up in a small community in north-central California, part of a Christian Reformed Church community; went to small Christian schools, a small liberal arts college in the same tradition, Dordt College; went to a small graduate school in the same tradition, ICS; I had lived my entire life in that environment.

Berlin was the first time I was out of that environment, and also in a foreign-language culture, being at these major universities on my own, without any support community intellectually. We did find spiritual support, but intellectually I was trying to find my way in this other tradition, which was really rich and detailed and exciting and important. So I had to struggle a lot.

The way I was trained at Dordt College and then also at ICS was a kind of hermeneutics of suspicion. Cal Seerveld had a way of using Vollenhoven's historiography of philosophy to indicate which "neighbourhoods" you should not live in. He called it "bad neighbourhood philosophy." You don't want to be a geneticist monist interactionist, or in any of all these different traditions, if you're going to do work as a Christian scholar. That's how I was trained. Initially when I was working on Adorno, I was trying to figure out how to characterize his position. And I still have many notes trying to figure out – is he really a dialectical thinker, a contradictory monist? Or is he more of a dualist, like Kierkegaard was? He goes both ways; if you try to classify him with that system, you're probably going to miss something. So finally I said, I can't worry about that.

What I had to do is understand his stuff from the inside out, and this was reinforced early on. I was at a party for graduate students of Carl Dahlhaus [...] This was during the first year I was there, so I was still struggling to speak in German. I felt like a child. What I thought and how I could speak were completely out of sync. I was trying to explain to one of the graduate students there what I hoped to do in my study of Adorno. I made the mistake of saying I was trying to work from a Calvinist standpoint.

And this guy went ballistic. He was so hostile. He said, "You can't be working from a *standpoint*! You have to be part of the *dialectic*!" Completely hostile. And then he just walked away from me. Later, because I was new and didn't know people, I was standing by myself, working out who I should talk to next. I'm not particularly gifted at that kind of small talk. He comes over to me, and he says to me, in German, "So, still standing on your Calvinist standpoint?"

Well, that really set me back. I thought, what have I said that is so offensive? Then I realized, what he was reacting to was any assumption that you have things cased already, and that you can put everyone else into your case. And I thought, even though it was painful, there's something right about what he was saying. So I actually started trying to think differently about the whole project of Christian scholarship, especially the project of trying to understand another scholar's work.

This was really intense. I was taking on very difficult texts, without a whole lot of secondary literature out there. Most of the secondary literature I could access was in German. There was hardly any in English, and not very many works of Adorno had been translated into English. I was immersed in a difficult German project. Towards the end of my stay there, I remember distinctly (I kept a diary the whole time we were there) a dream I had in which Adorno figured. He kept saying over and over "Die Wiege des Wankels." Now that's sheer nonsense in German. Maybe the closest you could come is "The cradle of oscillation," or "The cradle of going back and forth," something like that. When I woke up, I thought, oh yeah, I have to approach a dialectical thinker dialectically. That's the only way to do it. So that's what I ended up doing, working from the inside out, trying to go as far as possible along the path that Adorno mapped out, and then at the end of that coming up with my own rearticulation both of the insights and of the limitations.

That was a new way of working, for me. It marked a break with the reformational tradition as I had received it. However, the person I ended up working with at the Free University of Amsterdam, Johan van der Hoeven, was very sympathetic to this approach. He read texts that way. So I found a compatible adviser, one of the leading figures in that generation of reformational philosophy – not a well-known figure now, but he was appointed to the chair of systematic philosophy at the Free University of Amsterdam – and an extremely gifted reader of texts. He knew the Marxist tradition, he knew the phenomenological tradition, he had read Adorno, so he could help me quite a bit, mostly in the last stages when I spent about four months in the Netherlands rewriting the dissertation. I would meet with him a day at a time. We would meet in his office, haul out cigars, and go through the chapters [...]

There's an essay in my *Religion, Truth, and Social Transformation* book on metacritique.[11] I first wrote that essay in the early 1980s to present at ICS. What I didn't include in the book's explanatory notes is that it was a speech I gave when I was being considered for a position in the history of philosophy at ICS. (My good colleague at The King's University College at the time, Bill Rowe, got that position, and that's when I went to Calvin College instead.) It was actually an interview piece. In that essay I laid out the way I would approach the history of philosophy, showing also how that relates to but departs from the more Vollenhovian problem-historical method, which is what I was trained in.

As you know [Dean], from taking reformational philosophy with me, the issue of the antithesis is a huge issue. I had already come to my own understanding of that issue by the time I finished my dissertation, and it changed the way I do philosophy.[12] For me there is an antithesis, it's an antithesis between spirits, but it's not to be thought of as an antithesis between a particular religious tradition or a particular philosophical tradition and some other. It doesn't go quite to the same textured level that it does in Vollenhoven and Dooyeweerd.

Dettloff: And that's how you, as a Christian scholar, can read someone like Adorno and also maintain something of a standpoint?

Zuidervaart: Yes, and for me this question goes back to Henk Hart's work – where is the spirit of truth? And the spirit of truth moves in mysterious ways. It shows up in Adorno's work, it shows up in Heidegger's work, it shows up in Vollenhoven's work. It's a bit risky: you can end up just saying the spirit of truth is whatever I want it to be. But I think, if you are a careful scholar, and are serious about the project, you can't get away with that.

Dettloff: Let's talk a little more about reformational philosophy, especially because you just had the first volume of essays on reformational philosophy come out[13] and now the second volume is coming out.[14] What do you think is the future for reformational philosophy? Are there concepts or commitments in reformational philosophy that you think deserve a wider hearing or have some staying power? Are there others that maybe need to be retooled?

Zuidervaart: The reformational tradition as a philosophical tradition provides what I call a "holistic pluralism" that's very hard to find anywhere else. On the one hand, it emphasizes the integrity of all things, how they hang together, which goes back to passages like Colossians 1:17, how everything hangs together in Jesus Christ. That's the impetus for it. That means absolutely everything is interconnected. You can formulate this in ways that become ecologically wishy-washy stuff, but the tradition goes way beyond that. It also goes on to say how these interconnections *look*, systematically. You try then to give an account of that. I think that's extremely valuable, and really contrary to so much of twentieth-century and twenty-first-century philosophy, which has become more and more fragmentary, more and more specialized, more and more insular. That's one thing.

With that goes a very strong emphasis on pluralism. Initially it was a kind of structural pluralism, and an emphasis on the pluralism of religious commitments, those two. So a structural and a religious pluralism. This emphasis on pluralism can be expanded to include all the kinds of pluralism that have become important in the latter part of the twentieth- and early part of the twenty-first century – racial, ethnic, gender, sexual, etc. It has the potential to take on many contemporary issues that perplex other philosophies that [...] zero-in on one kind of pluralism and emphasize this without thinking about the rest. Those two things, holism and pluralism, are also what I'm trying to work out in the context of truth. It's a holistic pluralism.

The third thing I would emphasize that I think is extremely valuable from the reformational tradition, which gives it a leg up on almost any other religious philosophy that I know of, is an emphasis on how this holistic plurality is unified in the spirit; the fact that the spiritual direction of things is all-pervasive, completely inescapable, and fundamental to existence. But without turning that into a kind of spiritualism, an escapism, where you think things of the spirit are superior to things of the non-spirit, or what we have to live for is the things of the spirit, so you have to downplay the corporeal, all that stuff that's part of the Western tradition and part of the Christian tradition. I don't know how this happened, but it's exactly what the reformational tradition has been able to offer. It's hard to find it anywhere else. There is a kind of emphasis on pluralism and holism and spirituality that's fundamental in the Catholic tradition, but it's usually combined with a kind of dualism, of sacred and secular, spiritual and natural, and so on and so forth. You can find it in the Lutheran tradition too, and you can certainly find a creation spirituality in the Orthodox tradition. But all these three things together: for me, that's the heart of the reformational tradition as a philosophical tradition.

Along with this goes the social, cultural tradition that informs the reformational tradition and insists on people of faith contributing to society and making a difference in society. This also means, if you're in philosophy, you're going to try to contribute to philosophy, and by way of philosophy to the rest of society, and try to make a difference in philosophy. It means you're never just doing a job; you're never just marking your time as a professional, never just trying to gain a reputation. There's a really strong sense of calling, which I've had […]

And in all this I haven't gotten into any technical details. I mean, for me, for example, the modal theory of Dooyeweerd and Vollenhoven remains one of the most important contributions to an ontology of creation that I know of.[15] I don't work with it in the same kind of detailed, technical way that I used to, but it's still in the background, it's always there. I know with Henk Hart it's the same thing, it's always there. Because it's a way of reminding ourselves, there's more to the world than is dreamt of in most philosophies. It's a way of reminding ourselves of the very important, inherent, good diversity of human life in society and culture, structurally.

Dettloff: I think that's right, to identify those three things as not just uniquely articulated by reformational philosophy but uniquely available to it, allowing for other work to be done, even if it's not paying lip-service to those ontological programs right up front. There have been a few generations now of reformational thought, and it seems to me one of the interesting challenges is how to keep communicating those commitments. Sometimes that involves working out those ontological programs such that they could be internalized and put to work. Sometimes that involves not putting them so heavily on the table but just articulating the spirit or something. As new generations are trying to wrestle through what this tradition is going to mean for them in a contemporary world, how do you think scholars might be able to take it up and make use of it? What are the live issues in reformational philosophy that remain to be worked out and brought into new discourses?

Zuidervaart: I'm a firm believer in revisiting the classics of a tradition. Even though I haven't done as much as I could have in encouraging this in my own teaching, I did find occasions, both at King's and at Calvin, where I was teaching undergraduates, for some of my students to work in the classic texts of Dooyeweerd and Vollenhoven, particularly Dooyeweerd. And also to work in the next-generation texts, Henk Hart's *Understanding Our World* in particular, which is a marvellous rearticulation of the reformational tradition of philosophy in language that is fresh.

So I think it's important for people to go back to the sources and work their way through them. That's a big task. Dooyeweerd was a very ambitious thinker, but he was not a very good writer. Well, I should say the translation is not very good. Actually he's a good writer in Dutch. The translation/paraphrase/expansion that we have available is a hard read. It's a lot of work to go through that. But I still think people should be reading the *New Critique* if they're serious about the whole tradition.[16] Now there's more stuff available from Vollenhoven. Vollenhoven is actually easier to read, I find. It's just that he's cryptic: it's not always clear what he means. It's clear though that he was a better philosopher; I mean, he was trained as a philosopher. Dooyeweerd was trained as a legal theorist.

And I think it's really important for people to take up the next generation's work. There are some key texts there, one of them being Henk Hart's *Understanding Our World*, which did not receive the kind of attention that I thought it should have when it came out. I know there are many issues in that book, and I've tried to identify some of them,[17] but the reason they're important is because they're central issues in the tradition. Hart is wrestling with things having to do with laws and structures and how they relate to existence, how we could ever talk philosophically about God, issues that are indigenous to the tradition. These are big issues.

But then there are things that the tradition, as I received it, had not really gotten around to talking about. One of the things I've said before is that the classics of the tradition, Dooyeweerd and Vollenhoven, never made the linguistic turn or the hermeneutical turn. Twentieth-century philosophy went down a path that left them behind. Now there's the cultural turn, all these turns you have to keep up with somehow. I think that means people have to read the classics on the one hand and read more contemporary formulations on the other hand and try to think these things together on their own.

There also are big questions of life and society that the tradition was not able to take up, particularly issues having to do with ecology and the sustainability of the economy. If you think about political and legal philosophy, the tradition is a statist tradition. The question of how to think about governmental organization in the aftermath of the welfare state and the nation state, which is the space we're in right now – we have to do a lot of new work in order to take that up. Also to take up questions of international law and international governance; without them, we're not going to be able to properly address the environmental crisis. Who knows whether capitalism in its global form will ever implode, but people need to think about what comes next, so we're not just scrambling in the dark as the world falls apart around us.

5. REFORM OR REVOLUTION?

Dettloff: Yeah, maybe we can talk about that tension in the reformational tradition. The Kuyperian motif that sets everything off is sphere sovereignty, and Abraham Kuyper's own participation in governance. That has created a climate for creative political thinking, but it also hamstrings certain discussions about real, transformative change. It almost freeze-frames a certain political ontology, where politics becomes a matter of getting all the parts moving in the right way, but it precludes thinking about massive change. There's a tension between the revolutionary and reformational spirits generally in politics, and reformational philosophy takes its side. Having been formed by reformational thought and revolutionary traditions like Marxism, how do you see that tension working out?

Zuidervaart: One of the big eye-openers for me in studying Adorno was how the revolutionary tradition of Marxism came to an impasse, and that impasse emerged in the 1920s and 1930s. Adorno and his compatriots – Horkheimer, Marcuse – were well aware that there was no revolutionary alternative, no *viable* revolutionary alternative, in Europe, by the time they reached the 1930s. The real revolutionaries were fascists. So you don't have a revolutionary alternative on the left, you don't have a working class that's going to rise up because all it has to lose is its chains. You also don't have a kind of coalition of intellectuals, students, professionals, and so on, who understand the need for dramatic change. What do you do? Where do you turn? What do you point to as a hope for some kind of significant change in the long run?

They were at an impasse and honest enough to recognize this, and not simply wave their hands saying, well it will happen, somehow. Adorno, of course, has been labeled a pessimist, and blamed for not being revolutionary enough. When you look at his diagnosis of late capitalism and the possibilities for political change in that environment, I think you have to say he's mostly right. Habermas probably came to that conclusion at a certain point when he was closer to

Adorno's way of thinking and decided, well, we can't keep making all these noises about the working class and about the proletariat and about revolution being on the horizon. We have to think differently about social change. Now, I feel that Habermas has given up too much from the revolutionary spirit of the Marxist tradition, which means that he has accepted too readily the economic and administrative state systems that are in place, without sufficient critique of those systems *as systems*, and the damage that they cause to human life, to the environment.

I've had to go to the Critical Theory tradition to think about such matters because it actually addresses these issues. The reformational tradition for the most part does not address them. I'm sort of between Adorno and Habermas. On the one hand, I think Adorno's right about the depth of the problems and how difficult it is to envision a society-wide transformation. On the other hand, I think Habermas is right about the importance of the differentiation that we've achieved, and how there are really positive achievements in law, in government structures, in democratic potential at least in the public sphere, and so on, that one wants to hang on to.

But in the end, I come down saying the change that's needed is a change that must go up and down, across and beyond, society as a whole.[18] The only way I can think about the kind of change that's needed is in terms of a transformation that applies to society as a whole but occurs in a differentiated way, so it occurs politically, economically, in civil society, in the arts, and so on. Once you go to that, what I call differential transformation, things get really messy. There's no place you can point and say that's the fulcrum, that's where the change is going to start, that's where revolution is, right there. You can't do that anymore. So I don't know how to classify my approach. I call it transformational. It's not "reformational," because it's not gradualist. But it's also not revolutionary.

Dettloff: I wonder what you make, given your perspective, of the current political climate, which is seeing a resurgence of reactionary populism. In the United States, workers don't identify with leftist movements, and are even antagonistic to them. How does your work as an American scholar translate into that present moment?

Zuidervaart: I'm a bit at a loss with respect to American politics. My first instinct after the 2016 election was to start rereading things that

Adorno had written in the 1930s, 40s, and 50s about American culture. There's actually a book out on Adorno and democracy that does quite a bit of work to show he was concerned about tendencies in American society that were deeply anti-democratic.[19] Of course, what he considered to be genuinely democratic would also find very little room in the American political system, the way it has emerged, because the system doesn't have the depth of representation that I think most Marxists expect. Marxism is a very mixed tradition. There are some people who are more comfortable with representational democracy and others who are more into participatory and deep democracy, radical democracy, so there are variations in the tradition. I think Adorno, although he wrote very little directly on politics, directly on governance and the like, had syndicalist leanings. So he would think that genuine democracy would have to emerge from worker cooperatives, for example. In any case, my first instinct was to start reading some of that stuff again, which I did a little bit, and that's my first instinct simply because I think the Frankfurt School actually had its finger on many of the cultural and political tendencies in North America at the time that have continued and have not been well-identified and well-addressed.

There's a kind of apolitical politics in the US. In a sense, most Americans don't give a shit about politics or government until it directly affects them in one way or another. There's a kind of naïveté about what makes for a good society politically, and also a naïveté about how deeply things can go wrong. The Frankfurt School was writing about anti-Semitism. *Studies in Prejudice* was an entire series of studies at the time, and the Frankfurt School, Adorno particularly, were involved in a huge social-psychological study on *The Authoritarian Personality*.[20] All their data came from American culture, American citizens, and they were able to spell out some of the psychological traits of people who tend to support fascists in America. If you go to the "F-scale," the famous "fascist scale," it makes a whole lot of sense.

Adorno also did an entire study on the radio speeches of Martin Luther Thomas.[21] Thomas was a fundamentalist radio preacher during the 1930s in southern California, where Adorno was living. So Adorno would listen to all these radio broadcasts, and then he'd do a content and rhetorical analysis, and he was able to identify all the rhetorical tricks of the fascist orator in this radio preacher. Well he's just one radio preacher of a whole host of very influential radio preachers – [Charles E.] Coughlin, Paul Harvey, I mean this stuff has been going on, in terms of an ideological stance on the world that has political ramifications, for generations already in the US, combined with a very deeply anti-intellectual cultural strand. Climate change denial and anti-science and all the stuff that has come to the fore in a very dangerous way: it's always been there; it's just that the constellation of these things now has a kind of legitimacy simply because a leading figure who endorses that stuff got elected president.

Beyond that I just don't know where to go. When you look at my work, I'm really a philosopher's philosopher. Except maybe in my *Art in Public* book, I don't go into the details of political movements, political problems, and the like. So I feel a bit out of my element there. That's not a satisfactory answer, but that's where I'm at.

Dettloff: That's not an uncommon position, though. Even among career activists this feels like a massive defeat, and it is.

Zuidervaart: We are connected to a number of people in Grand Rapids who care deeply about what has happened, and we had one meeting before the 2017 presidential inauguration to talk about what we should do. Many of the people in that network are college professors. The thing that I said was, I feel as if there's been a massive failure on the part of college and university educators, and I include myself, to reshape political discourse and to create opportunities for people of different persuasions to have meaningful dialogue and debate. Somehow, we have missed that opportunity. The US higher education system is one of the best in the world, and it has not had a significant impact on political discourse in the US. It's baffling. When you look at the people who form the governments, and I'll just go back to the Obama administration, these are highly educated people. They're well-trained. They know what they're talking about. And yet, somehow, they're not able to give leadership in a way that speaks to the ordinary folks who are upset about things.

I can understand it from a distance. I can understand how higher education has become hyperspecialized; how it's become isolated from the rest of society, despite all the rhetoric about community engagement and so on; how within disciplines people have become more and more insular and just talk to each other. But I still think *we're educators*. We're teaching undergraduates and graduate students. These are people at a very important turning-point in their lives, when they're becoming adults in their own right. How is it that we –

especially my generation, the anti-Vietnam War generation – how did we just mess up?

6. SERVICEABLE SCHOLARSHIP

Dettloff: What do you make of ICS's involvement in this situation? As a graduate student here, the sense I get is that the Institute has its feet in both worlds, in a way, because it's supported largely by non-academic people, people who have interest in academics and appreciate it but nevertheless aren't doing that kind of work as a profession. Yet on the other hand, ICS puts out good scholarship and tries to make itself accountable. That seems to be something the reformational tradition is sort of birthed in, ontologically, by privileging naïve experience, which can be broken theoretically, but in the interest of coming back to that experience.

Zuidervaart: Yes, that's right. It's always been a tension at ICS because ICS has wanted to do everything – continuing education, adult education, worldview education, high-powered graduate education, MAs, PhDs – and a small institution can't do all those things well. So there's always been a tension about where you put your energies. But the impetus has always been right, and the impetus has always been that scholarship is for the sake of life and ordinary people.[22] It's hard to say exactly what that means, when you're actually writing a dissertation on Adorno's aesthetic theory, as I was, but that's always been the litmus test. Cal [Seerveld] always talked about philosophy as the "janitor of the sciences," and he always talked about "serviceability." In the end, scholarship has to be serviceable. That's very much part of the Kuyperian tradition, because Kuyper's movement was a movement of the *kleine luyden*, the little people, who were just ordinary folks, farmers, small-business owners, and so on, who cared about being good Calvinists in society and making a difference that way.

So the Institute has always been different in this way from most graduate schools and most universities; it's always had that sense of doing scholarly work as well as possible but for the sake of ordinary folks, society, and culture. That's part of its really valuable legacy, even though, when push came to shove, I was always on the more "scholarly" side, saying the priority should be the PhD and the MA programs. I understood the importance of worldview formation and did a little of that myself, but I always thought, if you're going to make a difference in the long run, it has to make a difference in the academy, because that's what we're good at and called to. This might not be satisfying for folks who didn't go to graduate school and don't necessarily understand all this philosophy, postmodernism, Critical Theory – the people actually paying our bills! Still, that's what we're called to, to make a difference in the academy with a view to making a difference beyond the academy. That's been one of the reasons ICS has remained such a central institution for me. It's been one of the few places I know of where this connecting of scholarship with ordinary life is indigenous to the institution; it's not something you add on, saying we've got to show that we're relevant to get government funding or whatever.

Dettloff: We haven't talked much about your books *Artistic Truth* and *Art in Public* except tangentially, and you're working on this new manuscript on truth, so perhaps we could circle back to the beginning of our conversation and talk about this sort of "apex" moment in your work. How does this new research on truth relate to these other projects, and could you say more about those projects?

Zuidervaart: In 1991, Joyce, our dog Rosa, our cat Ebony, and our best friend – my best friend – Ron Otten, all lived together in Toronto for a semester, because I was substituting for Cal Seerveld. Cal was on sabbatical, so I taught at the Institute as a visiting professor for a semester. I taught a seminar in aesthetics, and I taught the interdisciplinary seminar, which was really interesting because we were dealing with questions of creation order, a hot topic at the time that led to a famous conference in 1992 where everything hit the fan[23] [...]

So 1991, we're in Toronto, I'm living with my best friend, Ron, who had just finished his MFA in theatre at York University in the acting program. And he and a woman from Quebec had set up a little alternative theatre company called Jokerman Theatre Company, "Jokerman" coming from the song by Bob Dylan; Ron and I were both big fans of Bob Dylan. It was during the first Gulf War. We watched the nightly news, seeing this shock-and-awe bombing of Baghdad and feeling totally depressed about what was going on. But we had each other, and we talked a lot about politics, culture. At the time [...] Ron was working at TV Ontario. So he was very much connected to the media world. We talked about everything, and that was the context – teaching at ICS and living with my friend, Ron – where I first got the idea of a project in which I would talk about the arts in a much more broadly cultural way in relationship to politics, and at the same time work out a notion of truth in art.

At the end of that time, I think in July, when we had just moved back to Grand Rapids, I wrote a prospectus, a four-page description of a book I was going to write, called *Cultural Politics and Artistic Truth*. It talked about how I would draw on the German tradition and interact with more contemporary scholarship in order to work out a conception of the role of art in society, especially with regard to politics, and a notion of how that role is informed by the capacity of art for truth. That was 1991. Well this just happened to be right around the time when a huge battle was going on over funding for the NEA [National Endowment for the Arts], the late 80s and early 90s, a constant battle over whether there should *be* an NEA, to what extent we should fund controversial shows or works like the Serrano *Piss Christ*, and all that was part of the conversation Ron and I were having.

I wanted to make the case that art is important in society. Most of the stuff being done by professional aestheticians wasn't really addressing those issues. In those days, aesthetics in North America was a hyperspecialized, insulated field where people worked on old chestnuts and kept roasting them over the same fire: emotion and music, fiction and nonfiction, a lot of things that for me are very uninteresting, even though that's one of my professional associations (I've been a member of the American Society for Aesthetics since the mid 1970s) [...] I thought some of us philosophers should be addressing these big issues of the role of art in society because that's where the discourse is, that's where the controversies are.

I set out to do that, and of course I did it in the typical Zuidervaartian fashion. I was going to work my way from Hegel to Gadamer, you know, the entire list of usual suspects, primarily in the German tradition, to work out a notion of artistic truth. Then I was going to take up the major figures in political theory and economic thought. But the more I got into it, I realized this is an unending project, I'll never get finished. About this time, I became active with the Urban Institute for Contemporary Arts (UICA)[24] as president of the board and co-chair of their capital campaign, in which capacity I had to do a lot of public presenting to raise money, to explain to politicians why this is important, etcetera, etcetera. I did a lot of public speaking about the arts and started to understand what some of the dynamics were, what some of the issues were, what the arguments against government funding were.

So I got a lot of good practical experience, and the more I did that the more I thought this typical Germanic scholarly route is just not going to cut it. I'm going to have to do some of that, but I can't spend all my time working in and out of the German tradition. I've got to broaden my horizons. I've got to take on some of the key figures in Anglo-American aesthetics, who have boxed that tradition in so that it cannot meaningfully address these kinds of issues. I have to understand why people in the analytic tradition don't think that truth and art have much to do with each other; so I have to work in their texts and figure that out. I have to understand why the few things that have been written by American aestheticians on government funding for the arts and art politics are so thin. That was all new stuff I had to work on. At a certain point, about '95 or '96, I decided there's too much here to do in one book, and I had to split it into two books.

That was a relief, because then I could do more of what philosophers typically do, at least those who are continentally trained, in the *Artistic Truth* book, where I worked out my conception of artistic truth dialoguing with major figures, including Monroe Beardsley, who was the godfather of American aesthetics from the 1950s to the 1960s, and then some more contemporary figures, including Nicholas Wolterstorff and Nelson Goodman, who were big figures in American aesthetics. But then also Heidegger, Kant, Adorno to a certain extent, Habermas to a certain extent. Heidegger became the biggest figure in the book. It probably draws more on his thought with respect to art and truth than Adorno's. As I said before, the further I got into that work, I realized okay, now I really owe it to myself, and to anyone else who's interested, to work out a general theory of truth. I flagged that in the book, and I knew that was going to be the next big project.

Then I still had all this stuff on the politics and economics of art, and the question of government funding for the arts, to work out to my own satisfaction. I finished the manuscript for the *Artistic Truth* book during the summer (2002) when we moved to Toronto from Grand Rapids for me to take up the position in systematic philosophy at ICS. The book came out two years later, but the work was completed right at the beginning of my stay at ICS as a Senior Member. For the next several years after that I worked on the *Art in Public* book, and the more I got into it, the more I realized this is a huge project too. I was foolhardy enough to say I'm going to provide an alternative political philosophy, and I'm going to provide an alternative way of thinking about economic theory. Well, I'm not trained in those areas. And

I'm going to spell out a different approach to cultural policy, all in one book! That's nuts. But I did it, and the only way I could do it finally was to start laying out in a more systematic way a social philosophy, a theory of economic system, a theory of political system, a theory of civil society, a theory of the public sphere, and an account of the importance of a not-for-profit economy. That all came together because the book forced me to think these things through.

By the time I finished *Art in Public* I realized, now I have a second major project that in a sense I've committed myself to, and it has to do with the role of civil society in a global context. I talk about this a bit near the end of my *Social Philosophy after Adorno* book, the importance of civil society as a generator for political change and economic alternatives.[25] What I want to contribute – I don't know whether I'll ever write this second book, but that's the one that awaits me right now after the truth project is done – is a book where I try to spell out the normative potential of civil societal structures on a global scale, and the contributions that can be made in that context by traditions of spirituality and religion. So all this stuff about interfaith dialogue and so on, for me it's important because there's a potential there for addressing the world's deepest ills in a way that makes for long-range change, that contributes to what I call "interconnected flourishing." This can happen only by way of civil society. It also has to happen at the level of political systems and economic systems, but it can't simply start there or be restricted to those levels. It has to be in civil society as well. And that's of course where you can have genuine democratic participation too, so you can involve ordinary people. That's the second book. It's going to be about global ethics and global civil society.

Dettloff: I really hope you get to that book.

Zuidervaart: The reason I'm hesitant is partly because these big projects take a lot of time and a lot of energy, but partly because the more I get into the truth project the more I realize my own limitations. I don't know the history of thought about truth the way I would like to, and I'm not addressing medieval thought, I'm not addressing the Greek tradition, I'm not addressing non-Western traditions at all. I have a nagging sense that this is incomplete. I really need to look at the broader truthscape more historically than the way I'm doing now. That actually might be a subsequent book, but I don't know yet; I haven't decided. If I were Bob Sweetman, I would go the other way. I would do the historical groundwork first. I love history, and I try to work in a historically informed way, but I'm not a historian, and I work much more systematically.

Dettloff: Even systematically, though, you write across philosophical traditions in a lot of your work. How did that come about?

Zuidervaart: When I moved to Calvin College in 1985, it was a different game altogether, because Calvin was a big college, and it had a well-established philosophy department. I was one of the few continental philosophers in the department, so I had to learn to interact with analytic colleagues. That was a challenge, but from there I got the passion to address analytic philosophers and to try to write in a way that's accessible to people who are not trained in continental philosophy. We had a colloquium that met every week, and we would present our work there. I was presenting my work in Adorno because I was turning my dissertation into a book. Well, some of my colleagues didn't know much about Adorno, or about Marx or Hegel or Freud either, for that matter. I ended up having to explain all kinds of stuff. That gave me a sense of context, and how important it is to translate in ways that make sense to people who aren't part of your own tradition or your own kind of exposure. So I took it on as a challenge, I became pretty good at it, and I really enjoy it.

Dettloff: Is there anything else you would like to say, anything we haven't touched on?

Zuidervaart: The one thing I'm thinking about, because of last night [at the celebration of Lambert's retirement from ICS], is the importance of having really gifted, engaged, caring students. I've had them from the very beginning of my teaching career [...] My first full-time teaching gig at the college level was at King's. It was a small place; we had ten full-time faculty and 110 students, and adjuncts. I got to know all the students, of course. I was hired primarily to teach two interdisciplinary courses that were at the centre of the curriculum, one called "Perspectives on Life and Society," and the other called "Central Issues in Academic Disciplines." That teaching assignment set the trajectory of my work from then on [...] And I had some really, really good students [...]

Over the years, as part of my mission as a philosophy professor, I've tried in particular to encourage women students to flourish, as women, as students, and, if they were so inclined, as philosophers. And that came out last night. Allyson Carr talked about her formation with me at Calvin College and then at the Institute. Shannon Hoff, same thing. There were a number of other women PhD recipients at the reception last night. So that's been really important. And I've had very good students.

9

Revolution Isn't What It Used to Be

1. POST-TRUTH POLITICS

Dettloff: Last night you gave your exaugural address at the Institute for Christian Studies (ICS) in Toronto.[1] In that lecture, you said something about post-truth politics, the situation we find ourselves in today. What does that situation mean to you? How should we relate to a post-truth political world, and how did we get here?

Zuidervaart: I'll talk about how we got here, and maybe we can go into what to do about it later. One could see the clouds on the horizon years ago if one was paying attention. Those clouds were in the intellectual world to begin with. It really goes back to a shift away from a certain narrow understanding of truth, which equates it with factual accuracy, and thinks that's all that matters and all we need to achieve when we acquire knowledge. That emphasis has a label: positivism. There was a turn against positivism in the 1960s already, a move toward post-positivism in the philosophy of science and a development of alternative emphases in philosophy and other fields. It really gathered steam in the 80s and 90s with the development of so-called postmodernism, which put a very strong emphasis on the relativity of any truth claims, and the fact that there's always going to be power mixed into the claims that people make. Now it has really exploded into mainstream culture, to the point where ordinary folks think that either there's no factual truth to be established or, if there is, it really boils down to one person's opinion against somebody else's.

When that gets parlayed into politics, it becomes very dangerous, because there no longer is a basis on which people can debate public policy or take certain kinds of evidence seriously, and it's used by people in various political camps as simply a way to dismiss facts, to dismiss accuracy. If that becomes the mode of operation, it really means that whoever has the power carries the day. As we know, going back to Plato's *Republic*, if that's the way you think politics needs to operate, then you no longer have any possibility of striving for justice, and for equity and the like; justice, equity, solidarity, all those values, simply become matters of opinion, and whoever has the power carries the day. That's where we're at. It's a problem for everybody, for Republicans, Democrats, and progressives aligned with a different kind of party.

Dettloff: Do you think this is a case where some intellectuals were exhibiting symptoms of something coming, or have they shaped discourse in a certain way? Do you feel the loss of a naïve belief in truth in a sort of positivist sense is an inevitably net bad? Is there something to the way that postmoderns continued to think about things like justice or solidarity without that heavy-handed concept?

Zuidervaart: I think factual accuracy and making correct assertions are still very important. To dismiss or minimize them is problematic. But if you're going to have factual accuracy and "assertoric correctness," as I describe it, as part of what you emphasize in a culture, then you also need, at the philosophical and scholarly level, some account for it and for why it's important. That's what we're lacking now. We don't have a good account of that kind of truth or why it's important. Without an emphasis on factual accuracy and the correctness of assertions, the academic enterprise itself loses its entire reason for existence. I mean, the academic enterprise has to be about more than achieving factual accuracy, but *minimally* it has to be about achieving factual accuracy. If that goes out the window, we don't really have a rationale for academic work or universities or scientific research, and these things, despite all the problems attached to them, are crucial in the kind of society we inhabit. It's very disturbing to see politicians simply dismiss the careful, laborious, painstaking, self-sacrificial work that people have done in biology, physics, chemistry, psychology, and so on to understand what's at stake in the things going on in our society.

Dettloff: One thing I found very interesting as your student at the Institute is that I'm young enough that my points of contemporary reference are so-called postmoderns – Derrida, Foucault, and the rest of them. When I took your seminar on theories of truth, I thought, I never felt like this was a problem for me. Things like justice and power were problems, and that's why I wanted to sideline truth in my own work. Anytime someone says they have the facts, I thought, they're making a power move. I'm a Foucaultian, I guess, in that way. How would you speak to that anxiety, where people are nervous about talking about truth as another mask for power?

Zuidervaart: I understand that worry. Foucault himself, I think, is ambivalent about these matters. At different times in his life he said different things about truth and how it's mixed up in power. So I don't think Foucault is very clear on these matters. Yet there's a way of reading Foucault, which has become the dominant way of reading him, that hears a power play behind every truth claim.

Anyway, if there *is* a power play involved in every truth claim, that means there's a power play involved in every appeal to any value whatsoever. If that's the case, then there's really no basis for a critique of society, at least not a normative critique. All you can do is get upset about power. But why? What's wrong with it? Or, if you don't think power in itself is wrong, *what is* the problem? At what point does power become illegitimate? In order to answer that, you have to have some strong notion of justice or solidarity, and you have to be able to make truth claims with respect to those values. There has to be a way to get out of simply suspecting power all the time, to get to a point where you can critique power, illegitimate uses of power; and that requires strong truth claims.

2. SOCIAL CRITIQUE

Dettloff: That's a great segue to talk about what we should do in such a society, of where and how we might make such a critique, or where there's any hinge from which to do that. So here we are, in a post-truth society. The Democrats didn't save us from Donald Trump. What are we to do?

Zuidervaart: [Laughs.] I work at the level of generality, for the most part, so I have very little to advise about specific measures to take. But

I could say something in a general way that would be relevant to the more particular actions people need to take. I think at this point, at least in American society, the real alternatives are to be found not in formal politics, but in what I call civil society. All these organizations and movements and so on that are up in arms, resisting, protesting, organizing – that's where the movement toward a new politics can emerge, and it will take years and years for that to take shape in formal politics. The dominant political parties have been entrenched for so long that it will take a long time for them to be unentrenched, but it will happen, eventually. For that to happen, there must be a continual surge in civil society toward something different, which I think has to involve primacy given to concerns of ecology and, I'll say, income inequality, but it's bigger than that: an economy that, in order to operate, must continually channel public goods, collective goods, into the pockets of people that are already wealthy. It's a systemic problem, not a matter of making a few adjustments in the tax code or something. So those two things at least, an ecological concern and a concern about the very structure of capitalism, have to be at the centre of a new politics that must emerge out of the informal political sphere and finally take shape in a more formal way.

Dettloff: I want to circle back to that, but let's stay with these general problems and levels for a moment. You've done a lot of work creating vocabularies by which we *can* talk about systemic problems, and you think there needs to be an "architectonic critique" of society.[2] To get into this expansive project, perhaps we could simply start with what you call "societal evil," which is related. What do you mean by that?

Zuidervaart: The notion of societal evil is one I developed in order to get at the kind of problem that Adorno and Horkheimer were addressing in the *Dialectic of Enlightenment*. It's a problem that Adorno continued to struggle with right through the 1950s and 60s, until he died in 1969. He agonized about how to do philosophy after Auschwitz, about whether we can write poetry after Auschwitz. "After Auschwitz" becomes a kind of moniker for the situation he thinks society in the West finds itself in. The Holocaust, as a large-scale atrocity, is very difficult to understand. How could it occur? Why did people do it? Whom do you hold responsible for it, and how?

In order to account for something at that level, you have to be able to talk about how certain patterns of conduct, attitude, disposition, behaviour, all come together and entrench themselves in a society, in what I call cultural practices and social institutions. They become so enmeshed in the very fabric of society that it's (1) hard to recognize, (2) hard for anybody to take responsibility, because it's basically like the air we breathe, and (3) hard for anybody to resist. And that's what I'm trying to get at.

For me, the kind of patterns we have in place with respect to the so-called environment, our biosphere, is a manifestation of societal evil. It's such a deeply entrenched set of patterns that it's extremely difficult to recognize, take responsibility for it, and effectively resist. Same thing with the capitalist economy. The disparities in the economy between those who have and those who have not, and the way the economy depends on that disparity, are so entrenched that it's very hard for anybody to take any personal or even collective responsibility for it. But somebody's got to be responsible for it, right? Otherwise, it's just a fate that we live with, and we throw up our hands.

Dettloff: That's what I find so helpful about your approach. Intuitively, as a student or emerging adult, you slowly learn about all the ways in which you're part of a society that doesn't affirm any equitable life. And when you do, you feel paralyzed by the magnitude of the problem, and the ways in which you're involved in that problem, contributing to it, reproducing it. And you couldn't do otherwise, because the mode of production is organized in a specific way. *Your* approach helps to avoid a certain kind of cynicism, because it lets one actually *think* about what's going on. There's a temptation among the left generally to say if you're just thinking and not doing, then you're perpetuating the problem. But what you say is, if you're not thinking about it, then your doing will just get stuck in the same patterns. So maybe you could say more about how to think through critiquing something like societal evil, such that it doesn't just lodge you in an attitude that says as long as you know better then you've done enough.

Zuidervaart: Right, and this is where Adorno and I part company. The famous phrase from Adorno, an inversion of Hegel, is "The whole is the false."[3] Well, if the whole is the false, then the question is, what are the alternatives? Everything is false. Yet I don't think Adorno meant everything is false. Within the whole that is false, there are traces of something else, and you have to find those traces. But even that, to me, is insufficient. Traces of the good aren't good enough. I have a more robust view of what's good in society, and where the alternatives can emerge. I've tried to develop an approach where I can point to how existing institutions and structures, despite and amid the distortions, nevertheless have the potential for something better, *if* in fact they are redirected. But then there has to be a way of saying *how* they should be redirected, and for that you can't just have a pragmatic answer, of what works. It has to be normative in some way.

I've tried to develop a way of talking about the state, the economy, and civil society as three macrostructures, each of which has a certain task to be pursued, each of which is also failing, adequately, to perform that task because of normative deficiencies. To make it too simple, the normative deficiency of the administrative state is that it is not truly an institution for justice in the public realm. That's its task, but more often than not if fails to carry out that task and ends up being simply an institution that distributes and enforces power relations. Same with the economy. The capitalist economy, as the mainstream economy, has as a normative task taking care of the resources of our lives and creation in a way that contributes to flourishing across the board. It does some of that, but it does it inadvertently, because what it's really aimed at is private profit and efficiency. So there's a distortion of its normative calling. And yet, in that, it's still taking care of some things, sometimes better and sometimes worse, so it's not completely caught up in a societal evil that makes it irredeemable. And the same with civil society, which has a lot of problems; whereas it should be inculcating a robust solidarity towards others, it tends to emphasize a kind of charity and tolerance, and that's not enough.[4]

Once you recognize that there's something good to be said about each of these structures, and also something to be said in a critical vein, then you can start talking about how to work for the good of these structures and how to mitigate what's not so good. Of course, the other part of it is that change in one of those structures can happen only when change in the other structures also occurs, so it has to happen somehow in sync. Here I use the language of differential transformation. That's where you get to a very large-scale picture that most people find unrealistic, or utopian. Well, I admit, if this is going to happen, it will take generations to happen. But given the level at which the problems are pitched, how entrenched the societal evil is, I don't see any alternative. I think long-term change is required.

3. REVOLUTION AND ESCHATOLOGY

Dettloff: Well, that makes me wonder about certain expected leftist worries about that kind of approach, which can come off as a kind of reformist, patient process. In some ways the strength of it is that it's honest about the challenges present in society. But you can imagine a Leninist, for example, saying you're not going to change these big things through bourgeois means. I wonder about that sometimes with your work. We have things like the bourgeois state and capitalist economy, but is there a sense in which we shouldn't necessarily be beholden to these things that have emerged? Maybe we might even be better off without some of them, or with a complete and radical restructuring of them.

Zuidervaart: Yeah. Well, revolution isn't what it used to be. [Both laugh.] That was what the Frankfurt School was wrestling with in the 1920s and 30s already, after the imperialist war, the First World War. Once you have a capitalist economy that is sophisticated, complicated, interwoven with the academy, with people's ordinary lives, heavy consumption and so on – it's not the kind of economy you can just overthrow, no matter what kind of political moves you make. That's the problem.

Marx himself, when he tried to understand social revolution, taking the French Revolution as his primary example, indicated that economic revolution is a very slow process. There comes a point, in his language, where the relations of production and forces of production are so out of sync with each other that there's a possibility for dramatic change, but to get to that point takes hundreds of years.[5] It's not clear to me that we're anywhere close to that point in the global capitalist economy. So that's part of the problem: how to theorize revolution. A political revolution will be only as good as conditions for it are ripe economically. And I don't see it. That's where we can have a discussion. People on the left need to have that discussion.

But the other part of the discussion has to be: a revolution to what end? What is the societal good or what is the good society the revolution is for? It can't just be overthrowing what's bad. You also need to have a vision of what's good. That's what I'm trying to offer when I talk about the way these various institutions need to play a role in a way that contributes to interconnected flourishing.

Dettloff: Another thing that's helpful about your approach is that you try to do the very hard work of building an alternative that seems reasonable, no matter how far off it might be, so that at least you could think really hard about it, and that would set us up to have conversations about whether or not bourgeois means are a way to get there. How do your Christian convictions play into that approach? You don't always wear those on your sleeve, perhaps strategically, but there's a deep eschatological pulse in your work.

Zuidervaart: There are two very fundamental convictions – I'll call them theological, though I don't usually talk the language of theology – but there are two theological convictions that sustain all of my social philosophy. One is that, in principle, the creation is good. Or to put it more theologically, God created the heavens and the earth and declared them good. That's a strong theological conviction. The other is that where history is headed, in the long term, is toward the new heaven and the new earth. That, for me, is not "pie in the sky in the sweet by and by." That's really a vision of a new society. I think that's also the case in the Hebrew scriptures, in what we could call the messianic condition. There's a really strong sense in the chronologically later writings in scripture that everything is headed toward the messianic condition, when the wolf and the lamb lie down together.

Part of the task of the Christian social philosopher is to try to envision what a new earth would be like, given current conditions, given the kind of society we're in now – what would a new earth look like if we could move from where we are now to something that is better for everyone and everything? For clues about that, of course I'll pay attention to what philosophers and political theorists and economists and so on have said about what makes for human and creational flourishing. But I'm also going to take seriously what I can find in the scriptures of the Hebrew and Christian traditions. My talking about justice, solidarity, and resourcefulness comes out of scriptural sources, even though I don't always indicate that. *Resourcefulness* is my way of translating a notion of stewardship that is very strongly articulated in the work of Bob Goudzwaard, a Dutch Calvinist social and economic philosopher, and a trained economist.[6]

That notion of stewardship has currency now, more broadly, among Protestants, Catholics, and people in the Orthodox tradition as well. Yet I find the term *stewardship* itself problematic, partly because it sounds sectarian, although now even corporations talk about stewardship. (They never miss an opportunity to tie into what seems to have cachet!) *Resourcefulness*, too, has problems. If you're a Heideggerian, you think, "You're just talking about *Gestell*, the enframing of everything; everything's been turned into resources for a technological society."[7] That's obviously not the way I mean it. I haven't been able to find a single term to do what needs to be done. But this sense of taking care of creatures is very strong in Hebrew scripture. It's part of what the Children of Israel were mandated with, and it gets down to very concrete things like not overworking the soil, giving it a rest, which now is coming back into organic farming. So picking up this ancient wisdom is a way of finding alternatives to highly industrialized and polluting agribusiness.

Dettloff: The way you draw from those scriptural sources also sets up your eschatological sympathies in a way that's very different from Adorno and Horkheimer. For them, the messianic condition provides some glimmer of hope, but it also becomes a depressive realization, it's a lost messianic state that they want to believe in but can't for a variety of reasons. In your work, I detect something less depressive, that the messianic state is more encouraging, inspiring rather than something to mourn because it's not here.

Zuidervaart: Adorno uses the language of traces, a bit like Derrida actually – the justice that is still to come.[8] I think the reason he and Horkheimer both have such thin views of this nevertheless necessary future is because they don't have a robust normative account of society in the present. They don't have a robust notion of justice or solidarity. They never formulated that kind of robust normative stance to support the critique they launched, so they also were not able to project beyond current conditions to a condition where those normative expectations could be realized. For me, it's a problem of normativity, and it's a problem in the Marxist tradition more broadly. There's a lot of debate about whether Marx can be read to have an ethical stance or not. I understand well why Marx did not want to talk that language, because the people who *were* talking that language tended to be Idealists who thought simply having the right ideas or values would be enough to change society, and of course that's complete nonsense. But, going in the historical materialist direction and emphasizing the importance of economic and technological change, he did not work out a very thick normativity to support his critique of capitalism.

4. A CHRISTIAN LEFT?

Dettloff: Having talked about both your Christianity and a bit about the left, I wonder, do you think there's such a thing as the "Christian Left," or is there a way of sorting out how Christianity might relate to leftist politics in general? How are these related in your own life?

Zuidervaart: I don't think there's a Christian Left. I think there are many ways in which Christians have found themselves aligning with forces on the left. When I was a young college professor in the 1980s, liberation theology coming from South America was really powerful and attractive for Christians who aligned with the left. In Edmonton, Alberta, where I started my postsecondary teaching career at King's University (it was King's College then), I quickly found myself affiliated with progressive Catholics who were very much informed by liberation theology. I found myself comfortable with those folks. They were the folks I hung out with.

In fact, Joyce and I were part of a co-op house in the inner city in Edmonton, and some of our progressive Catholic friends were part of another co-op house. We joined forces, and I was the founding president of a new co-op called Inn Roads Housing Co-op, making inroads in the inner city, which was controlled by absentee landlords. Seventy per cent of the people living in the inner city were tenants, and most of them rented from absentee landlords who were not taking care of their property and were charging exorbitant rents. So we founded a housing cooperative that incorporated these two freestanding cooperative houses, and then started acquiring or building more property. And the housing co-op is still there, still going. It was the progressive Catholics and progressive Calvinists, if you wish, who started it, because what mattered to us was a liberating of people who were oppressed and on the margins; that's where we needed to put our energy in a very specific way in the geography where we found ourselves.

But these things come and go, especially in North America. Fads come and go really quickly. The language of liberation theology seems to have faded from people's consciousness, and they have gone towards other liberatory movements. Feminism has been an important movement that has attracted people to a kind of left formulation of theological convictions (I'll just use shorthand); gay liberation has been another. Part of what I find disturbing in North America is that such identity politics keeps people from seeing a bigger picture. They seem to line up with this cause or that cause, this group or that group, and it's hard for people to see a bigger picture about how in the end we are dealing with an underlying pattern, oppression, power, that affects everyone. That's also part of what makes it difficult for there to be a Christian Left, because Christians jump on one bandwagon or another, and they tend to dissipate their energies in that way.

5. KUYPERIAN POLITICS

Dettloff: This reminds me a bit of Jacques Ellul. I'm struck by how, in his book *Anarchy and Christianity*, there's a lot about his Christianity but not a lot about his commitment to anarchist labour causes. There's always an anxiety on his part whether he's being Christian enough, but never an anxiety about whether he's helping workers enough; so there's a strange Christian identity politics at work there. That's one interesting thing about ICS's brand of Calvinism, it seems to me. On the one hand, it has a very strong identity. In the Netherlands it comes out of arguably a certain kind of identity politics; they wanted their own political party, social institutions, etc. But at the same time, ICS's way of taking that up has been not so anxious about getting involved in these other kinds of movements. How have you navigated that tradition, as received and advanced by ICS?

Zuidervaart: I grew up as part of a Dutch immigrant culture in northern California without knowing much about what I'll just call the reformational movement. I was a member of the Christian Reformed Church (CRC) all my life until much later; I went to schools that were part of that religious culture, including college and graduate school; and I got my PhD from the Free University of Amsterdam. All of that was in the context of a Dutch Calvinist upbringing.

Once I went to Berlin, I was exposed to a very different religious culture and a very different *kind* of left politics. You talk about Marxists and anarchists, well they were *there*, and they were serious. They would disrupt classes. It wasn't just armchair politics. That opened my eyes to a much bigger world, and a much bigger sense of what the issues are.

When I came back to North America, I wasn't ready to just self-identify again with all the institutions I grew up with. I'm not dismissive at all; obviously, I've lived my whole life and continue to live my life in the schools that come out of that tradition, and very happily so. Yet the emphasis on having all the manifestations of your Christianity channeled through organizations that self-identify in a certain way has become much less important for me. In terms of my own practicing of Christianity, I have not been a member of the Christian Reformed Church for many, many years. I found myself much more comfortable in the United Church of Canada, which, among Canadian Protestant denominations, is known as a social justice church. Now, in the States, I'm in the Presbyterian Church (U.S.A.), which also is on the more progressive side, politically, among Presbyterians. Among Presbyterians and United Church folks, there's never been the same kind of emphasis on having Christian schools, Christian labour associations, Christian political organizations, and so on. They don't have that emphasis. They have a very strong emphasis on bearing witness in society to the Prince of Peace, if you want to put it that way, but they don't have the same understanding of how that has to happen.

Dettloff: That's also interesting because your own work is so invested in these Dutch Calvinist thinkers, but in practice you found a home in these other traditions. I'm not a Calvinist myself; I grew up Roman Catholic and wandered through a variety of Protestant denominations, and now I'm back in the Catholic Church. When I tell people that I go to the Institute for Christian Studies, a Calvinist school, and when people know about my *revolutionary* sympathies and that this school comes out of a *reformational* tradition, people are often surprised. But I like to emphasize that there's a very unexpected kind of leftist strand in Calvinism generally, even as mediated through the reformational tradition. Why might people be surprised that there are leftist Calvinists, and how do you think that's possible?

Zuidervaart: Well, the rap on Calvinism in North America is that it's Puritan, right? So it's highly moral and highly judgmental and constraining; in American society, I suppose you could explain a lot of things that have happened in the twentieth and twenty-first centuries as a rebellion against Puritanism. There's that public image of what Calvinism is all about, which is hard to counteract.

But more specifically, in the Dutch Kuyperian movement, which is where I come from intellectually, the folks who came out of that and settled in the United States ended up mostly being Republicans. That happened for various reasons, but I think it had to do with a certain translation of the notion of sphere sovereignty, that each social sphere has its own authority. They thought the state should not be controlling civic life. And they thought that the Democratic Party tended to go in that direction, particularly after the Roosevelt era, when "big government" really took shape. Ideologically, many of them were small-business people or farmers, so they had a strong sense of being independent and not having their lives dictated by government. Anybody who knows about the Christian Reformed Church will realize that the default position, politically, of the CRC in the United States is Republicanism of one sort or another. Not necessarily libertarian Republicanism; although some of the more politically prominent people, like Betsy DeVos, end up being libertarians, many others in the CRC are not libertarians.

In Canada it has been more of a mixed bag, because a lot of the people who came from the Netherlands and settled in Canada arrived in the 1950s rather than the 1920s or earlier in the States. Those folks often were more open to having government prominently involved in adjudicating matters of social justice and providing for social welfare, because they had already experienced that as a good thing in the Netherlands, supported by their own political party. But even in Canada, a wing of the CRC gravitated toward the Reform Party, which ended up being the dominant strand of the Conservative Party that former Prime Minister Stephen Harper came out of. So there's a split among CRC folks in Canada as well. You can even see it among the organizations that came out of the Dutch immigration. On political issues, the Christian Labour Association of Canada (CLAC) tended to be much more conservative than Citizens for Public Justice (CPJ). In fact, CPJ in a sense broke away from the CLAC; they're on different pages, politically.

Dettloff: So Calvinism is a complicated thing, politically, like anything else.

Zuidervaart: Yes, exactly, it is [...]

6. WHAT IS TO BE DONE?

Dettloff: Let's bring some of these things together to close. To circle back like I said I would earlier, I'll ask you to do the thing you're not really supposed to ask theorists to do, which is to see if you might have some more advice, having inculcated a long spirit of Christian sources, leftist sources, philosophical sources, etc. You've also been involved in real organizing on the ground, not just in the housing co-op you mentioned, but a variety of things, like the Urban Institute for Contemporary Arts (UICA) in Grand Rapids, which is at least in part a political body. For Christians today, dissatisfied with what's on offer, and those worried about the state of politics, what are we supposed to do? The standard leftist wisdom is to say don't worry about upcoming elections, get busy somewhere else. What do you think?

Zuidervaart: I guess it was Jacques Ellul who said think globally and act locally. I think that's still good advice. I think it's really important to get involved in something local that you can see is making a difference, but also is aligning in a helpful way with larger patterns beyond the local scene, whatever that means: whether it's community agriculture, social work, whatever. That gives you a way to contribute in a specific locale to some kind of change. That's part of it. But I think acting locally needs also to be done for the sake of what's global. It's easy to just get caught up in activism and of what needs to be done because the tasks are right in front of you and so obvious. Especially for people who are intellectuals or cultural leaders of some sort, however, their involvement needs a more global horizon to it, and that's tricky.

    I kept reminding myself, when I was involved at UICA, this is *one* institution in *one* city. Yet what we're doing here could have significance beyond it, for better or worse, and we need to keep that in mind. It was obvious that we influenced patterns on the local scene. That entire area of Grand Rapids was pretty run-down, and a lot of people wouldn't go there because they felt it was dangerous. By virtue of our creating an arts centre, that has changed. We weren't the only organization, but we were an anchor organization. All kinds of good things have happened there. But of course, now real estate values have gone up and a lot of homeless and street people are no longer comfortable there.

    That's one of the things we were aware of when we put our arts centre together: there's got to be a way, somehow, to include the folks who are on the margins, and to make our organization welcoming and interactive for them. That affected the design of the building. We found out that buildings with an imposing facade or steps leading up to them are less inviting for street people; they won't go into them, they don't feel safe. So we made sure to have a street-level entrance, glass so you could see what you're walking into, all that stuff. We hired teams of local people to do mosaic work, with the guidance of a fine mosaic artist, in the sidewalk outside. We were very aware what we were doing would create patterns that could be unhelpful for people on the margins. We also were aware that some of that's out of our control, real estate markets being what they are. This pattern repeats itself over and over again. Artists go into rundown areas, property values go up, and then the development starts, so people who could live there because the real estate values were down in the dumps are forced out.

Act locally, then, but with a global sense of why what you're doing is important and how you might contribute, whatever that means in specific circumstances.

10

Pursuing Truth
in a Post-Truth Society

I. BUILDING BRIDGES

Dettloff: Concerns about truth and epistemology have become central themes in your research. This is difficult not only because of the historicizing you do of the concept of truth, but also because theories of truth have a niche character, whether you're talking about "analytic" philosophy or "continental" philosophy. Philosophers are often in silos maintained not just by their partisanship, but by increasingly detailed articulations of problems within problems. What I find interesting in your approach is that you have a commitment to get out of those silos and to build bridges between them. As you put it in an essay, "My response is deliberately to cross philosophical divides: divides between analytic and continental philosophy, and, within continental philosophy, between Heideggerian thinking and Critical Theory."[1] I want to talk about how you negotiate those divides in a moment, but to start perhaps you could say something about why you think those divides exist in the first place, since you have done so much work now trying to understand their historical development.

Zuidervaart: That's a very interesting question. I don't know quite where to touch down historically in answering it. Most recently, I've been doing a lot of work in analytic philosophy, and I've been trying to figure out what the historical origins are for contemporary accounts of truth in analytic philosophy. That has driven me back to the early twentieth century and the development of logical positivism. What I'm now trying to understand historically is, what fuels or feeds the rise of logical positivism? It happens at the same time as the rise of phenomenology and its spin-offs. In my reading of this history, the two spin-offs that are most important are Critical Theory and Heidegger's work; I see both of those coming out of phenomenology.

Phenomenology and logical positivism develop at the same time, and there's even some conversation across the line between the phenomenologists and logical positivists. Particularly, there's quite a bit of conversation between Gottlob Frege (who's really hard to classify, but he's the godfather of so much analytic philosophy) and Edmund Husserl (who's the godfather of phenomenology). Plus, Bertrand Russell, who is a very important figure in the rise of logical positivism, was in conversation with Gottlob Frege.

What really binds these three together as part of the historical moment is that they're all trying to work out a new philosophy of logic, trying to work out a way of thinking about logic that would also then unravel problems in the other disciplines, particularly in mathematics. Husserl had a grounding in the philosophy of arithmetic, the subject of his first major publication.[2] Frege, same thing, he was actually a philosopher of mathematics and a logician.[3] And Russell, one of his first major publications was *The Principles of Mathematics*.[4] You get this groundswell of interest in logic, and a new development of logic to address lasting problems in the disciplines, again especially in the mathematical disciplines. So that's part of the technical side, if you will, to the development that I'm trying to come to grips with.

The more cultural and sociological or even political side to it is of course much more expansive. There, I try to think about how European culture and politics developed in the nineteenth century, and then how American culture and politics (which were really distinct and yet, at the intellectual level, very oriented toward the European scene) gradually started to break away and become their own thing in the twentieth century. What I think intellectually unites the two sides, what I'll call the American and European right now, is a struggle over cultural authority. Which experts, or which leaders and which enterprises, are going to have cultural authority? You can see that battle going on already at the end of the eighteenth and beginning of the nineteenth century, where it has to do primarily with whether science, in a very broad sense, will have the voice of authority, or religion, that is, traditional religion, organized religion. That's one of the big conflicts, politically, not only in the Enlightenment but also in the French Revolution.

Soon after that, there's a new conflict between what we could call science and art, where art is seen as somehow giving us access to an intuitive understanding of things that is "more true" than the kind of access that science gives us. Art becomes a third party in the struggle over cultural authority. At the same time, of course, a whole lot of stuff is happening politically, with a more democratic understanding of how we should organize ourselves politically, and ongoing responses to the industrial revolution and the supercharging of capitalism as an economic system.

It takes a lot to try to think all that together, and see how it goes together, but one way to do it is to use Dooyeweerd's notion of the "ground motive" of nature and freedom as an organizing trope. This is surprising to me, because I haven't thought that Dooyeweerd's way of doing the historiography of philosophy is all that helpful. He says most of European philosophy, from the time of the Renaissance and Reformation onwards, is driven by the struggle between Nature and Freedom: "Nature," not as the non-human, natural world, but as the control of nature by way of scientific and technological expertise, versus "Freedom," as the freedom and personality of the individual, who cannot be so controlled or should not be so controlled.

That dynamic or conflict between nature and freedom very clearly surfaced in Kant's writings. On the one hand, his account of knowledge is really an account of knowledge as a scientific enterprise, and, on the other hand, his account of morality is an account of the free individual who is not going to be controlled by science, or by the patterns that science explains. So you have a tension between freedom, Kantian freedom, and nature, in the sense of the world of nature as understood by scientific knowledge.

I think that dynamic, you could call it the Kantian dynamic, is very strong in European culture, and it also gets picked up in American culture. If you look at John Dewey's work, you can see much of it as an attempt to get out of that bind or go beyond it. He also has enough Hegel in his background to know that there *is* a way to get out of that bind, a Hegelian way. I can't go all the way into the fate of Hegel; Marx comes out of Hegel obviously, and he sees Hegel as a better way to deal with political and economic issues than Kant, even though Marx is a severe critic of Hegel. But the attempt to synthesize nature and freedom, which you get in Hegel, breaks apart as the nineteenth century goes on. Finally, when you get to the early part of the twentieth century, all the attempts to keep it together (let's call them the Hegelian or neo-Hegelian attempts) are discredited. And all the other attempts to split the difference (let's call them the neo-Kantian attempts), to say you have to pay attention to facts in a certain way (that's the role of the natural sciences) and you have to pay attention to values in a different way (that's the role of the *Geisteswissenschaften*, the social sciences and the humanities) – these sorts of compromises saying you have to have two different enterprises, as it were, and each is legitimate – also seem no longer to be persuasive.

Then people like Frege, Russell, and Husserl, who are all trying to do something new, decide they're not going to be Hegelians. Russell especially is very clear: he's an anti-Hegelian who started out as a Hegelian, influenced by F.H. Bradley and the whole neo-Hegelian English way of thinking about things. He broke with that and gave up on it, really rejected it and came up with another way of thinking about things, where getting clearer about facts and language became the important thing, and making sure that logic has the upper hand rather than the huge, synthetic, and non-verifiable statements that the Hegelian tradition is reputed to engage in.

That's part of it [...] There are at least two more things I want to mention. One is, I suspect (I haven't been able to do the historical research; I always say I'm not a historian, just interested in history) that in the early twentieth century there's also a frustration with the imperialism of the regimes that controlled Europe at the time. In Germany there's a frustration with a Prussian imperialism, in England there's a frustration with, let's call it, a Victorian imperialism. The grandeur of it, the claims being made, the kinds of neo-gothic and neo-baroque buildings being put up, the imposition of the state on culture and human life – many intellectuals are frustrated with this. You certainly pick that up in the arts, and I suspect in philosophy, too, though I haven't been able to document it. So part of the gesture of rejecting the synthesis of Hegel and his followers, and the dissatisfaction with the compromise of the neo-Kantians, is, I think, also a dissatisfaction with the imperialist state and its control of public life. Obviously, by the time you get into the 1920s, there's a real dissatisfaction with these imperialist states that went to war together and murdered and controlled the fates of so many thousands, indeed millions of soldiers and civilians who were killed in the First World War.

What does truth have to do with that? Truth becomes something that is no longer thought of globally, the way the Hegelians think about it. It gets thought of in a much more specialized way. Truth now pertains to that which we accomplish in logic and in the hard sciences. It no longer pertains, at least on a certain reading of all three of these figures – Frege, Husserl, and Russell – to what the arts and religion, maybe even politics, might offer. It becomes a much more specialized concept, and the project of figuring out what truth is becomes a much more specialized project as well.

There's also a rejection of that specialization, and a challenging of it, in both Heidegger and Critical Theory. They say, wait a minute, truth has much more to do with how we live, or what the quality of life is, and is not simply to be aligned with science. Science has its own problems and is connected to problematic political and economic structures, in the case of Critical Theory, or it's connected to a kind of technologizing, if you will, of human life and existence, in the case of Heidegger's diagnosis. So I don't want to make this too simple. Yet there's a kind of turn in the early part of the twentieth century among some of the leading figures – leading especially for a certain kind of analytic philosophy as well as phenomenology – a turn towards a specialized notion of truth that has to do with the relationship between propositions and facts, to use one terminology, and simultaneously also a turn toward truth as something pertaining to life in a more general way. I don't know how to put all these threads together, but these are threads I consider when I think of the historical background to the nest of issues I'm dealing with now.

2. THE IDEA OF TRUTH

Dettloff: We'll find some ways to pull those threads together here. This is a good place-setting of the context, and the fact that there are so many threads to pull together in a simple theory or story is something I hoped we could illustrate, since it helps to make sense of the concepts you use in your own constructive work. There are a lot of moving parts in your conception of truth, but you also work very hard at summarizing that conception in a number of places. Perhaps you could give another summary here?

Zuidervaart: Okay. You started this conversation talking about how I try to bridge divides between analytic and continental philosophy, and then between Heideggerian thought and Critical Theory. That might be a good way to introduce my general conception, which tries to take the best insights of these three traditions – maybe others, but these are the three I'm most familiar with now – and work them into a comprehensive idea of truth. From the analytic side, one can give a very intense, focused discussion of the notion that I call "propositional truth." What makes for true propositions, sentences, statements, beliefs – from that side you can give a strong account of this. I think it's too thin, and I think there are lots of problems with it, but nevertheless there's very good attention paid to propositional truth in the analytic tradition. Also, a rejection of propositional truth in that tradition, which I think becomes very problematic in the contemporary setting. There's a wealth of information, argument, and reflection on propositional truth in the analytic tradition. With the analytic tradition I want to say, yes, propositional truth is important. What I don't want to say with the analytic tradition (although very few people will actually say it this way) is that propositional truth is all-important.

From the side of Critical Theory, I want to say that truth has very much to do with the way a society is organized, and I want to ask, what happens when power becomes the possession of the few, and many people are oppressed? Or when wealth becomes the possession of the few, and many people are impoverished? And so on. Truth has to do with that. And from the side of Heidegger, I take the insight that truth in its core meaning has to do with the opening up of things to potentials and possibilities that they could achieve.

All of that comes together. It's not like I sat around thinking about which pieces of these traditions I should put together, but all of these inform my notion of truth. What I've tried to come up with is a general conception of truth within which I can locate a notion of propositional truth, and then show how propositional truth is related to other sorts of truth, such as artistic truth and religious truth and the like. The general conception I have is of truth as a process, not a property or a thing, in which two poles continually inform each other. I talk about this process as a dynamic correlation between, on the one hand, human faithfulness to societal principles, and, on the other hand, a life-giving disclosure of society. The notion of disclosure: that comes from Heidegger. I work in the notion of a life-giving opening-up of society: that comes much more from Critical Theory. I work in the notion of faithfulness to societal principles, which, I think, could be said to be a background intuition in all the emphases on propositional truth in the analytic tradition, although very few people in that tradition would actually say this. And, of course, the notion of faithfulness to societal principles also gives a kind of weight to the reformational tradition that I'm trained in, where having a proper response to what God calls us to is central to what it means to be human.

That's the way I bring these various strands together into my own conception: a dynamic correlation between human fidelity to societal principles and life-giving disclosure of society. What does that have to do with propositional truth? I have just finished a chapter in which I try to say what my notion of propositional truth is. What's been important for me to do in this chapter is to lay groundwork for showing that the structure of propositional truth reiterates the structure of truth as a whole. I even use a term that people like Russell use to talk about the structure of propositional truth, although I use it differently: *isomorphism*. For Russell, at least in certain stages of his writing, the isomorphism has to be between the structure of the belief or the proposition, on the one hand, and the structure of the fact, on the other. Those two structures have to be lined up with each other.

That's not how I'm using the term, however. I'm talking about how the structure of propositional truth has to line up with the structure of truth as a whole, and, in lining up with the structure of truth as a whole, it also echoes the structure of other sorts of truth. So, the structure of propositional truth is going to mime or echo the structure of artistic truth, religious truth, and so on. And all of those manners of truth, in their structural similarity, are part of the structure of truth as a whole. The isomorphism is between different domains of truth, and from those domains to truth as a whole. That's how, finally, I've come up with a vocabulary to show that it's not completely ludicrous to think that propositional truth is important as part of truth as a whole, nor is it stupid to think about truth as a whole as somehow the umbrella under which to think about propositional truth, scientific truth, religious truth, and so on. It allows me to say propositional truth has structural similarity to other domains of truth, and that also makes it possible for me to say in more detail why propositional truth is both important and also not all-important. If you limit truth to propositional truth, you'll miss so much of what's important in the rest of culture and society, because there are other sorts of truth that have to be given their due.

Dettloff: It's fascinating to hear you talk about this with all that weight of modern philosophy behind it. I can't help but think of the way Alasdair MacIntyre famously opens *After Virtue*[5] with a parable of people who find various fragments of rules to a game. They want to play this game, but they can't, because they don't have the fullness of the rules, only bits and pieces. What would you do in such a situation? In many ways that strikes me as an apt metaphor for what you're working with as well, of course not in the Aristotelian or Thomist direction that MacIntyre goes, but in an attempt to pull all these fragments together and say, well, maybe there actually is a game that could be played. Some people found this ruleset, others found that ruleset. How would you talk about that situation, the fragmentation of society and truth?

Zuidervaart: Fragmentation of society occurs right within the university and within philosophy as a discipline, so what we have is a flywheel effect. There's a continual push to specialize and define expertise ever more narrowly, and that affects all disciplines. At the same time, of course, the authority, if I may use that word, or the credentialing of these people with expertise becomes more and more questionable, because their expertise becomes more and more unintelligible to ordinary, plain folks, people who are not scientists or professionals. The more specialization you have inside the academy, the more the academy becomes distant from the rest of society. At the same time, so many of the problems that we're dealing with as a society, as a global society, cannot be dealt with except through the expertise of folks who have academic training or are in the academy fulltime. This is a big issue.

You see this flywheel effect inside philosophy when it comes to the topic of truth as well, particularly in analytic philosophy, where the debates become more and more narrowly focused and the vocabulary more technical, and the "payoff" of the conversation becomes less and less accessible to anyone who's not highly trained already. Once you get in a situation where, in general, the culture has its questions about truth – whether it's important, whether there *is* truth, who can get away with claiming to speak the truth, and so on – many philosophers are at a loss as to how to address that. They're spending their time on very technical problems and debates without dealing with the broader implications of those debates, without seeing they need to offer something to the culture as a whole on the topic of truth, as well as the topic of justice and so on. I'm not sure if that answers your question, but your question at least prompted these thoughts.

Dettloff: We can talk more about the contemporary situation in a moment. I can imagine, too, that as you're trying to pull these things together, one of the challenges of speaking across specializations is that you can't really make everyone happy by virtue of just crossing that bridge and translating beyond those technical discourses. Someone will always be upset that this or that aspect of propositional truth is insufficiently dealt with, or someone might be suspicious of turning philosophy into an abstraction from ideological or political problems. How have you found a way to build a conciliatory approach here? The definition you just gave to me about truth, involving terms like fidelity, disclosure, life, etc. – that seems like something that, if you said it at a conference to many philosophers, you would get a lot of different questions about working parts of that theory. How do you negotiate those differences?

Zuidervaart: Well, we'll see [...] The very thought that there could be more to truth than propositional truth is like a stopping point rather than a starting point for many analytic philosophers. It's something that, I have to say in all honesty, creates a great deal of anxiety. I want my work to be read and responded to in a constructive manner, but if it's just rejected out of hand, at the outset, then a lot of this work is in vain. The other anxiety is the anxiety of being regarded as an amateur or dilettante in the literature that I'm dealing with, because of course I can't go into all the details [...] There's no way to satisfy all the potential critics in advance. The only way you can start to satisfy them is to respond to questions that come up, and hopefully they're good questions and don't just lead to the embarrassed silence of someone farting in a public forum.

But I've tried to remind myself – it's taken me a long time to get to this point – in the end, I'm not writing for any particular audience, in a sense. I'm writing for the sake of the idea I'm working with, and hopefully that's going to be an idea that other people can take up and find helpful. I can't tie myself up in knots thinking about the particular audiences that might reject it out of hand, or ridicule it, or completely misread it. If I did that, I'd have to stop writing now.

3. HOLISTIC ALETHIC PLURALISM

Dettloff: Well, I think anybody who has spent any significant time with your work would have a hard time accusing you of any kind of amateurism. You definitely do your homework, and that comes through. And you've changed your position over time through that work, deepening and expanding it. Perhaps we could track some of that development. About a decade ago, you described your project as developing a "critical hermeneutics."[6] More recently, you suggested the label "holistic alethic pluralism." Is that a significant change of vocabulary? A translation for an audience? How has your position changed over the last ten years or so?

Zuidervaart: The first description of my approach comes from a stage in my writing where I was still sorting out how I relate to these various traditions, and "critical hermeneutics" is really a summary of a way of approaching other philosophers. It's approaching them through immanent criticism with what I call "metacritical intent." I try to find the good insights that are there by engaging in a critique of the positions they develop, with a view to other positions that are in conflict with their positions, and with a hope that out of this dialectical process something good will emerge. So that's a way I approach other philosophers and negotiate different traditions.

In the meantime, of course, having done that negotiation for quite a while, I've come up more clearly with my own articulation of the central idea I want to put forward, the idea of truth. When I try then to summarize the position I've arrived at, or am arriving at, through the process of critical hermeneutics, that is when I use the label "holistic alethic pluralism." I finally came up with that label when, at the encouragement of a few colleagues at DePaul University, where I presented a paper on Husserl, I gave up the plan to write a book that laid out my conception of truth through a series of dialectical dialogues between analytic and continental philosophers. They said, you have enough of a notion of truth on your own that you don't need to do this. Besides, it's a huge and laborious thing to go about laying out your own ideas. I said to myself, maybe they're right; I should abandon the project as I've conceived it up to now, and just lay out what I'm trying to do in an introduction to a new book. So I did that.

That introduction is the article titled "Holistic Alethic Pluralism."[7] In writing it, I finally established how my conception is both in line with and different from the other conceptions that I'm dealing with. Unlike most analytic philosophers, I have a holistic conception of truth. Unlike many continental philosophers, I have a pluralist conception of truth. Alethic pluralism is in fact one strain of analytic philosophy now. The kind of pluralism the alethic pluralists embrace is really a pluralism with regard to propositional truth, not a pluralism that entails both propositional truth and other kinds of truth. So I think it's a pretty good label for my conception: holistic alethic pluralism. Once you know what alethic means (and philosophers use that all the time when they refer to truth), it's a holistic pluralism with regard to truth.

It's also very much in line with what I take to be the genius of the reformational tradition, which I became clearer about when I was working on *Religion, Truth, and Social Transformation*. I needed to write an introduction positioning my work with regard to my own tradition and summarizing what were the most important parts of that tradition.[8] There, it became clearer to me that there's a kind of holistic pluralism with regard to societal structures, with regard to knowledge, and with regard to what it means to be human that's really at the core of the tradition and turns out to be at the core of my notion of truth as well. So there's a nice resolution for several different things I needed to deal with, one of them simply having to do with strategy, with how I might write a book.

After I'd finished writing "Holistic Alethic Pluralism," I started thinking, what about all this stuff I've already written on continental philosophy? That's when I decided to put it together in a book on its own. That became *Truth in Husserl, Heidegger, and the Frankfurt School*, in which I already signal what the main lines of my conception of truth are and show how those main lines emerge in part from a critical retrieval of different theories in continental philosophy.

4. SCIENTIFIC TRUTH

Dettloff: That helps, and makes sense, too, of how you're borrowing from vocabularies of people you're working with but subtly challenging them in your borrowing from them. That's a clever way of pulling people into the conversation. Let's talk also about one thing in your theory of truth that might rub up against certain philosophers, maybe especially analytic philosophers, and that's your application of your theory of truth to other domains, namely, the sciences and the arts. In both cases, you situate these disciplines in a wider social context, arguing against deflationary accounts of truth and in favor of truth as "disclosure."[9] I think it's probably easier to see how a disclosive account of truth would go a long way in talking about artistic truth, but science seems like a harder sell. People don't like to think of science as contextual or disclosive. What do you think your attention to disclosure does to help illuminate truth in the sciences?

Zuidervaart: Well, I have to write that chapter yet, so we'll see whether I can actually make this bear out. But I have written the chapters on propositional truth, and that's the key, I think, to thinking about scientific truth. You must have an account of propositional truth that actually is robust enough to support an account of scientific truth, and if you engage in deflation with regard to propositional truth, I think the next move is also to engage in deflation with regard to scientific truth. Propositional truth is broader and wider, more common in life in general, than scientific truth is, but scientific truth is basically a hyperbolic version of propositional truth. So to account for scientific truth, you have to have a robust account of propositional truth. I think I have that now.

My account of propositional truth puts together two notions that come out of Heidegger (although not quite in his vocabulary) and that are often not put together in philosophy of science, or in epistemology more broadly. Those notions are *disclosure*, which we're talking about, and *decontextualization*. I try to show in my account of propositional truth that if you want to think about it with sufficient depth, you have to situate propositional truth in the practices of life, where we go about having beliefs and forming beliefs, often without ever articulating them in language and not asserting them as propositions. We just "have" beliefs. We don't need to articulate them. Beliefs, for me, are insights into practical affairs; they're insights we have in the normal practice of life. I think there's a kind of truth to beliefs at that level of, simply, ways of having insight that you could talk about as *reliability*. Beliefs that really do the work that they're supposed to do in ordinary life are reliable beliefs, and they're true in that sense. You can count on them. This is not so far from Dewey and

James and the pragmatists with respect to truth. I think they were onto this in their accounts of truth. But, when you want to move from that notion of the truth of beliefs to the truth of assertions, you have to start talking about facts.

Facts, for me, are specific ways in which practical objects, the objects that we are engaged with in our practices, disclose themselves to us. That's where the notion of disclosure starts playing an important role. Practical objects disclose themselves, and they do so as we engage in language usage and make assertions with respect to them. I try to give an account of what that disclosure involves. It already involves a decontextualization of the object and the practices themselves, because you're already focusing on the object under language, specifically by making reference to the object and engaging in predication with respect to the object. At that level, a "fact" is what I call the predicative self-disclosure of the object; it's the object disclosing itself in a certain way. Once you move from there to the truth of propositions, you get to another level of both disclosure and decontextualization. So there's a continuum of both disclosure and decontextualization that provides the framework for the truth of propositions.

Now, if that's right (and I'm doing this all a little too quickly), then I can go on to talk about scientific truth as a further refinement of both the disclosure and the decontextualization that's characteristic of propositional truth in general. I touched on this a bit in the essay "Science, Society, and Culture" in my book *Religion, Truth, and Social Transformation*, but now I need to work it out in a much more detailed way. In that essay, I talk about how what's crucial for the truth scientists seek is a kind of discursive reflexivity in the scientists' practices, a highlighting of the making, testing, and debating of assertions, and being aware that this is exactly what you're doing; you're not just making statements, you're actually putting statements out there to be tested and contested, etc. It's a discursive reflexivity: you're aware of doing this while you're doing it. On the side of the object, there is what I call a "virtualized predicative self-dis/closure," because the object is no longer just an object in practice, no longer a practical object, no longer even an object that is self-disclosing as a fact, but now it's an object that's been isolated in a certain way, singled out, put under a certain microscope, if you will. It's been framed in a certain scientific language and so on and so forth. So it has been virtualized. In that virtualized setting, the fact that you're after is going to be a much more specialized fact. You could call it a state of affairs instead of a fact. In any case, those two things go together. On the one hand, the discursive reflexivity on the part of the agent approaching the object, and, on the other hand, virtualized predicative self-dis/closure on the part of the object in relation to the agent, that is, the scientist who is trying to approach it.

Now, of course, all that emphasis on decontextualization raises the question of how science ties into a wider context, and there I have to give a much broader account of science as a social institution, or maybe the academy as a social institution. Because you can see, if that's what science is like, then it easily becomes isolated from a democratic populace. There's a kind of intrinsic pressure, not just a systemic pressure from the way the economy works or the way technology works, but a kind of intrinsic pressure within science itself, when it's working well, to isolate itself from the rest of life. And that has to be counteracted within science itself, not just from the outside.

5. CRISIS OF TRUTH

Dettloff: That's a good way to start talking about a certain crisis of science, or a crisis of truth more generally. When you mention facts, it's hard not to think of things like "alternative facts." It may be easy to look at some of these more intricate or abstract theories of truth and say these are part of a glass bead game, something intelligent people do when they get together like playing chess, and maybe some of those theories are actually just that. But looking around at contemporary society, which some people describe as being "post-truth," and you've used that language as well, truth is hardly something we can just take for granted. You don't have to be a Foucaultian anymore to say that truth is political. That's especially after the Trump administration's reliance on alternative facts, but also after the "March for Science" in 2017 that occurred in over 600 cities. Scientists aren't usually the kinds of people who go out and march for their discipline itself. Such a public demonstration signals that truth is up for grabs, conceptually or otherwise. How does your research relate to this political environment? Do you see a connection at all between your work on truth and the mass confusion of contemporary capitalism?

Zuidervaart: I think so. I hope to address these issues in the book that I'm writing, although it won't be accessible to a general audience, or to Donald Trump, or to my brother and sister, and so on. But I intend a chapter on politics and truth, and hopefully I can work out these issues there.

Let me just make a few observations about the condition that we're in right now. For a long time, in North American culture and maybe more broadly in Eurocentric culture, science and scientists were in positions of authority. They were regarded as experts, and their pronouncements were considered to have great weight. That's no longer the case. I think there have been many different ways in which the authority of science and scientists has been undermined. When you don't have them as authorities, that opens the gate for other authorities to replace them. What kind of authorities will those replacements be? Religious authorities? Moral authorities? Political authorities? Artistic authorities? I think we're in a real struggle now over who's going to have authority and what kind of authority it is going to be.

The danger we have is that the struggle for authority is mixed up with a populist reaction to globalization, which often takes a nationalist flavour that sometimes can be a racist nationalist flavour, like white nationalism. These are very dangerous times. When there's a crisis of authority, that means simply speaking the truth is not enough. You have to have a way of actually backing up the truth that you speak in ways that are convincing. Scientists are in a very shaky position, because they have a hard time backing up the truth they speak in a way that's convincing to a populist-minded population. People like Donald Trump are very clever at exploiting this problem and putting themselves in the judgment seat, if you will, and posing as the authorities on everything, whether it be on scientific, political, or technological questions, whatever. In claiming authority, they also claim to speak the truth, but now in such a way that it just is whatever they say. In other words, their authority is the authority to speak whatever truth they happen to find worth saying. That way of thinking about truth, as whatever some person says or some community says, is intrinsically, I think, opposed to truth as such. It's not just post-truth; it's anti-truth. There's an anti-truth disposition on the part of significant public figures.

That has happened for various reasons. One, I would think, is there's been a gradual collapse of public culture in North America due to systemic pressures that come from the economy and the administrative state. The ability to engage in debate about issues becomes more and more narrow and undermined. I touched on that a bit in my book *Art in Public*,[10] but the trends I pointed to in that book have become more pronounced. Among those who politically resist both the populist turn and the authoritarian turn, there's a very thin normative language. It's almost assumed that of course you would understand that you're supposed to be a democratic citizen, or that you can't just take people who pompously proclaim things as speaking the truth. But what sort of normative backing do you have for that? What's your normative set of reasons for subscribing to democracy, or thinking truth is important, and so on?

I touched on the isolation of expertise before. I think that's another problem. We don't have good fora, good settings in our academies and our other cultural institutions, for people with expertise not just to *speak to* a general public but to *hear from* a general public and *learn from* it, to take what a general public is concerned about under advisement and to work with it in their own thought and scientific experimentation and so on, the way they design their research projects.

Another reason: we have been in what I would call a condition of cultural relativism for a long time, a culture where people have thought that whatever is true is true for you and not for me, or true for my group and not your group. That's fed in part by identity politics, where each marginalized or oppressed group thinks its truth is the most important truth. As soon as you talk that language, my truth and your truth, you're engaged in a relativist project. I think good ol' American or North American individualism plays into this too, where each individual is somehow sacrosanct and doesn't need to be held accountable to a wider forum. We've been in a relativist culture for a long time.

I think postmodernism in the academy has contributed to that. I'm not going to say postmodernism is the source of relativism, but it contributes to it, because it has become sceptical about truth claims. You mentioned Foucault. I think Foucault is a very complex thinker, but there's a danger in how Foucault is read as saying all truth claims are power moves. As soon as you think truth is just a power move and nothing more, you can no longer treat it as a truth claim. You're giving up the idea of truth. This is exactly what the Trump people have done, talking about alternative facts, fake news – they're just saying it's all politics, that is, it's all power machinations, and may the most powerful win. There is no truth, I think, on that account; there are no facts, there are no truth claims, just power moves. I could get myself into a lot of trouble by saying Trump is the ultimate pseudo-

Foucaultian, but still there's a continuity between pointing out that there are power moves made when truth claims are asserted and thinking that's *all* that's happening when someone makes a truth claim.

These are loose thoughts, but when you put them all together, we're in a real spiritual crisis, about which direction our society should head in, and how in that direction we could actually achieve something that's good for everybody. I think for a lot of people that question doesn't even come up anymore, but I think it's a question that has to be asked. I think we're in a spiritual crisis, not just a political crisis [...]

6. TRADITIONS OF TRUTH

Dettloff: To round this conversation out, we should talk about a connection you made about truth as a strange problem both for philosophy and for Christians engaging philosophy. On the one hand it seems that it should be a natural investigation for "lovers of wisdom" to determine what the truth is and how to comport ourselves in the world in light of truth. Yet as you note in a recent essay,[11] Christianity and the wisdom tradition of philosophy both converge and diverge on the question of truth and comportment. As a Christian philosopher studying truth, how do you see these traditions intersecting and departing?

Zuidervaart: That's a terrific question, and in trying to answer it I will probably find a better way of articulating the whole problem I'm engaged with. Here's a first attempt at trying to answer it. I think what's common to what I will call the "biblical wisdom tradition," by which I mean the Hebrew and Christian wisdom traditions, and what I will call the "Greek wisdom tradition," the one that gets articulated and refined in Greek philosophy, can be concepts of faithfulness, which are intrinsic to my own conception of truth. So it's nice, because I'm finding a way to bring my own conception into touch with both these strands, which are the most important strands in the development of Western philosophy and culture.

What is the notion of faithfulness? I talk about fidelity to societal principles. I think there's a strong emphasis on faithfulness in the very origins of the Greek wisdom tradition, in Parmenides for example, but there what you are faithful to is the real, that which does not change, is eternal, and so on and so forth. That kind of faithfulness to the real is a strong motivating factor in the Greek tradition and all the way through to twentieth-century analytic philosophy in particular. An emphasis on accuracy, correctness, being true to the facts – that's just a much more thinned-out articulation of what Parmenides was concerned about way back in the sixth century before the Common Era.

In the biblical tradition, there's also a notion of faithfulness, but there it's a faithfulness in relationship with the other. The other is a calling that comes to us, and the other with whom we are in relationship. The other can be the neighbour, other creatures, the divine – the other is a very broad concept. That's really a different kind of faithfulness, but it's faithfulness, nevertheless. So you have a competition between two kinds of faithfulness that are found in two different traditions for thinking about truth.

The other side of it is the other axis that I emphasize in my own conception, the emphasis on disclosure. Heidegger was right in saying, when you go back to the Greeks, what they are thinking about in truth is the disclosure of being or reality, not simply a corresponding with reality. It's an opening up of being that's important. That's also in Parmenides; it just so happens that being for him is eternal, unchanging, and doesn't have any kind of time or transition or relationships built into it. It's more like mathematical numbers. In the Greek tradition, it's primarily a disclosure of being or reality; in the Hebrew tradition, it's a disclosure of life and creation, and creation is understood as dependent on a Creator – there is no sort of "Being," if you will (I take this especially from Dooyeweerd), to which we have to be faithful, that has to be disclosed.

These two notions, faithfulness and disclosure, which I'm still working with, you can find articulated differently in these two traditions. The one strand leads to a certain emphasis on propositional truth, the other strand, which is much less articulated in our overall tradition, leads to an emphasis on a holistic notion of truth. I'm trying to put these two things together. I will never insist on a faithfulness to the real as the *key* to truth, but I understand the appeal of that. When you get to that level of truth, to propositional truth, there is something like being faithful to the real, being faithful to the object as it discloses itself to you. Anyway, those are my thoughts right now. This is a way of saying the two traditions have more in common than you might think, though there's a real reason for their divergence, because of a difference between what we are faithful to and what we need to disclose.

Dettloff: It's interesting to think of that in light of people like Hadot or Foucault, who were trying to find the continuities between ancient philosophy and its inheritance in Christian philosophy. That seems right; the continuity is precisely the faithfulness, but the discontinuity is what one wants to be faithful to.

Zuidervaart: Yes. But this also puts me in conflict with Critical Theory, particularly Adorno and Horkheimer's account of the dialectic of enlightenment,[12] because they read what I call the biblical wisdom tradition as simply part of an overall tradition of emphasizing instrumental reason and reducing the scope of rationality. My account actually claims differently, that there are resources within our overall tradition, both on the Greek side and on the biblical side, for a more capacious notion of rationality and of what truth comes to. Someday I'll have to work out that disagreement with Critical Theory as well.

Dettloff: Let's end with one final note along these lines. What resources do you think are still available in both the Christian and philosophical traditions to address a moment characterized by "anti-truth" politics and overly specialized academic disciplines?

Zuidervaart: That's a great question! There's so much one could say in reply, but let me give a brief response. To borrow a distinction from Terry Eagleton, the resources available in these traditions help make me hopeful but not optimistic.[13] I am hopeful because so many leaders in the arts, education, religion, and even government recognize that anti-truth politics and hyperspecialized expertise are unsustainable in the long run. If we care about the future – and I believe many leaders do care – then the global scale of economic injustice and environmental destruction does not let us fiddle while Rome burns. I'm hopeful because ordinary folks of many different backgrounds and persuasions still hear the calls to justice and solidarity and stewardship that echo from their religious and cultural traditions, even when we don't always know how to translate what we hear into suitable policies and practices. I'm hopeful, too, because so much resistance has built up to the sheer stupidity and malevolence of those who would reduce democratic governance and education to a zero-sum game of thrones.

Even though Christianity and philosophy often have been at odds, sometimes for very good reasons, both of them harbor abundant resources of normative reflection on what makes for goodness in human life and society. For someone who takes these resources seriously, the challenge is to draw on them while rearticulating a hopeful vision of truth-telling politics and of ethical scholarship for the common good.[14] That's what my current work on the idea of truth tries to do. I'm hopeful – albeit not optimistic – this work will bear good fruit.

Publication Information

Note: This list provides information about the sources for all chapters within this volume, in their order of appearance.

1 "Philosophy, Truth, and the Wisdom of Love." *Christian Scholar's Review* 48, no. 1 (Fall 2018): 31–43.
2 "Holistic Alethic Pluralism: A Reformational Research Program." *Philosophia Reformata* 81, no. 2 (2016): 156–78.
3 "Distantial Ways of Knowing: Doug Blomberg's Proposal for a Reformational Epistemology." *Philosophia Reformata* 84, no. 1 (2019): 58–78.
4 "Social Domains of Knowledge: Technology, Art, and Religion." *Philosophia Reformata*, 84, no. 1 (2019): 79–101.
5 "Transformational Social Critique and a Politics of Hope." Posted online as "Reformational Social Philosophy" and "Toward a New Politics," in response to a Ground Motive Book Symposium on *Religion, Truth, and Social Transformation*, ICS, Toronto, 30 May 2016 and 1 June 2016; http://www.groundmotive.net/2016/05/reformational-social-philosophy.html and http://www.groundmotive.net/2016/06/toward-new-politics.html.
6 "Reformational Philosophy Revisited." Posted online as "Philosophy, Art, and Religion" and "Dooyeweerd, Truth, and the Reformational Tradition," in response to a Ground Motive Book Symposium on *Religion, Truth, and Social Transformation*, ICS, Toronto, 2 June 2016 and 3 June 2016; http://www.groundmotive.net/2016/06/philosophy-art-and-religion.html and http://www.groundmotive.net/2016/06/dooyeweerd-truth-and-reformational.html.

7 "Hegel, Malick, and the Postsecular Sublime." In *Immanent Frames: Postsecular Cinema between Malick and von Trier*, edited by John Caruana and Mark Cauchi, 47–67. Albany: State University of New York Press, 2018. Expanded and revised.

8 "Toronto to Berlin and Back Again." Interview with Dean Dettloff, conducted in Toronto on 11 March 2017. Previously unpublished.

9 "Revolution Isn't What It Used to Be." Interview with Dean Dettloff, recorded in Toronto on 13 May 2017, and podcast on *The Magnificast*, 20 May 2017; https://themagnificast.wordpress.com/2017/05/20/ep-8-revolution-isnt-what-it-used-to-be-w-lambert-zuidervaart/.

10 "Pursuing Truth in a Post-Truth Society." Interview with Dean Dettloff, conducted via Skype on 27 July 2018. Previously unpublished.

Notes

INTRODUCTION

1 Arendt, "Truth and Politics," 545–6. Arendt wrote this essay in response to controversies over her book *Eichmann in Jerusalem* and first published it in the *New Yorker* on 25 February 1967.
2 See Zuidervaart, *Social Philosophy after Adorno*, 6–7.
3 Arendt, "Truth and Politics," 562–3.
4 Ibid., 570–1.
5 Ibid., 571.
6 Arendt's understanding of impartiality does not assume, however, that the truthteller should occupy a position of abstract detachment from the political realm, a position from which to leverage power without regard to actual human interests. For more on Arendt's critique of this "Archimedean norm" in much of Western philosophy and political thought, which regards power as leverage and assumes that knowledge requires *abstract* impartiality, see Disch, *Hannah Arendt and the Limits of Philosophy*.
7 Dooyeweerd, "The Dilemma for Christian Philosophical Thought," 267, a translation by Chris van Haeften of Dooyeweerd, "Het dilemma voor het christelijk wijsgerig denken."
8 See "Introduction: Transforming Philosophy," in Zuidervaart, *Religion, Truth, and Social Transformation*, 3–22, and "Introduction: 'The Point Is to Change It,'" in Zuidervaart, *Art, Education, and Cultural Renewal*, 3–24.
9 For a comprehensive and lively introduction to Kuyper's life and work, see Bratt, *Abraham Kuyper: Modern Calvinist, Christian Democrat*.

10 For details about their contributions, see especially Tol, *Philosophy in the Making*, and Chaplin, *Herman Dooyeweerd*.
11 The story of ICS's founding and its first forty years is told by VanderVennen, *A University for the People*.
12 Arendt, "Truth and Politics," 559–60. The same proscription would apply, of course, to any attempt to erect such a tyranny with the help of a despot who is *not* philosophically inclined.
13 Exceptions to this pattern include the essays in Part Two ("Truth and Politics") of *Truth Matters*, edited by Zuidervaart et al., 101–71, as well as the writings of my ICS colleague Ron Kuipers. See, for example, Kuipers, *Richard Rorty*.
14 Without being thematized as such, questions about truth and politics do come up in the writings of feminists who have studied or taught at ICS, the VU Amsterdam, and related schools. A reverse chronological sample of such ICS-related writings would include Carr, *Story and Philosophy for Social Change*; Hoff, *The Laws of the Spirit*; Wesselius, "A Responsible Philosophy"; and Guen Hart, "Power in the Service of Love." For an illuminating personal reflection on why first-generation reformational philosophy can lead one to resist rather than embrace feminism, see Botha, "On Being a Christian Philosopher and Not a Feminist."
15 See especially chapters 1, 2, and 10 in the current volume as well as "Unfinished Business: Toward a Reformational Conception of Truth," in Zuidervaart, *Religion, Truth, and Social Transformation*, 277–97, and Zuidervaart, *Truth in Husserl, Heidegger, and the Frankfurt School*.
16 Arendt, "Truth and Politics," 545–6.
17 Ibid., 564, 573.
18 See chapters 1, 4, and 5 in Zuidervaart, *Religion, Truth, and Social Transformation*.
19 Here, and throughout this book, I use "art" and "the arts" to refer to the full range of artistic practices, products, and events: not only the visual arts but also dance, film, literature, music, theatre, and the like.

CHAPTER ONE

1 Miriam Pederson, "Hold Your Horses," one of three poems, accompanied by images of three sculptures by Ron Pederson, in a collaboration titled "Conversations," in Acero Ferrer et al., eds, *Seeking Stillness*, 313.
2 See Hadot, *Philosophy as a Way of Life*, and *What Is Ancient Philosophy?* Robert Sweetman uses Hadot's notion of spiritual exercise to help make sense of various traditions of Christian scholarship in *Tracing the Lines*.

3 For a survey of these traditions, see Huston Smith, *The World's Religions*, a completely revised and updated edition of Smith's pathbreaking *The Religions of Man*. Smith emphasizes the notion of "wisdom traditions" in this revised edition, which presupposes *Forgotten Truth*, his attempt to see what the world's religions hold in common and what the modern West is in danger of forgetting. See also Smith, *Why Religion Matters*, where he tries to address the "spiritual crisis" that has arisen, he claims, from the West's writing "a blank check for science's claims concerning what constitutes knowledge and justified belief" (4). I would argue that the deposit on which this scientistic check is drawn stems from a Greek philosophical wisdom tradition at odds with many religious wisdom traditions.

4 The historical record is more complicated than this suggests, of course. In *Philosophy as a Way of Life*, for example, Hadot argues both that the Patristics Christianized spiritual exercises inherited from Greek and Hellenistic philosophy and that medieval Scholasticism, in distinguishing theology from philosophy and privileging theology, "emptied [philosophy] of its spiritual exercises" (107), thereby setting the stage for a predominantly theoretical and systematic emphasis in modern philosophy.

5 Unless noted otherwise, all Bible translations are from the New Revised Standard Version (NRSV).

6 For an exploration of the relation between the truth of assertions and the truth of actions in the history of Western thought, see Campbell, *Truth and Historicity*. Campbell subsequently argues in *The Concept of Truth* that truth is primarily an attribute of actions rather than of linguistic items; that assertions are primarily actions; and that assertions, like other actions, are true as achievements. Other than reformational scholars such as Hendrik Hart and Calvin Seerveld, Campbell is one of the few contemporary philosophers who highlight the Hebrew concept of truth as relational faithfulness (*emeth*) and who consider it a better clue to the nature and value of truth than a Greek concept of truth as unchanging correctness (*aletheia*). See, for example, Campbell, *Truth and Historicity*, 434–9, and Campbell, *The Concept of Truth*, 100–24.

7 Seerveld, "A Concept of Artistic Truth Prompted by Biblical Wisdom Literature," 296.

8 Here I barely hint at a response to Clarence Joldersma's eloquent call, in "Earth's Lament: A Friendly Supplement to Zuidervaart's Societal Principles in an Era of Climate Change," to let Earth's lament be heard in its own nonhuman voice, such that the gift of Earth's "primordial call to

responsibility, from a time immemorial," receives normative weight (330). I find Psalm 85:11 intriguing in this connection – "truth will spring up from the earth" – but right now I do not know quite how to incorporate these matters into a conception of truth. Still, I recognize the need to do so, and thereby to give credence to the strong sense I've had for years that nonhuman creatures have their own integrity out of which they address us and through which God speaks. Janet Wesselius captures this sense in her moving meditation "The Patient Hope of Rosa: Reflections on Dog-Kissed Tears," for example: "Animals ... show us a different way of being in the world ... Given our linguistic and rational abilities ... we sometimes need animals for God to break into our awareness and for us to listen to God's voice" (12). See also Sue Sinclair's "Adorno Poems," where, despite societal evil, beauty on Earth is not simply "false consolation" but a promise that "even loneliness" is "no longer truly lonely" (101). All three contributions are in Acero Ferrer et al., eds, *Seeking Stillness*.

9 Wolterstorff, *Justice in Love*.
10 Duck, "Come and Seek the Ways of Wisdom," v. 1.
11 Strictly speaking, one should refer to Jewish wisdom *traditions*. Even among the wisdom books of the Hebrew Bible known as "Writings" – Proverbs, Job, Ecclesiastes, and the Song of Songs – one can detect different emphases, historical settings, and literary forms. See Fontaine, "Wisdom Traditions in the Hebrew Bible."
12 Duck, "Come and Seek the Ways of Wisdom," v. 2.
13 Hart, "Filled with All God's Fullness," in Acero Ferrer et al., eds, *Seeking Stillness*, 22. Hart's hunch is borne out by Lester J. Kuyper, "Grace and Truth," 3–19. Kuyper argues in lexicographical detail that "full of grace and truth" in John 1:14 translates a Greek rendering of central Old Testament language for God as, for example, "abounding in steadfast love [*chesed*] and faithfulness [*emeth*]" (Exod. 34:6).
14 Olthuis, "Creatio Ex Amore." Olthuis shows how a theology that begins with "God as love" is, and must be, dramatically different from one that begins with God as (a) Being – what one could call the pervasive Parmenidean legacy in Western theology. This difference also affects how one thinks about truth, as I hope to show.
15 Not only philosophy, however, but also such fields as art, science, politics, and education. See, for example, Doug Blomberg's attempt to work out the implications of such a "wisdom perspective" for schooling in *Wisdom and Curriculum*.
16 On the importance of Parmenides for the entire Western alethic tradi-

tion, see chapter 3 ("Truth as Divine Norm") in Campbell, *Truth and Historicity*, 18–39. Campbell summarizes the Parmenidean concept of truth as "faithful adherence to the Real" (32), and he says it set Western philosophy firmly on the path to both depersonalizing and dehistoricizing truth.

17 Parmenides, "Poem of Parmenides," fragment 8, 174.
18 Joshua Lee Harris, "Parmenides' Challenge and Zuidervaart's Stereotheticism: A Project both Ancient and Original," in Acero Ferrer et al., eds, *Seeking Stillness*, 56–73, illuminates this problem of an absent "middle" (*metaxy*) as a perennial challenge posed by Parmenides and addressed by holistic alethic pluralism in the reformational tradition.
19 Such recognition of temporality and relationality is built into Franz Rosenzweig's concept of revelation, it seems to me. See Karin Nisenbaum, "Zuidervaart in Conversation with Rosenzweig: Artistic Truth, Life-Giving Disclosure, and Revelation," in Acero Ferrer et al., eds, *Seeking Stillness*, 260–84.
20 See Zuidervaart, "Truth and Goodness Intersect." For a more elaborate account, in response to twentieth-century German philosophy, see chapter 8 ("Conclusion: Truth and Goodness Intersect") in Zuidervaart, *Truth in Husserl, Heidegger, and the Frankfurt School*, 175–85.
21 Seerveld, "A Concept of Artistic Truth," 297.
22 Not all fibs are simple, of course, and the question of what counts as a lie is not always easy to settle. See in this connection the illuminating essay by Martin Jay, "Can Photographs Lie? Reflections on a Perennial Anxiety," in Acero Ferrer et al., eds, *Seeking Stillness*, 285–306.
23 The Lie is very closely connected to what I call "societal evil." See, for example, "Earth's Lament: Suffering, Hope, and Wisdom," in Zuidervaart, *Religion, Truth, and Social Transformation*, 319–21. I take up this connection in the next section.
24 "Post-Truth," https://www.oxforddictionaries.com/press/news/2016/12/11/WOTY-16; accessed 19 April 2017. For a succinct study of the origins and ramifications of contemporary post-truth politics, see Lee McIntyre, *Post-Truth*.
25 Frankfurt, *On Bullshit*, which distinguishes "bullshit" from actual lies. Unlike the liar, who knows a factual truth and tries to deceive someone about it, bullshitters do not care whether what they say is factually true or false: "It is just this lack of ... concern with [factual] truth ... that I regard as of the essence of bullshit" (33–4). Or, as Frankfurt puts it a little later, "the essence of bullshit is not that it is [factually] *false* but that it is *phony*" (47). Unlike liars, then, bullshitters try to hide their own lack

of concern about factual truth. Because of this, says Frankfurt, "bullshit is a greater enemy of the [factual] truth than lies are" (61). One sees this, I think, in the notion of a "post-truth" world. Frankfurt's sequel *On Truth* says why, despite the bullshitters, all of us should care about factual truth.

26 Arnold De Graaff, *The Gods in Whom They Trusted*, argues that, at root, contemporary environmental degradation and societal violence stem from a global economic system and the "neoliberal ideology" that directs it. He shows in great detail how an alternative, holistic understanding of economic life and human knowledge, directed by the vision of love and truth in the Hebrew scriptures, can support a radically different way of living and thereby a transformed society.

27 Acknowledging limits to our resistance should not encourage passivity. Instead it should spark both focused creativity and long-range vision in our resistance. See in this connection Allyson Carr's discussion of One Billion Rising's public choreographed piece "Break the Chain" as a truthful way to challenge sexual violence and gendered oppression, in "Social Philosophy after Trauma: Art for Dialogue in the Public Square," in Acero Ferrer et al., eds, *Seeking Stillness*, 130–48.

28 To borrow words from the letter to the Ephesians, those who resist societal evil do not simply struggle "against enemies of blood and flesh" but against "cosmic powers of this present darkness" and against "the spiritual forces of evil" (Eph. 6:12). Famously this letter then urges its readers to strap on "the belt of truth," "the breastplate of righteousness," and the sandals of the "gospel of peace" (Eph. 6:14–15) – recalling the confluence of truth, justice, and *shalom* in Psalm 85 and elsewhere.

29 Cockburn, "Grim Travellers."

30 See "Earth's Lament," where I call for a philosophy that embodies "patient hope for a new Earth, and comprehensive wisdom about the shape of the old" (318).

31 See "Macrostructures and Societal Principles: An Architectonic Critique," in Zuidervaart, *Religion, Truth, and Social Transformation*, 252–76.

32 I follow Terry Eagleton, *Hope without Optimism*, in sharply distinguishing genuine hope from "the banality of optimism." Correctly noting that there is "surprisingly little philosophical reflection on what hope consists in" (38), Eagleton devotes an entire chapter to Ernst Bloch, whom he calls "*the* philosopher of hope" (90). Bloch's too-often neglected three-volume magnum opus on the topic was published in German in the 1950s and did not appear in English translation until 1985. See Bloch, *The Principle of Hope*. On the importance of a partially Bloch-

inspired theme of hope in Theodor W. Adorno's negative dialectical conception of truth, see Zuidervaart, *Social Philosophy after Adorno*, 48–76, and my essay "History and Transcendence in Adorno's Idea of Truth."

33 See Hart, "Filled with All God's Fullness," which comments on Ephesians 1–3 and explores the importance of openness to spiritual reorientation for both the practice and the theory of truth.

34 "Unfinished Business: Toward a Reformational Conception of Truth," in Zuidervaart, *Religion, Truth, and Social Transformation*, 284.

35 Given this description of truth, I think recent attempts to derive an ethics from the appeal to personal authenticity in Martin Heidegger's *Being and Time* are bound to fail: they cannot do justice to the interrelational character of truth as involving both societal principles and societal disclosure. In this connection, see the illuminating essay by Lauren Bialystok, "Authenticity, Ethics, and Truth: Zuidervaart and Heidegger in Reverse," in Acero Ferrer et al., eds, *Seeking Stillness*," 240–59.

36 I discuss some of these complications in "History and Transcendence in Adorno's Idea of Truth."

37 As is apparent from earlier references, the primary inspiration for reconceiving factual truth within a broader, reformational conception of truth stems from my graduate studies and subsequent teaching at the Institute for Christian Studies in Toronto. I am especially indebted to the pioneering work of Hendrik Hart, who has argued for years that truth and knowledge are "totality concepts" to which narrow conceptions of fact/assertion correspondence and justified true belief cannot do justice. See in particular chapters 7 ("Knowledge") and 8 ("Theory of Analysis, Thinking and Theory") in his *Draft for Proposed ICS Syllabus for Systematic Philosophy*, 357–612; his essay "The Articulation of Belief"; and the brief subsection on "Knowledge and Truth" in Hart, *Understanding Our World*, 355–7. I examine some issues in Hart's epistemology in chapter 4 of the current volume. See also chapters 6–8 in Zuidervaart, *Religion, Truth, and Social Transformation*, 133–82.

38 Although my broader conception is at odds with the standard Western philosophical concept of truth, it is not incompatible with alternatives to this standard concept in the Western tradition. I discuss some of these alternatives in *Truth in Husserl, Heidegger, and the Frankfurt School*. One can find a similar emphasis on living the truth in Catholic moral theology. See, for example, Josef Pieper, *Living the Truth* and Klaus Demmer, *Living the Truth*.

39 I discuss what this emphasis on the call to love implies for a philoso-

pher's vocation in "Spirituality, Religion, and the Call to Love," in Zuidervaart, *Art, Education, and Cultural Renewal*, 180–96.
40 "The Call," by the metaphysical poet George Herbert (1593–1633), as set to music by Ralph Vaughan Williams in *Five Mystical Songs* (London: Stainer & Bell, 1911), 21–2.

CHAPTER TWO

1 Detailed presentations of results from this research program occur in two monographs, one focused primarily, but not exclusively, on continental philosophy, and the other primarily, but not exclusively, on analytic philosophy. The first volume has been published as Lambert Zuidervaart, *Truth in Husserl, Heidegger, and the Frankfurt School: Critical Retrieval* (Cambridge, MA: MIT Press, 2017). The second volume, not yet published, has the tentative title *Social Domains of Truth: Science, Politics, Art, and Religion*.
2 Stich, *The Fragmentation of Reason*, 123. Stich gives the example of "poor Harry" who had the true belief that his flight was scheduled to leave at 7:45 a.m., caught it on time, and died when the airplane crashed. For a perceptive challenge to Stich's background assumptions and in defense of Donald Davidson's primitivist position, see Ellefson, "Cognitive Diversity, Conceptual Schemes, and Truth."
3 Quine, *Pursuit of Truth*, 80. Quine does grant, however, that the truth predicate is needed to talk about "sentences that are not given" and to generalize over a large number of sentences (80–1).
4 Rorty, *Truth and Progress*, 41.
5 Originally the term *critical theory* referred to a research program associated with the Frankfurt School of Western Marxism (Adorno, Horkheimer, Marcuse, Habermas, etc.), and it continues to get used in this way. In its broader contemporary usage, it also refers to such projects of social critique as feminism, postcolonialism, queer theory, and critical race theory. I distinguish these two usages by capitalizing "Critical Theory" when referring to the Frankfurt School tradition.
6 Foucault's own writings can be read as supporting such a position, but they do not need to be read in this way. In one of his most-cited reflections on "Truth and Power," for example, Foucault says the following: "'Truth' is linked in a circular relation with systems of power which produce and sustain it, and to effects of power which it induces and which extend it. A 'regime' of truth." Foucault, *Power/Knowledge*, 133. What does

it mean to say that "truth" induces effects of power and that the effects of power extend "truth"? It could mean that, as an ordered "economy" of statements, the entire complex of truth claims and their justification unavoidably plays a role in the way power operates within a society. That seems right to me, and it need not entail a problematic instrumentalizing of truth. But it could also be taken to mean that truth claims are *no more than tools* – i.e., that the only way in which the "economy" of truth plays a role in society is via the operation of power. Foucault's identifying a "circular relation" between "truth" and "systems of power" suggests that truth claims are not simply power moves, but his description of this circular relation leaves unclear what truth claims are or do beyond their role in the operation of power.

7 Frankfurt, *On Bullshit*.
8 I discuss two of the most important anthologies in the next section. A representative, chronological list of English-language books on truth since 2000 written by philosophers for a non-specialist audience would include Engel, *Truth*; Williams, *Truth & Truthfulness*; Lynch, *True to Life*; Blackburn, *Truth: A Guide*; Frankfurt, *On Truth*; and Campbell, *The Concept of Truth*.
9 Adorno, *Against Epistemology*, 72.
10 As René van Woudenberg has pointed out in comments on an earlier version of this chapter, the position that *truth in general* resists a real definition need not entail that *propositional truth* resists a real definition. I agree. In fact, I believe much can be learned from the project of specifying necessary and sufficient conditions for propositional truth. Yet I doubt whether such attempts at giving a real definition can do justice to either the internal complexity of propositional truth or its interlinkage with other domains of truth.
11 Kirkham, *Theories of Truth*, 20.
12 See especially the diagram in Lynch, ed., *The Nature of Truth*, 4.
13 Lynch, ed., *The Nature of Truth*, 5.
14 Medina and Wood, eds, *Truth: Engagements across Philosophical Traditions*, 3.
15 Alcoff, "Reclaiming Truth," 336–7.
16 The work of William P. Alston, a Christian philosopher in the analytic tradition, is quite instructive in this regard. His book *A Realist Conception of Truth* devotes seven chapters to articulating and defending alethic realism and rejecting epistemic conceptions of truth. In chapter 8, however, he says why truth is important, and in the epilogue he suggests the

primary difference between his alethic realism and the anti-realist positions he rejects might stem from their "intolerance of vulnerability" (264) – a suggestion very similar to Herman Dooyeweerd's challenge to the "pretended autonomy of philosophical thought." See Dooyeweerd, *In the Twilight of Western Thought*, 1–60.

17 See Zuidervaart, *Truth in Husserl, Heidegger, and the Frankfurt School*, 112–17.
18 Zuidervaart, *Artistic Truth*, 6.
19 Aristotle, *Poetics* X.1–9, in S.H. Butcher, *Aristotle's Theory of Poetry and Fine Art*, 34–7. See also Butcher's chapter on "Poetic Truth," 163–97.
20 Anselm, "On Truth."
21 I discuss Hegel's conception of absolute spirit in chapter 7 below.
22 See in this connection Taylor, *The Ethics of Authenticity*.
23 See in this connection Zuidervaart, *Truth in Husserl, Heidegger, and the Frankfurt School*.
24 In a chapter titled "Acting Truly," Richard Campbell provides an extended analysis of what it means to call someone a "true friend." See Campbell, *The Concept of Truth*, 100–24.
25 See especially "Macrostructures and Societal Principles: An Architectonic Critique," in Zuidervaart, *Religion, Truth, and Social Transformation*, 252–76.
26 See especially Putnam, *Reason, Truth and History* and Alston, *A Realist Conception of Truth*.
27 For a representative collection of essays in this field, see Pedersen and Wright, eds, *Truth and Pluralism*. Prominent writings by Crispin Wright include *Truth and Objectivity*, "Truth: A Traditional Debate Reviewed," and "Minimalism, Deflationism, Pragmatism, Pluralism." See also the strong case against deflationism and in favor of "truth pluralism" in Edwards, *The Metaphysics of Truth*.
28 In particular, Lynch, *Truth as One and Many*.
29 This approach has resonance with the argument in van Woudenberg, "Truths That Science Cannot Touch," that there are, and we can know, truths that science cannot touch. Unlike van Woudenberg, I think there is an *institutional* way to demarcate science from non-science, even though I agree with him that truth (a certain type of truth, in my account) is the primary goal of science.
30 See "Living at the Crossroads: Ethical Scholarship and the Common Good," in Zuidervaart, *Art, Education, and Cultural Renewal*, 170–9.
31 I wish to thank Joshua Harris and René van Woudenberg for their very helpful comments on an earlier draft of this chapter.

CHAPTER THREE

1 Blomberg, "The Development of Curriculum with Relation to the Philosophy of the Cosmonomic Idea."
2 Hart, *Draft for Proposed ICS Syllabus for Systematic Philosophy*.
3 Hart, *Understanding Our World*.
4 Blomberg did spend a year at the Institute for Christian Studies (ICS) in Toronto (1975–76), however, and his dissertation cites several publications by Arnold De Graaff and James Olthuis, who were faculty colleagues and close collaborators with Henk Hart at ICS in the 1970s. Blomberg reports that he had intended to study with Hart in 1975–76, but learned too late that Hart was on sabbatical, no doubt working on his *Draft Syllabus*, which he first finished in 1976.
5 The context for these two chapters on epistemology lies in a larger research project on the idea of truth, as described in the previous chapter.
6 See, for example, Vollenhoven, *Reformed Epistemology*, 8–10, 21, and 75. This is a translation of Vollenhoven's 1926 inaugural lecture *Logos en ratio*, where the equivalent passages occur on 11–12, 20, and 59. Although Vollenhoven subsequently dropped the *logos* theme, so prominent in this publication, John Kok observes that *Logos en ratio* "remained on Vollenhoven's list of required examination literature well into the 1950s." Kok, *Vollenhoven: His Early Development*, 233. Anthony Tol notes that, prior to 1926, Vollenhoven used the Dutch terms *kennen* and *weten* to mark the distinction between psychical knowing and analytic knowing, respectively. Tol, *Philosophy in the Making*, 103–4, 188–97, and 251n54.
7 See, for example, Vollenhoven, *Hoofdlijnen der logica*, 47, where Vollenhoven says the trustworthiness (*betrouwbaarheid*) of God is "the final ground for our faith, for our faith-knowledge [*geloofskennis*]."
8 Mekkes, "Knowing," 317.
9 Popma, *Inleiding in de wijsbegeerte*, 110–11. Whereas here Popma tends to characterize the distinct ways of knowing as modes of *consciousness* – juridical *rechtsbesef*, aesthetic *schoonheidsbesef*, and *technisch besef*, for example (112) – in the essay "Knowing" Mekkes characterizes them as ways of *acting*. As will become apparent later, my own approach, with its emphasis on practices and institutions, is closer to Mekkes in this regard. See also Mekkes, "Methodology and Practice," which emphasizes the priority of "practical distinguishing as caught up in communal action" over "theoretical systematizing" and places both theoretical and practical knowledge in service of "life-disclosure" (82–3).

10 van Woudenberg, "Theorie van het kennen," 29–37, 74–80.
11 Dooyeweerd, *A New Critique of Theoretical Thought*, vol. 2, 427–598. For a critical exposition focused on these pages, see "Dooyeweerd's Conception of Truth," in Zuidervaart, *Religion, Truth, and Social Transformation*, 54–76.
12 Vollenhoven, *Calvinism and the Reformation of Philosophy* (1933), excerpt, 27–9. See also the illuminating essay by Kok, "Vollenhoven and 'Scriptural Philosophy.'"
13 In "Dooyeweerd's *Gegenstand* Theory of Theory," Hendrik Hart affirms certain insights within Dooyeweerd's Gegenstand theory but considers Dooyeweerd's formulations highly problematic. The insights have to do with three distinctions: between (multidimensional) knowing and (analytically qualified) thinking, between (law-side-oriented) theoretical thought and (subject-side-oriented) nontheoretical thought, and between (theoretically integrating) philosophy and (theoretically specializing) other academic disciplines. Once one works through Hart's criticisms, however, it seems that such insights are available not so much *because* of Dooyeweerd's formulations as *despite* them. One should also compare this essay with the much longer discussion in Hart's 1979 *Draft Syllabus*, 614–62, which takes up the criticisms of Dooyeweerd's theory of theory by Hendrik Van Riessen and Danie Strauss. See also the discussion of Vollenhoven, Dooyeweerd, and Van Riessen on the distinction between theoretical and nontheoretical knowledge in van Woudenberg, "Theorie van het kennen," 37–48.
14 Although not opposed to such an approach, Hart's 1979 *Draft Syllabus* is more cautious about claiming there are multiple ways of knowing. His fundamental position is that knowing "is characteristic of ... all doing, all acting, all practice, when it is integral, both with respect to its own calling and in its service to the rest of human life" (562). In other words, "knowledge" is a totality concept, pertinent to the full range of human practices. This position leaves open the question of whether and how to distinguish different ways of knowing. The syllabus only begins to address that question when, for example, it distinguishes faith as "sure knowledge" from reason ("analytic knowing," in Hart's terminology) as "distinct knowing" (563–4). A few years later, however, Hart elaborates this faith/reason distinction – in relationship to a holistic conception of knowledge – in his essay "The Articulation of Belief." I discuss this essay in the next chapter.
15 Here *science* has the broad nineteenth-century sense of *Wissenschaft* or *wetenschap*, and it includes mathematics, the natural sciences, the

humanities, and the social sciences. Because this term has become closely identified with the natural sciences and with the empirical side to the social sciences, I often use terms like *academic endeavours* and *academic disciplines* instead to indicate the full range of the "scientific" enterprise.
16 Blomberg, "The Development of Curriculum," xii.
17 Seerveld's lectures, given at study conferences in Unionville, Ontario and Banff, Alberta during the summers of 1962 and 1963, were published together in Seerveld, *A Christian Critique of Art and Literature*.
18 Ibid., 70.
19 Ibid., 70–1.
20 Blomberg, "The Development of Curriculum," 171. Blomberg's dissertation follows Dooyeweerd's modal order rather than Seerveld's, and it also prefers Dooyeweerd's characterization of the aesthetic mode in terms of "harmony" to Seerveld's emphasis on "suggestion," "allusivity," "nuancefulness," and the like. This raises a host of interlinked issues in modal theory, not least of which, in the current context, is whether Seerveld's account of "imaginative knowing" would make much sense if one followed Dooyeweerd's modal theory with respect to the aesthetic. In this connection, see "Dooyeweerd's Modal Theory: Questions in the Ontology of Science," in Zuidervaart, *Religion, Truth, and Social Transformation*, 77–109.
21 Blomberg, "The Development of Curriculum," 193–4.
22 Ibid., 206.
23 Ibid., 194–5.
24 Dooyeweerd, *A New Critique of Theoretical Thought*, 2: 185.
25 Blomberg, "The Development of Curriculum," 173.
26 Ibid., 187–8; italics in the original.
27 Ibid., 189.
28 Ibid., 472.
29 Ibid., 575.
30 Blomberg, "Toward a Christian Theory of Knowledge," 52, 42. This essay also appears as a reprint in the collection *Voices from the Past: Reformed Educators 1992*, ed. Donald Oppewal (Grand Rapids, MI: Calvin College, 1992), 185–92.
31 Ibid., 44.
32 Ibid., 46.
33 Ibid., 52.
34 Ibid., 53.
35 Ibid., 52–5.
36 Ibid., 56.

37 Ibid., 57–9.
38 See Zuidervaart, *Art, Education, and Cultural Renewal*, 181–4, and Zuidervaart, *Religion, Truth, and Social Transformation*, 12–13, 216–18, and 238–41.
39 Blomberg, "The Development of Curriculum," 300.
40 See Zuidervaart, *Artistic Truth*, 62–5 and passim; also Zuidervaart, *Art, Education, and Cultural Renewal*, 106–8, 111–12.
41 Blomberg, "The Development of Curriculum," 295, 300.
42 Olthuis, *Facts, Values and Ethics*, 191–3.
43 Ibid., 196.
44 In this connection, see also the brief comment on Olthuis's dissertation in Hart's *Draft Syllabus*, 624–5, where Hart cites a proposition (*stelling*) accompanying Olthuis's dissertation that said "the so-called 'Gegenstand-relation' of theoretical thought is nothing other than the (opened-up) logical subject-object relation" (quoted in Hart, *Draft Syllabus*, 625). Hart notes, however, that Olthuis appears to have changed his mind about these matters in the 1970s.
45 Hart, *Draft Syllabus*, 556–65. Actually, Vollenhoven's preferred term is "analytic coming to know" (*het analytische leren kennen*). Vollenhoven is not entirely clear about the modal "location" of knowing, however. In *Isagôgè Philosophiae / Introduction to Philosophy*, for example, he says "coming to know differs modally according to the law spheres within which it takes place" (111), but then he "temporarily" confines his discussion to the analytic law-sphere and subsequently says very little about knowing that takes place supra-analytically. Citing other of Vollenhoven's writings from the late 1930s and early 1940s, Kok says that Vollenhoven recognizes different modally qualified kinds of nonscientific knowledge, of which faith-knowledge is one (Kok, "Vollenhoven and 'Scriptural Philosophy,'" 118–19). But again, it is not clear whether such kinds are really distinct from analytic knowing or are simply examples of analytic knowing within primarily nonanalytic contexts. No doubt it is so, as Kok reports Vollenhoven to have claimed, that the knowing involved in children's respect for their parents has a different character than that involved in citizens' respect for their government (119), but does this difference occur because the "knowings" are qualitatively different or because the institutional contexts are qualitatively different?
46 Blomberg, "The Development of Curriculum," 119.
47 Although Blomberg's dissertation does not intend his descriptions of concrete experience to evoke empiricism, his initial examples are mostly perceptual ones, and he even invokes the phrase "knowledge by

acquaintance" – albeit purportedly cleansed of "its Empiricist assumptions" – that Bertrand Russell and other logical empiricists made famous. See Blomberg, "The Development of Curriculum," 24–6, 93–6. Immediacy and passivity are, of course, hallmarks of experience under empiricist descriptions, unlike emphases on the historical and cultural mediation of experience among more Hegelian thinkers. See, for example, the account of "hermeneutic experience" in Gadamer, *Truth and Method*, 265–379.

48 Blomberg, "Ways of Wisdom," 134. Much of this essay is incorporated into chapter 9 ("The Getting of Wisdom") in Blomberg, *Wisdom and Curriculum*, 149–63.

49 Blomberg explains that he borrows this phrase from Nicholas Maxwell, *From Knowledge to Wisdom*, and he intends it to mean both *understanding* and *implementing* "what ought to be accomplished" (Blomberg, *Wisdom and Curriculum*, 5). *Value* is a synonym for *normativity* in Blomberg's usage; it means that which is (properly) of value. In various places, this book characterizes *wisdom* both as the "realization of value" and as the "realization of normativity," with *realization* understood as an active, interactive, responsive, and participatory process. See especially chapter 5 ("The Realization of Value") in *Wisdom and Curriculum*, 85–93. By uniting understanding and implementing in the concept of realization of value, Blomberg appears eager to avoid his earlier divide between (closed) concrete experience and (opened) norm-oriented distantial knowing.

50 Blomberg, "Ways of Wisdom," 139, 131.

51 Blomberg, *Wisdom and Curriculum*, 162.

52 This is the famous example of an aesthetic experience used in Edward Bullough's equally famous essay "'Psychical Distance' as a Factor in Art and an Aesthetic Principle," which Seerveld cites in *A Christian Critique of Art and Literature*, 71n6. I discuss the social and political context and implications of Bullough's essay in Zuidervaart, "The Politics of Aesthetic Distance."

53 Vollenhoven, *Isagôgè Philosophiae*, 135–8.

54 I wish to thank Doug Blomberg, Peter Enneson, Henk Hart, and Cal Seerveld for their helpful comments on drafts of this chapter.

CHAPTER FOUR

1 Blomberg, "The Development of Curriculum with Relation to the Philosophy of the Cosmonomic Idea."

2 In this chapter I do not discuss the abilities of nonhuman animals to

know, which Vollenhoven rightly recognizes but, in my view, mistakenly assigns a "purely emotional character." See *Isagôgè Philosophiae / Introduction to Philosophy*, 108–9.

3 Sometimes the knowable is itself capable of knowing the knower (e.g., when one person knows another), and sometimes it cannot (e.g., a knowable rock does not know the geologist who studies it, at least not on a plausibly circumscribed conception of knowledge).

4 This is how I formulate the crucial insight, articulated by Vollenhoven and Dooyeweerd, and characteristic for the reformational tradition, that all knowledge is inescapably "religious." I do not use *religion* and its cognates in this connection because I use them to refer to organized faith and worship as a distinct social domain (what Vollenhoven and Dooyeweerd typically refer to as faith, faith-life, etc.). Instead I speak of the spiritual direction to all knowledge, its being inescapably spiritual. Hendrik Hart has knowledge's holistic and spiritual character in mind when he calls knowledge a totality concept.

5 Because, like Hendrik Hart, I regard the idea of knowledge as a whole as a totality concept, the structure of knowledge as a whole cannot be a *typical structure* with, for example, qualifying and founding functions. That, however, leaves open the possibility that different domain-specific types of knowledge (e.g., artistic, scientific, and religious knowledge) do have typical structures that can be specified, at least in part, in terms of qualifying and founding functions. In the discussion that follows, the dominant knowledge practices in different social domains point to distinct qualifying functions, but I do not address the question of founding functions.

6 Vollenhoven, *Hoofdlijnen der logica*, 47.

7 Vollenhoven, *Isagôgè Philosophiae*, 134.

8 Ibid., 111.

9 There is, of course, considerable controversy over the standard definition, much of it sparked by the so-called Gettier problem that Edmund Gettier's classic little paper raised in 1963 – see Gettier, "Is Justified True Belief Knowledge?" In *Warrant: The Current Debate*, for example, Alvin Plantinga argues that the (primarily) internalist notion of *justification* is both confused and inadequate. He proposes instead an externalist notion of *warrant* that employs the concepts of proper function and design plan – see Plantinga, *Warrant and Proper Function*. So, strictly speaking, Plantinga characterizes knowledge as *warranted* true belief rather than as *justified* true belief. In other respects, however, he retains the standard definition of knowledge, as does Reformed Epistemology

Notes to pages 71–4

in general. Much of reformational philosophy, by contrast, begins with a considerably broader idea of knowledge, and it tends not to emphasize either justification/warrant or belief. That difference helps explain difficulties in communication between these two schools of Reformed thought, despite their common roots in the Kuyperian tradition. For a useful survey of the standard definition and controversies about it, see Ichikawa and Steup, "The Analysis of Knowledge."

10 One also needs to spell out a holistic conception of truth within which propositional truth is important but not all important, as I have indicated in chapter 2.

11 "Wij staan voor de vraag 'wat is kennen'; en als de vraag 'wat is dat' in haar volle zwaarte genomen wordt, moet het antwoord luiden: dat weten we niet. Een deel van het zijnde is kennende, en wat zijn is weten we evenmin als we kunnen doorgronden wat kennen is." Popma, *Inleiding in de wijsbegeerte*, 116. ("We confront the question 'What is knowing'; and if the question 'What is that' is taken completely seriously, then the answer must be: We do not know. Part of what has being is [capable of] knowing, and we do not know what being is any more than we can fathom what knowing is.")

12 Unlike Blomberg's dissertation, I do not restrict the term *insight* to a reflective awareness of norms. Although norms (societal principles, in my own vocabulary) are knowable, there is much more to the knowable than norms, and insight into the knowable encompasses much more than a reflective awareness of norms. For a discussion of Blomberg's understanding of normative insight, see the previous chapter.

13 Zuidervaart, *Religion, Truth, and Social Transformation*, 293–7; Zuidervaart, *Truth in Husserl, Heidegger, and the Frankfurt School*, 4–6, 96–101, and passim.

14 "Science, Society, and Culture: Against Deflationism," in Zuidervaart, *Religion, Truth, and Social Transformation*, 310.

15 Zuidervaart, *Artistic Truth*, 57–62, 127–34.

16 Elsewhere I describe the scientific stance as "a discursive reflexivity that doubles the universalizing and decontextualizing impetus of assertoric activities." "Science, Society, and Culture," in Zuidervaart, *Religion, Truth, and Social Transformation*, 309.

17 Seerveld, *A Christian Critique of Art and Literature*, 70–1.

18 Seerveld proposes the following intermodal order: numerical, spatial, kinetic, physical, bio-organic, psychical, technical, aesthetical, lingual, analytical, social, economic, juridical, ethical, confessional. Dooyeweerd, by contrast, proposes the following: numerical, spatial, kinematic, physi-

cal, biotic, psychical, analytical, historical, lingual, social, economic, aesthetic, juridical, moral or ethical, pistic. I discuss issues that arise from such differences in intermodal order in "Dooyeweerd's Modal Theory: Questions in the Ontology of Science," in Zuidervaart, *Religion, Truth, and Social Transformation*, 77–109.

19 *Familial* is a broad term to encompass not only families but also patterns of marriage, kinship, and friendship. In the past, reformational philosophers have used the term *ethical* to designate this domain, but the contemporary philosophical usage of *ethical* to mean "moral" or, more broadly, "normative" seems to preclude using the term in that way now – it creates too much confusion.

20 See Parry, "*Episteme* and *Techne*."

21 Some instruments are capable of what could be called secondary or tertiary knowing, insofar as they are designed to make things or solve problems "on their own." The explosion of research and production in robotics and artificial intelligence opens many new issues to consider in this connection.

22 Vollenhoven circumscribes *know-how* (*technê*) as "being practically active in the relationship of subject to object within the historical sphere, with the goal of satisfying practical-historical needs by working up materials" (Vollenhoven, *Isagôgè Philosophiae*, 139; translation modified). Like Seerveld, and unlike Vollenhoven and Dooyeweerd, I do not regard "the historical" as a modal sphere. I prefer to speak of a technical sphere and of technology as (perhaps) a social institution.

23 The classic discussion of this distinction is Gilbert Ryle's "Knowing How and Knowing That," chapter 2 in *The Concept of Mind*, 25–61. For an extensive review of the literature on this topic, see Fantl, "Knowledge How."

24 As was mentioned in an earlier note, I use the term *spiritual* for what Vollenhoven and Dooyeweerd discuss as *religious*. When I consider the relation between analytic and religious knowledge in what follows, I wish to illuminate the relation *between* two modally delimited sorts of functioning and *between* two sorts of social domains – *within* the overarching context of spiritually directed knowledge as a whole. Both religious knowing and analytic knowing are spiritually directed, as are all other sorts of knowing.

25 "Religion in Public: Passages from Hegel's *Philosophy of Right*," in Zuidervaart, *Religion, Truth, and Social Transformation*, 237–51, especially 238–41.

26 I do not use terms like *believing worshippers* and *believers* in this context,

in order to avoid confusions between belief as a stance or activity of trust in someone or something and belief as a propositional attitude.
27 I put "God" in quotation marks in order to indicate a functional rather than a prescriptive characterization. Not all religions are monotheistic, and some have divinity concepts that are hard to render in standard "God-talk."
28 Hart, *Draft for Proposed ICS Syllabus for Systematic Philosophy*.
29 Hart, *Understanding Our World: An Integral Ontology*.
30 Hart, "The Articulation of Belief: A Link between Rationality and Commitment," 215–16. In focusing on this essay from the early 1980s, I do not mean to suggest that Hart continued to hold the same positions in later writings. Especially instructive on that score are his dialogue with Kai Nielsen in Nielsen and Hart, *Search for Community in a Withering Tradition*, and the Festschrift essay by Stoffel N.D. Francke, "In the Face of Mystery."
31 See especially the essays "God, Law, and Cosmos: Issues in Hendrik Hart's Ontology," "Artistic Truth, Linguistically Turned: Variations on a Theme from Adorno, Habermas, and Hart," and "The Inner Reformation of Reason: Issues in Hendrik Hart's Epistemology," all collected in Zuidervaart, *Religion, Truth, and Social Transformation*, 133–82.
32 Hart, "The Articulation of Belief," 221.
33 Ibid.
34 Ibid., 220, 222.
35 Here Hart implicitly takes issue with Vollenhoven, who, in his later writings (after 1939 or so), says both God and God's law are analytically knowable: God, to the extent that God has revealed Godself, and God's law, "by the light of the word of God from the cosmos" (Vollenhoven, *Isagôgè Philosophiae*, 123). Vollenhoven also does not restrict the analytically knowable to structures, patterns, and the like. He has no qualms about saying one can (analytically) know an individual entity and understand both its differences from and its connections with other individual entities. Insofar as they concern earthly creatures, primary concepts, which Vollenhoven regards as results of analytic knowing, can pertain to "realms," "individual things," and "structures," according to his *Hoofdlijnen der logica*, 59. For a perceptive discussion of the epistemological issues raised when reformational philosophers construe human knowledge as limited by God's law(s), see van Woudenberg, "Theorie van het kennen," 67–74.
36 Hart, "The Articulation of Belief," 220, 222.
37 Ibid., 222.

38 Ibid., 226.
39 Ibid., 226–9.
40 Ibid., 230.
41 Ibid., 231.
42 Hart's position that confessional statements and creedal beliefs are not propositional is, of course, controversial; I lay out my disagreements with this position below.
43 Hart, "The Articulation of Belief," 230.
44 See Dooyeweerd, *A New Critique of Theoretical Thought*, 2: 185–92.
45 Hart, *Draft Syllabus*, 308–19.
46 Hart, *Understanding Our World*, 264. For an insightful and creative extension of Hart's appropriation of Dooyeweerd on this topic, see Nicholas Ansell, "Foundational and Transcendental Time."
47 Hart, "The Articulation of Belief," 231–2.
48 Ibid., 232.
49 Ibid., 233.
50 In the modal terms that Hart uses, one would say they are qualified or led by different functions – analytic and fiduciary functions, respectively.
51 Tellingly, in a footnote to an early passage that objects to the narrowly propositional view of knowledge as "justified true belief," Hart exclaims: "The whole enterprise of the justification of 'belief' seems irrational to me" (Hart, "The Articulation of Belief," 237n6). He does not seem to recognize that justification is intrinsic to analytic knowledge, that justification has counterparts in other sorts of confirmation within other types of knowledge, and that confirmation as such is one of several necessary ingredients to knowledge as a whole. If the enterprise of justifying belief were irrational, there would be no point to explicating what Plantinga calls "warranted Christian belief" – see Plantinga, *Warranted Christian Belief*.
52 On my view, beliefs have content – they are about something – but, in contrast to much of the literature in analytic epistemology, I think beliefs need to be articulated in language in order for that content to be propositional. The reason for this is that the occurrence of propositions presupposes reference and predication, and reference and predication occur in linguistic utterances or speech acts. Propositions are the assertible content of speech acts, and they are most readily displayed by assertoric speech acts (assertions, statements, and the like). Behind this view lies a Seerveldian understanding of intermodal order in which technical and lingual functioning precede analytic functioning – see note 18

above. There also lies an emphasis on linguistic practices similar to the "relational linguistic approach to the conceptual" pursued by Robert Brandom, *Articulating Reasons*, 6. For more on the distinctions among beliefs, assertions, and propositions, in relation to the topic of truth, see Zuidervaart, "How Not to Be an Anti-Realist"; also contained in Zuidervaart, *Truth in Husserl, Heidegger, and the Frankfurt School*, 103–21.

53 Zuidervaart, *Truth in Husserl, Heidegger, and the Frankfurt School*. See also Zuidervaart, *Religion, Truth, and Social Transformation*, 287–94.

54 See the discussion of art talk in Zuidervaart, *Artistic Truth*, 68–73, 134–9.

55 Here I put "bodily" in quote marks because, like Dooyeweerd and Vollenhoven, I do not restrict the human body to that which is physical and organic but regard it as ranging across all levels of functioning and as encompassing all sorts of human practices. Nevertheless, much of the literature on bodily knowing and embodied knowledge focuses on bio-organic processes and patterns, and that is the literature I have in mind.

56 van Woudenberg, "Theorie van het kennen," 33.

57 To say linguistic knowledge is pre-propositional does not mean that speech acts and sentences lack propositional content, but it does suggest that the propositional content they have occurs in anticipation of logical or analytic functioning. Correlatively, the practices of analytic knowing, which result in propositions, presuppose linguistic functioning. Moreover, what Kristeva, *Revolution in Poetic Language*, labels *the semiotic* is more fundamental to language than a traditional focus on syntax and semantics can recognize. Admittedly, this is a controversial position, and it flies in the face of not only Vollenhoven and Dooyeweerd but also much of the Western philosophical tradition. The current chapter, however, is not the place to present the necessary details.

58 I wish to thank Henk Hart, Peter Enneson, and two anonymous *Philosophia Reformata* referees for their instructive comments on earlier drafts of this chapter.

CHAPTER FIVE

1 The symposium on *Religion, Truth, and Social Transformation* was organized by Dean Dettloff on behalf of ICS's Centre for Philosophy, Religion and Social Ethics (CPRSE). It can be accessed at http://www.groundmotive.net/2016/01/coming-up-ground-motive-symposium-on.html.

2 See especially Chaplin, *Herman Dooyeweerd: Christian Philosopher of State and Civil Society*.

3 Jonathan Chaplin, "Speaking Truth to 'Power,' Calling 'Truth-Tellers' to Account: Probing the 'Dialectical' Relationship Between Religion and the State," posted on 18 April 2016, at http://www.groundmotive.net/2016/04/speaking-truth-to-power-calling-truth.html.
4 Zuidervaart, *Religion, Truth, and Social Transformation*, 243.
5 Obviously this rough and ready formulation would require many qualifications and refinements – what about infants and children, what about immigrants and illegal aliens, etc. – but perhaps it will do as a first approximation.
6 Perhaps I am closer to Jürgen Habermas here than Chaplin considers warranted. In any case, recent battles over Supreme Court decisions and appointments in the United States clearly affect my perspective.
7 Jonathan Chaplin, "Probing the Contours and Foundations of a Reformational 'Architectonic Critique' of Society," posted on 25 April 2016, at http://www.groundmotive.net/2016/04/probing-contours-and-foundations-of.html.
8 For an instructive attempt to think through these relations, following the model of Hegel's *Philosophy of Right*, see Axel Honneth, *Freedom's Right*.
9 Zuidervaart, *Social Philosophy after Adorno*, 175–81.
10 See Brunkhorst, *Solidarity: From Civic Friendship to a Global Legal Community*.
11 Zuidervaart, *Religion, Truth, and Social Transformation*, 261.
12 Ben Fulman, "The Future of Critical Theory," posted on 29 April 2016, at http://www.groundmotive.net/2016/04/the-future-of-critical-theory.html.
13 See chapter 6 ("Countervailing Forces") in Zuidervaart, *Art in Public*, 170–203.
14 Clinton E. Stockwell, "Beyond Political Augustinianism," posted on 11 April 2016, at http://www.groundmotive.net/2016/04/beyond-political-augustinianism.html.
15 Hegel, *Phenomenology of Spirit*, 9.
16 Ruthanne Crapo, "Pluralism in a Multicultural Civil Society: Losing My Religion?" posted on 22 April 2016, at http://www.groundmotive.net/2016/04/pluralism-in-multicultural-civil.html.
17 See in this connection two talks given in 2008 by my colleague Bob Sweetman at *Another Brick in the Wall*, an ICS Worldview Conference: "Why We Don't Join Institutions Anymore" and "Will This Church Have Children?"

18 I addressed this topic years ago in an essay titled "Consuming Visions."
19 Farshid Baghai, "A Hope without a More Primary Hopelessness?" posted on 15 May 2016, at http://www.groundmotive.net/2016/05/by-farshid-baghai-this-post-is-part-of.html.
20 Zuidervaart, *Religion, Truth, and Social Transformation*, 239.
21 Michael DeMoor, "Deflation and Deliberation: Some Notes on Science in Public," posted on 9 May 2016, at http://www.groundmotive.net/2016/05/deflation-and-deliberation-some-notes.html.
22 Zuidervaart, *Religion, Truth, and Social Transformation*, 311.
23 See Zuidervaart, "After Dooyeweerd: Truth in Reformational Philosophy."
24 Zuidervaart, *Religion, Truth, and Social Transformation*, 311.
25 Ibid.
26 "Living at the Crossroads: Ethical Scholarship and the Common Good," in Zuidervaart, *Art, Education, and Cultural Renewal*, 170–9, a companion volume to *Religion, Truth, and Social Transformation*.
27 See Zuidervaart, *Art in Public*, 263–6.
28 Zuidervaart, "Living at the Crossroads," in *Art, Education, and Cultural Renewal*, 173.
29 Ibid., 172.

CHAPTER SIX

1 The complete symposium on *Religion, Truth, and Social Transformation* can be accessed at http://www.groundmotive.net/2016/01/coming-up-ground-motive-symposium-on.html.
2 Ronald A. Kuipers, "Beyond Belief? Reflections on 'God, Law, and Cosmos: Issues in Hendrik Hart's Ontology,'" posted on 2 May 2016, at http://www.groundmotive.net/2016/05/beyond-belief-reflections-on-god-law.html.
3 Hart, *Understanding Our World*, xvii–xxiii and passim.
4 Adrian N. Atanasescu, "Identity or Difference? From a Linguistically Turned Concept of Artistic Truth to a Linguistically Turned Concept of Religious Truth," posted on 14 March 2016, at http://www.groundmotive.net/2016/03/identity-or-difference-from.html.
5 Zuidervaart, *Religion, Truth, and Social Transformation*, 256.
6 This is not to deny that there is a distinct domain of kinship, friendship, and intimate partnerships – such as Dooyeweerd and Vollenhoven label "moral" or "ethical" – nor is it to deny that there is a social domain where the societal principle of justice sets the dominant tone – namely, the state and related institutions.

7 See chapter 7 ("Relational Autonomy") in Zuidervaart, *Art in Public*, 207–40, and Zuidervaart, "Creating a Disturbance: Art, Social Ethics, and Relational Autonomy."
8 See chapter 6 ("Countervailing Forces") in *Art in Public*, 170–203.
9 To be fair, here Habermas is saying that only morality, not either science or art, can replace the normative authority that once attached to religion. He also recognizes that morality is not as clearly differentiated as science and art are in the modern world. See Habermas, *The Theory of Communicative Action*, vol. 2, 91–2.
10 Zuidervaart, *Artistic Truth*. For a short summary of this book and of *Art in Public* that places them in the context of reformational aesthetics, see "Imagination, Art, and Civil Society" – chapter 7 in Zuidervaart, *Art, Education, and Cultural Renewal*, 103–25.
11 Zuidervaart, *Religion, Truth, and Social Transformation*, 175. See also the discussion of religious beliefs in chapter 4 of the current volume.
12 Hendrik Hart, "Reformational Reason Revisited," posted on 21 March 2016, at http://www.groundmotive.net/2016/03/reformational-reason-revisited.html.
13 Zuidervaart, "How Not to Be an Anti-Realist: Habermas, Truth, and Justification"; also in Zuidervaart, *Truth in Husserl, Heidegger, and the Frankfurt School*, 103–21.
14 The first monograph is *Truth in Husserl, Heidegger, and the Frankfurt School* (2017). The second, not yet published, is tentatively titled *Social Domains of Truth*. Their topics are summarized in "Holistic Alethic Pluralism" – chapter 2 in this volume.
15 I leave aside the complication that questions about goodness also figure into questions about legitimacy, and truth and goodness, albeit intimately connected, are not the same.
16 Zuidervaart, *Religion, Truth, and Social Transformation*, 177.
17 Ibid., 241.
18 Zuidervaart, "Spirituality, Religion, and the Call to Love," in *Art, Education, and Cultural Renewal*, 180–96. An earlier version, given as a lecture in November 2014 to the Scripture, Faith, and Learning seminar at ICS, is available online at: http://ir.icscanada.edu/icsir/handle/10756/337419. The formulation of God's calling, guiding, and inspiring stems from my reworking what an endnote to "Earth's Lament" describes as Vollenhoven's "Trinitarian distinction among three relationships that God sustains with creation" (*Religion, Truth, and Social Transformation*, 387). See

the entire note (387n19) for the details of this distinction and its relevance for thoughts about law and order.

19 Bob Sweetman, "Criticism after Dooyeweerd and Vollenhoven," posted on 8 February 2016, at http://www.groundmotive.net/2016/02/criticism-after-dooyeweerd-and.html.

20 Ben Hampshire, "The Possibilities of Authentic Philosophical Histories," posted on 3 April 2016, at http://www.groundmotive.net/2016/04/the-possibilities-of-authentic.html.

21 Perhaps I should add that I have found Frederick Copleston's *A History of Philosophy* to be a valuable resource for teaching undergraduate philosophy, even though I have never assigned its volumes as course texts. I may be wrong, but Copleston strikes me as an engaged reporter. Indeed, I regard his work in the history of philosophy as a successful synthesis of creative participation and faithful transmission.

22 Neal DeRoo, "It's Time for Reformational Philosophy," posted on 28 January 2016, at http://www.groundmotive.net/2016/01/its-time-for-reformational-philosophy.html.

23 *Religion, Truth, and Social Transformation* takes up these issues in chapters 1, 3, and 14; I return to them below.

24 Zuidervaart, *Religion, Truth, and Social Transformation*, 321.

25 Peter Wing-Kai Lok, "Beyond Humanism and Posthumanism: On Hendrik Hart's Philosophical Anthropology," posted on 5 April 2016, at http://www.groundmotive.net/2016/04/beyond-humanism-and-posthumanism-on.html.

26 Zuidervaart, *Religion, Truth, and Social Transformation*, 216.

27 Ibid., 217.

28 Jazz Feyer Salo, "Generative Problems or Dynamic Limits? Retrieving Dooyeweerd's Transcendental Critique of Theoretical Thought," posted on 1 February 2016, at http://www.groundmotive.net/2016/02/generative-problems-or-dynamic-limits.html.

29 Josh Harris, "Spectres of Nature-Grace: On Dooyeweerd's 'Religious Truth,'" posted on 16 February 2016, at http://www.groundmotive.net/2016/02/spectres-of-nature-grace-on-dooyeweerds.html.

30 Ansell, *The Annihilation of Hell*.

31 Dan Rudisill, "Dooyeweerd's Modal Theory: Hermeneutics in Action," posted on 22 February 2016, at http://www.groundmotive.net/2016/02/dooyeweerds-modal-theory-hermeneutics.html.

32 For a discussion of Husserl's account of categorial intuition and its

place in his conception of truth, see Zuidervaart, "Propositional and Existential Truth in Edmund Husserl's *Logical Investigations*"; also in Zuidervaart, *Truth in Husserl, Heidegger, and the Frankfurt School*, 19–45.

33 "In my view, critical realism should take up the following position: first of all, it presupposes a mind-independent cosmos [*een denkvreemden kosmos*], encompassing God's entire creation, including thought [*het denken inbegrepen*], ordered according to categories. But – and this against the reproach, from the idealist side, that realism renders itself guilty of an illogical duplication – these categories are not logical categories, but *cosmic*, that is to say, they are categories of a cosmic coherence [*eenheidsverband*], which no *logical* differentiation can disturb. This cosmic sphere is the determining ground [*rechtsgrond*] for Lask's objective Gegenstand sphere [*objectieve Gegenstandssfeer*], in which the method of eidetic intuition [*wezensschouwing*] finds its place. This Gegenstand sphere of pure meaning, which is not *knowable* [*kenbaar*] in itself but only *intuitable* [*schouwbaar*], supplies the material for purely logical thought, which, in its judgments, unfolds the pure primordial forms of thought." This is Peter Enneson's translation, which I have modified, of a passage from Dooyeweerd's unpublished manuscript "Normatieve rechtsleer. Een kritische methodologische onderzoeking naar Kelsen's normatieve rechtsbeschouwing" [Normative Legal Philosophy. A Critical Methodological Investigation of Kelsen's Normative View of Law], 45. Unlike Enneson, who translates "wezensschouwing" as "showing essences" and "schouwbaar" as "beholdable," I use terms that tie them directly to Husserl's notion of eidetic intuition. For an argument that such notions stem instead from Franz Xavier von Baader, see Friesen, "Dooyeweerd's Idea of Modalities: The Pivotal 1922 Article."

34 See Zuidervaart, *Artistic Truth*, 56–65.

35 Tricia Van Dyk, "Art in the Real World," posted on 29 February 2016, at http://www.groundmotive.net/2016/02/art-in-real-world.html.

36 Dooyeweerd, "Het tidjsprobleem en zijn antinomieen op het immanentiestandpunt."

37 Allyson Carr, "Critical Retrieval in Community," posted on 25 May 2016, at http://www.groundmotive.net/2016/05/critical-retrieval-in-community.html.

38 Doug Blomberg, "A Living Philosophical Tradition of Redemptive Hope," posted on 25 January 2016, at http://www.groundmotive.net/2016/01/a-living-philosophical-tradition-of.html; and "Responding Wisely to Earth's Lament," posted on 18 May 2016, at http://www.groundmotive.net/2016/05/responding-wisely-to-earths-lament.html.

39 Zuidervaart, *Religion, Truth, and Social Transformation*, 317.

CHAPTER SEVEN

1 Elkins, "Against the Sublime," 88.
2 Some of this chapter appeared previously in the essay "Art, Religion, and the Sublime: After Hegel" in *Owl of Minerva* 44, nos 1–2 (2012–13): 119–42. I thank the journal editor, Ardis B. Collins, for permission to use parts of that essay in this chapter.
3 Costelloe, "The Sublime: A Short Introduction to a Long History," 7.
4 Guyer, "The German Sublime after Kant," in *The Sublime*, ed. Costelloe, 109.
5 Ibid., 110. I say "purported" because, on my own reading, Hegel does not declare the death or end of art.
6 Kant, *Critique of the Power of Judgment*, §29, 149; V: 266.
7 Hegel, *Aesthetics: Lectures on Fine Art*, 2 vols; *Vorlesungen über die Ästhetik*, in G.W.F. Hegel, *Werke in zwanzig Bänden*, vols 13, 14, 15; cited as *Aesthetics*, followed by the volume and page in the English translation and the German edition, thus: *Aesthetics* I: 375; 13: 483.
8 Hegel, *Aesthetics* I: 155; 13: 205.
9 Hegel, *Aesthetics* I: 175; 13: 230.
10 Hegel's primary examples of the three subphases within the first phase ("Unconscious Symbolism") come from the ancient Parsi, Indian, and Egyptian religions, respectively. The three subphases within the third phase ("Conscious Symbolism"), by contrast, are not associated with religions but with three modes of "comparative" presentation: (1) fables, parables, and the like; (2) allegory, metaphor, and simile; and (3) didactic and descriptive poetry.
11 Hegel, *Aesthetics* I: 317; 13: 411–12.
12 Hegel, *Aesthetics* I: 318; 13: 412–13.
13 Hegel, *Aesthetics* I: 321; 13: 416.
14 Hegel, *Aesthetics* I: 320; 13: 415.
15 Hegel, *Aesthetics* I: 363; 13: 467.
16 Hegel, *Aesthetics* I: 363; 13: 468.
17 Hegel, *Aesthetics* I: 364; 13: 469.
18 Hegel, *Aesthetics* I: 365–6; 13: 471. That is why, Hegel claims in this passage, pure pantheism "can ... be expressed artistically only in poetry, not in the visual arts."
19 Hegel, *Aesthetics* I: 371–7; 13: 478–85.
20 Hegel, *Aesthetics* I: 372–3; 13: 480.
21 Hegel, *Aesthetics* I: 321; 13: 416–17.
22 Hegel, *Aesthetics* I: 379; 13: 487.
23 Hegel, *Aesthetics* I: 371–2; 13: 478–9.

24 Hegel, *Aesthetics* I: 375–7; 13: 483–5.
25 Hegel, *Aesthetics* I: 372; 13: 479.
26 Hegel, *Aesthetics* 1: 375–6; 13: 484.
27 Psalm 8 is of particular interest in this context. Although it begins and ends with paeans to God's majesty, within this envelope is a poetic letter attesting to the regal status of humankind.
28 Hegel, *Aesthetics* 1: 373; 13: 481.
29 Elkins, "Against the Sublime," 75.
30 Hegel, *Aesthetics* I: 101; 13: 139.
31 Hegel, *Aesthetics* I: 101; 13: 139.
32 Hegel, *Aesthetics* I: 103–4; 13: 142–3.
33 Hegel, *Aesthetics* I: 104; 13: 144.
34 Elkins, "Against the Sublime," 75.
35 Hegel, *Aesthetics* I: 303; 13: 393.
36 Hegel, *Aesthetics* I: 483; 14: 84.
37 Desmond, *Art and the Absolute*, 202n71.
38 Burke, "A Dialectical Approach to Aesthetics in the Age of Post-Metaphysical Modernity," 105. Although I think Burke overstates his case, he is right to call attention to the way in which Hegel's account of the sublime mimes the dialectical relation between art and philosophy in his aesthetics as a whole.
39 Adorno, *Aesthetic Theory*, 197. Adorno's account of the sublime is considerably more nuanced and dialectical than this brief quotation indicates, however.
40 As I explain elsewhere, societal evil is evil "that seeps into cultural practices and social institutions, gathers strength over the years, and comes to dominate an entire societal formation ... Societal evil cannot be explained away as a natural occurrence outside human control. Yet it also cannot be ascribed to specific individuals or groups, as if it were solely their responsibility. Societal evil is distinct from natural evil and moral evil, although not unrelated to them." Zuidervaart, "Earth's Lament: Suffering, Hope, and Wisdom," in *Religion, Truth, and Social Transformation*, 319–20.
41 Hegel, *Aesthetics* I: 371–7; 13: 478–85. Hegel's description of "unworthiness" is especially telling: "we find depicted in a penetrating and affecting way grief over nullity, and the cry of the soul to God in complaint, suffering, and lament from the depths of the heart." *Aesthetics* I: 376; 13: 485.
42 For a discussion of these issues in Adorno's *Negative Dialectics*, see Zuidervaart, *Social Philosophy after Adorno*, 48–76, 175–81.

43 Scott, "Heaven, Texas and the Cosmic Whodunit."
44 Rybin, *Terrence Malick and the Thought of Film*, xii.
45 Ibid., xxi.
46 Ibid., 176–7.
47 Patterson, "Introduction: Poetic Visions of America," 2.
48 Ibid., 10, commenting on essays by Stacy Peebles Power and Robert Silberman.
49 Arensberg, ed., *The American Sublime*. In the review cited earlier, A.O. Scott touches on this tradition when he suggests that *The Tree of Life* "shows a clear kinship with other eccentric, permanent works of the American imagination, in which sober consideration of life on this continent is yoked to transcendental, even prophetic ambition. More than any other active filmmaker Mr Malick belongs in the visionary company of homegrown romantics like Herman Melville, Walt Whitman, Hart Crane and James Agee."
50 Wilson, *American Sublime*.
51 See Crowther, *The Kantian Sublime*.
52 See, for example, Brennan, *Wordsworth, Turner, and Romantic Landscape*.
53 Rob Wilson's account is much more complicated than this summary can suggest, as one sees in the following complex two-sentence précis from the introduction to his book: "The [American] sublime, by converting powerlessness and a lurking sense of social self-diminishment – or historical guilt – into a conviction of dematerialized power awaiting national use, eventuated in a figure of 'self-reliance,' then, for whom power is not the capacity to act or to conjoin, but to convert such inaction or disjunction into tropes and compacts founded in vast scenes of dehistoricized willing. Flooded with energy and light, artistic aggression was sublimated into a national performance." Wilson, *American Sublime*, 5.
54 Weiskel, *The Romantic Sublime*, 22–33.
55 Ibid., 41, 83–106, 136–64.
56 Ibid., 37.
57 Wilson, *American Sublime*, 12.
58 Heidegger, *The Essence of Reasons*, trans. Terrence Malick.
59 Zuidervaart, *Artistic Truth*, especially 118–39.
60 "Religion in Public: Passages from Hegel's *Philosophy of Right*," in Zuidervaart, *Religion, Truth, and Social Transformation*, 237–51, especially 238–41.
61 Hegel, *Phenomenology of Spirit*, 38.
62 Adorno, *Aesthetic Theory*, 18–19, 260–1. In light of my previous comments

about Hegel's purported "end of art" thesis, which also troubled Adorno, let me quote two passages where Adorno offers his own response: "[Aesthetics today] must not play at delivering graveside sermons, certifying the end [of art], savoring the past, and abdicating in favor of one sort of barbarism that is no better than the culture that has earned barbarism as recompense for its own monstrosity" (*Aesthetic Theory*, 4). "Nor is it possible to sketch the form of art in a [future] changed society. In comparison with past art and the art of the present it will probably again be something else; but it would be preferable that some fine day art vanish altogether than that it forget the suffering that is its expression and in which form has its substance ... What would art be ... if it shook off the memory of accumulated suffering" (*Aesthetic Theory*, 260–1).

63 Adorno, *Negative Dialectics*, 17–18; translation modified.

CHAPTER EIGHT

1 See chapter 9 ("The Confirmation of Taste") in Zuidervaart, "Kant's Critique of Beauty and Taste," 325–466.
2 Zuidervaart, *Artistic Truth*.
3 Hart, *Draft for Proposed ICS Syllabus for Systematic Philosophy*.
4 For a glimpse into what this philosophy of music might have been like, see Zuidervaart, "Music."
5 Seerveld, *Benedetto Croce's Earlier Aesthetic Theories and Literary Criticism*.
6 Adorno, *Aesthetic Theory*. See also Zuidervaart, *Adorno's Aesthetic Theory: The Redemption of Illusion*.
7 Lukács, "Reification and the Consciousness of the Proletariat," in *History and Class Consciousness*, 83–222.
8 The first set of lectures was subsequently published in German as *Ästhetik (1958/59)* and in English as Adorno, *Aesthetics (1958/59)*.
9 See in this connection Zuidervaart, "Adorno's Critique of Heidegger: The Temporality of Truth."
10 At the time, Rolf Tiedemann was director of the archive and editor-in-chief of Adorno's collected writings. These lectures were subsequently published as Adorno, *Ontologie und Dialektik (1960/61)*, and in English as Adorno, *Ontology and Dialectics 1960/61*.
11 Zuidervaart, "Metacritique: Adorno, Vollenhoven, and the Problem-Historical Method," in *Religion, Truth, and Social Transformation*, 183–204.
12 See in particular sections 1.1 ("Third Reflections") and 6.3 ("Truth in Adorno's Aesthetic Theory") in Zuidervaart, "Refractions: Truth in Adorno's Aesthetic Theory," 2–7, 199–205.

13 Zuidervaart, *Religion, Truth, and Social Transformation*.
14 Zuidervaart, *Art, Education, and Cultural Renewal*.
15 See "Dooyeweerd's Modal Theory: Questions in the Ontology of Science," in Zuidervaart, *Religion, Truth, and Social Transformation*, 77–109.
16 Dooyeweerd, *A New Critique of Theoretical Thought*.
17 See "God, Law, and Cosmos: Issues in Hendrik Hart's Ontology," in Zuidervaart, *Religion, Truth, and Social Transformation*, 133–55.
18 See chapter 4 ("Globalizing Dialectic of Enlightenment") in Zuidervaart, *Social Philosophy after Adorno*, 107–31.
19 Mariotti, *Adorno and Democracy: The American Years*.
20 Adorno, et al., *The Authoritarian Personality*.
21 Adorno, *The Psychological Technique of Martin Luther Thomas' Radio Addresses*.
22 See in this connection VanderVennen, *A University for the People*.
23 Published in *An Ethos of Compassion and the Integrity of Creation*, edited by Brian J. Walsh, Hendrik Hart, and Robert E. VanderVennen.
24 UICA is a multi-disciplinary contemporary arts center in Grand Rapids, Michigan. See "The UICA Story" in *Art in Public*, 190–203.
25 See section 6.2 ("Social Ethics and Global Politics") in Zuidervaart, *Social Philosophy after Adorno*, 162–75.

CHAPTER NINE

1 See "Philosophy, Truth, and the Wisdom of Love" – chapter 1 in the current volume.
2 See, for example, "Macrostructures and Societal Principles: An Architectonic Critique," in Zuidervaart, *Religion, Truth, and Social Transformation*, 252–76.
3 Adorno, *Minima Moralia*, §29, 50. Hegel's dictum was "The True is the whole." See Hegel, *Phenomenology of Spirit*, 11.
4 For a more extensive account of normative deficiencies and the normative redirection of societal macrostructures, see chapter 5 ("Civic Sector") in Zuidervaart, *Art in Public*, 129–69.
5 See, for example, the famous summary Marx gives of the "guiding principle" to his historically informed study of political economy in the preface to Marx, *A Contribution to the Critique of Political Economy*, 19–23.
6 See, for example, Goudzwaard, *Capitalism and Progress*, and Bob Goudzwaard, Mark Vander Vennen, and David Van Heemst, *Hope in Troubled Times*.
7 See, for example, Heidegger, *The Question Concerning Technology and Other Essays*.

8 "Justice remains, is yet, to come, *à venir*, it has an, it is *à-venir*, the very dimension of events irreducibly to come. It will always have it, this *à-venir*, and always has." Derrida, "Force of Law: The 'Mystical Foundation of Authority,'" 27. Concerning Adorno on traces of hope and happiness, see chapters 2 ("Metaphysics after Auschwitz") and 6 ("Ethical Turns") in Zuidervaart, *Social Philosophy after Adorno*, 48–76 and 155–81, and Zuidervaart, "History and Transcendence in Adorno's Idea of Truth."

CHAPTER TEN

1 Zuidervaart, "Unfinished Business: Toward a Reformational Concept of Truth," in *Religion, Truth, and Social Transformation*, 278.
2 Husserl, *Philosophy of Arithmetic* (1891).
3 For a collection of Gottlob Frege's most important writings in philosophy of mathematics and logic, see *The Frege Reader*, ed. Michael Beaney.
4 Russell, *The Principles of Mathematics* (1903).
5 MacIntyre, *After Virtue: A Study in Moral Theory*.
6 Zuidervaart, "Unfinished Business," 278–9. See also Zuidervaart, *Artistic Truth*, 1–14.
7 Chapter 2 in the current volume, the revised version of an essay first published in 2016.
8 See "Introduction: Transforming Philosophy," in Zuidervaart, *Religion, Truth, and Social Transformation*, 3–22.
9 See "Science, Society, and Culture: Against Deflationism," in Zuidervaart, *Religion, Truth, and Social Transformation*, 298–313; and Zuidervaart, *Artistic Truth*.
10 See chapter 6 ("Countervailing Forces") in Zuidervaart, *Art in Public*, 170–203.
11 See "Philosophy, Truth, and the Wisdom of Love" – chapter 1 in the current volume.
12 Horkheimer and Adorno, *Dialectic of Enlightenment*.
13 Eagleton, *Hope without Optimism*.
14 See "Living at the Crossroads: Ethical Scholarship and the Common Good," in Zuidervaart, *Art, Education, and Cultural Renewal*, 170–9.

Works Cited

Acero Ferrer, Héctor, Michael DeMoor, Peter Enneson, and Matthew J. Klaassen, eds. *Seeking Stillness or The Sound of Wings: Scholarly and Artistic Comment on Art, Truth, and Society in Honour of Lambert Zuidervaart.* Eugene, OR: Wipf and Stock, 2021.
Adorno, Theodor W. *Negative Dialectics.* Translated by E.B. Ashton. New York: Seabury Press, 1973.
– *Minima Moralia: Reflections from Damaged Life.* Translated by E.F.N. Jephcott. London: NLB, 1974.
– *Against Epistemology: A Metacritique; Studies in Husserl and the Phenomenological Antinomies.* Translated by Willis Domingo. Cambridge, MA: MIT Press, 1983; c. 1982.
– *Aesthetic Theory.* Edited by Gretel Adorno and Rolf Tiedemann. Translated, edited, and with an introduction by Robert Hullot-Kentor. Minneapolis: University of Minnesota Press, 1997.
– *The Psychological Technique of Martin Luther Thomas' Radio Addresses.* Stanford, CA: Stanford University Press, 2000.
– *Ontologie und Dialektik (1960/61).* Edited by Rolf Tiedemann. Frankfurt am Main: Suhrkamp, 2002.
– *Philosophy of New Music.* Translated, edited, and with an introduction by Robert Hullot-Kentor. Minneapolis: University of Minnesota Press, 2006.
– *Aesthetics (1958/59).* Edited by Eberhard Ortland. Translated by Wieland Hoban. Cambridge: Polity, 2018.
– *Ontology and Dialectics 1960/61.* Edited by Rolf Tiedemann. Translated by Nicholas Walker. Cambridge: Polity, 2019.
Adorno, T.W., Else Frenkel-Brunswik, Daniel J. Levinson, and R. Nevitt Stanford, in collaboration with Betty Aron, Maria Hertz Levinson, and

William Morrow. *The Authoritarian Personality*. New York: Harper & Brothers, 1950.

Alcoff, Linda Martín. "Reclaiming Truth." In *Truth: Engagements across Philosophical Traditions*, edited by José Medina and David Wood, 336-49. Malden, MA: Blackwell, 2005.

Alston, William P. *A Realist Conception of Truth*. Ithaca, NY: Cornell University Press, 1996.

Ansell, Nicholas. "Foundational and Transcendental Time: An Essay." In *Philosophy as Responsibility: A Celebration of Hendrik Hart's Contribution to the Discipline*, edited by Ronald A. Kuipers and Janet Catherina Wesselius, 63-79. Lanham, MD: University Press of America, 2002.

– *The Annihilation of Hell: Universal Salvation and the Redemption of Time in the Eschatology of Jürgen Moltmann*. Eugene, OR: Cascade Books, 2013.

Anselm. "On Truth." In *The Major Works*, 151-74. Oxford: Oxford University Press, 1998.

Arendt, Hannah. "Truth and Politics." In *The Portable Hannah Arendt*, edited by Peter Baehr, 545-75. New York: Penguin Books, 2000.

Arensberg, Mary, ed. *The American Sublime*. Albany, NY: SUNY Press, 1986.

Aristotle. *Poetics*. In S.H. Butcher, *Aristotle's Theory of Poetry and Fine Art, with a Critical Text and Translation of The Poetics*, 1-111. New York: Dover, 1951.

Beaney, Michael, ed. *The Frege Reader*. Oxford: Blackwell, 1997.

Benjamin, Walter. "Theses on the Philosophy of History." In *Illuminations*, edited by Hannah Arendt, translated by Harry Zohn, 253-64. New York: Schocken Books, 1969.

Bloch, Ernst. *The Principle of Hope*. 3 vols. Translated by Neville Plaice, Stephen Plaice, and Paul Knight. Cambridge, MA: MIT Press, 1985.

Blackburn, Simon. *Truth: A Guide*. Oxford: Oxford University Press, 2005.

Blomberg, Doug. "The Development of Curriculum with Relation to the Philosophy of the Cosmonomic Idea." PhD diss., University of Sydney, 1978.

– "Toward a Christian Theory of Knowledge." In *No Icing on the Cake: Christian Foundations for Education in Australasia*, edited by Jack Mechielsen, 41-59. Melbourne: Brookes-Hall Publishing Foundation, 1980.

– "Ways of Wisdom: Multiple Modes of Meaning in Pedagogy and Andragogy." In *Ways of Knowing in Concert*, edited by John H. Kok, 123-46. Sioux Center, IA: Dordt College Press, 2005.

– *Wisdom and Curriculum: Christian Schooling after Postmodernity*. Sioux Center, IA: Dordt College Press, 2007.

Botha, M. Elaine. "On Being a Christian Philosopher and Not a Feminist."

In *Philosophy, Feminism, and Faith*, edited by Ruth E. Groenhout and Marya Bower, 243–59. Bloomington: Indiana University Press, 2003.

Brandom, Robert. *Articulating Reasons: An Introduction to Inferentialism*. Cambridge, MA: Harvard University Press, 2000.

Bratt, James D. *Abraham Kuyper: Modern Calvinist, Christian Democrat*. Grand Rapids, MI: Eerdmans, 2013.

Brennan, Matthew. *Wordsworth, Turner, and Romantic Landscape: A Study of the Traditions of the Picturesque and the Sublime*. Columbia, SC: Camden House, 1987.

Brunkhorst, Hauke. *Solidarity: From Civic Friendship to a Global Legal Community*. Translated by Jeffrey Flynn. Cambridge, MA: MIT Press, 2005.

Bullough, Edward. "'Psychical Distance' as a Factor in Art and an Aesthetic Principle." *The British Journal of Psychology* 5, no. 2 (1912): 87–118.

Burke, Donald A. "A Dialectical Approach to Aesthetics in the Age of Post-Metaphysical Modernity." PhD diss., York University (Toronto), 2011.

Campbell, Richard. *Truth and Historicity*. Oxford: Clarendon Press, 1992.

– *The Concept of Truth*. New York: Palgrave Macmillan, 2011.

Carr, Allyson. *Story and Philosophy for Social Change in Medieval and Postmodern Writing: Reading for Change*. New York: Palgrave Macmillan, 2017.

Chaplin, Jonathan. *Herman Dooyeweerd: Christian Philosopher of State and Civil Society*. Notre Dame, IN: Notre Dame University Press, 2011.

Cockburn, Bruce. "Grim Travellers." On the album *Humans*. True North Records, 1980.

Copleston, Frederick, S.J. *A History of Philosophy*. 9 vols. Westminster, MD: Newman Press, 1947–74.

Costelloe, Timothy M. "The Sublime: A Short Introduction to a Long History." In *The Sublime: From Antiquity to the Present*, edited by Timothy M. Costelloe, 1–7. Cambridge: Cambridge University Press, 2012.

Crowther, Paul. *The Kantian Sublime: From Morality to Art*. Oxford: Clarendon Press, 1989.

De Graaff, Arnold. *The Gods in Whom They Trusted – The Disintegrative Effects of Capitalism: A Foundation for Transitioning to a New Social World*. Norwich, UK: Heathwood Press, 2016.

Demmer, Klaus. *Living the Truth: A Theory of Action*. Translated by Brian McNeil. Washington, DC: Georgetown University Press, 2010.

Derrida, Jacques. "Force of Law: The 'Mystical Foundation of Authority.'" In *Deconstruction and the Possibility of Justice*, edited by Drucilla Cornell, Michael Rosenfeld, and David Gray Carlson, 3–67. New York: Routledge, 1992.

Desmond, William. *Art and the Absolute: A Study of Hegel's Aesthetics*. Albany, NY: SUNY Press, 1986.

Disch, Lisa Jane. *Hannah Arendt and the Limits of Philosophy*. Ithaca: Cornell University Press, 1994.

Dooyeweerd, Herman. "Normatieve rechtsleer. Een kritische methodologische onderzoeking naar Kelsen's normatieve rechtsbeschouwing." Unpublished manuscript, 1922. Dooyeweerd Archives 77, Box VN 38, Folder VIN 122.

– "Het dilemma voor het christelijk wijsgeerig denken en het critisch karakter van de wijsbegeerte der wetsidee." *Philosophia Reformata* 1, no. 1 (1936): 3–16.

– "Het tijdsprobleem en zijn antinomieen op het immanentiestandpunt." *Philosophia Reformata* 1, no. 2 (1936): 65–83.

– *A New Critique of Theoretical Thought*. 4 vols. Translated by David H. Freeman, William S. Young, and H. de Jongste. Reprint edition (1969). Philadelphia: Presbyterian and Reformed Publishing, 1953–58.

– *In the Twilight of Western Thought: Studies in the Pretended Autonomy of Philosophical Thought*. Nutley, NJ: Craig Press, 1965, c. 1960.

– "The Dilemma for Christian Philosophical Thought and the Critical Character of the Philosophy of the Cosmonomic Idea." *Philosophia Reformata* 83, no. 2 (2018): 267–78.

Duck, Ruth. "Come and Seek the Ways of Wisdom" (©1993). In *Glory to God: The Presbyterian Hymnal*, #174. Louisville, KY: Westminster John Knox Press, 2013.

Eagleton, Terry. *Hope without Optimism*. Charlottesville: University of Virginia Press, 2015.

Edwards, Douglas. *The Metaphysics of Truth*. Oxford: Oxford University Press, 2018.

Elkins, James. "Against the Sublime." In *Beyond the Finite: The Sublime in Art and Science*, edited by Roald Hoffmann and Iain Boyd Whyte, 55–63. Oxford: Oxford University Press, 2011.

Ellefson, Olaf. "Cognitive Diversity, Conceptual Schemes, and Truth." In *Truth Matters: Knowledge, Politics, Ethics, Religion*, edited by Lambert Zuidervaart, Allyson Carr, Matthew Klaassen, and Ronnie Shuker, 83–99. Montreal: McGill-Queen's University Press, 2013.

Ellul, Jacques. *Anarchy and Christianity*. Translated by Geoffrey W. Bromiley. Grand Rapids, MI: Eerdmans, 1991.

Engel, Pascal. *Truth*. Montreal: McGill-Queen's University Press, 2002.

Fantl, Jeremy. "Knowledge How." In Edward N. Zalta, ed., *The Stanford Encyclopedia of Philosophy* (Fall 2017 Edition), <https://plato.stanford.edu/archives/fall2017/entries/knowledge-how/>.

Fontaine, Carole R. "Wisdom Traditions in the Hebrew Bible." *Dialogue: A Journal of Mormon Thought* 33, no. 1 (2000): 101–17.

Foucault, Michel. "Truth and Power." In *Power/Knowledge: Selected Interviews and Other Writings 1972–1977*, edited by Colin Gordon, 109–33. New York: Pantheon Books, 1980.

Francke, Stoffel N.D. "In the Face of Mystery: Following a Spiritual Trace." In *Philosophy as Responsibility: A Celebration of Hendrik Hart's Contribution to the Discipline*, edited by Ronald A. Kuipers and Janet Catherina Wesselius, 81–98. Lanham, MD: University Press of America, 2002.

Frankfurt, Harry G. *On Bullshit*. Princeton, NJ: Princeton University Press, 2005.

– *On Truth*. New York: Alfred A. Knopf, 2006.

Friesen, J. Glenn. "Dooyeweerd's Idea of Modalities: The Pivotal 1922 Article." *Philosophia Reformata* 81, no. 2 (2016): 113–55.

Gadamer, Hans-Georg. *Truth and Method*. 2nd, rev. ed. Translation revised by Joel Weinsheimer and Donald G. Marshall. New York: Crossroad, 1989.

Gettier, Edmund L. "Is Justified True Belief Knowledge?" *Analysis* 23, no. 6 (1963): 121–3.

Goudzwaard, Bob. *Capitalism and Progress: A Diagnosis of Western Society*. Translated and edited by Josina Van Nuis Zylstra. Grand Rapids, MI: Eerdmans, 1979.

Goudzwaard, Bob, Mark Vander Vennen, and David Van Heemst. *Hope in Troubled Times: A New Vision for Confronting Global Crises*. Grand Rapids, MI: Baker Academic, 2007.

Guen Hart, Carroll. "Power in the Service of Love: John Dewey's Logic and the Dream of a Common Language." *Hypatia* 8, no. 2 (1993): 190–214.

Guyer, Paul. "The German Sublime after Kant." In *The Sublime: From Antiquity to the Present*, edited by Timothy M. Costelloe, 102–17. Cambridge: Cambridge University Press, 2012.

Habermas, Jürgen. *The Theory of Communicative Action*. 2 vols. Translated by Thomas McCarthy. Boston: Beacon Press, 1984, 1987.

Hadot, Pierre. *Philosophy as a Way of Life: Spiritual Exercises from Socrates to Foucault*. Translated by Michael Chase. Oxford: Blackwell, 1995.

– *What Is Ancient Philosophy?* Translated by Michael Chase. Cambridge, MA: Belknap Press of Harvard University Press, 2002.

Hart, Hendrik. *Draft for Proposed ICS Syllabus for Systematic Philosophy*. Toronto: Institute for Christian Studies, 1979.

– "The Articulation of Belief: A Link between Rationality and Commitment." In *Rationality in the Calvinian Tradition*, edited by Hendrik Hart, Johan van der Hoeven, and Nicholas Wolterstorff, 209–48. Lanham, MD: University Press of America, 1983.

- *Understanding Our World: An Integral Ontology*. Lanham, MD: University Press of America, 1984.
- "Dooyeweerd's *Gegenstand* Theory of Theory." In *The Legacy of Herman Dooyeweerd: Reflections on Critical Philosophy in the Christian Tradition*, edited by C.T. McIntire, 143–66. Lanham, MD: University Press of America, 1985.

Hegel, G.W.F. *Vorlesungen über die Ästhetik*. In G.W.F. Hegel, *Werke in zwanzig Bänden*, vols 13, 14, 15. Frankfurt: Suhrkamp, Theorie Werkausgabe, 1970.
- *Aesthetics: Lectures on Fine Art*. 2 vols. Translated by T.M. Knox. Oxford: Clarendon Press, 1974, 1975.
- *Phenomenology of Spirit*. Translated by A.V. Miller. Oxford: Oxford University Press, 1977.

Heidegger, Martin. *The Essence of Reasons*. Translated by Terrence Malick. Evanston, IL: Northwestern University Press, 1969.
- *The Question Concerning Technology and Other Essays*. Translated by William Lovitt. New York: Harper Torchbooks, 1977.
- *Being and Time* (1927). Translated by Joan Stambaugh. Albany: SUNY Press, 1996.

Herbert, George. "The Call." In *Five Mystical Songs*, composed by Ralph Vaughan Williams, 21–2. London: Stainer & Bell, 1911.

Hoff, Shannon. *The Laws of the Spirit: A Hegelian Theory of Justice*. New York: SUNY Press, 2014.

Honneth, Axel. *Freedom's Right: The Social Foundations of Democratic Life*. Translated by Joseph Ganahl. Cambridge: Polity, 2014.

Horkheimer, Max, and Theodor W. Adorno. *Dialectic of Enlightenment: Philosophical Fragments* (1947). Edited by Gunzelin Schmid Noerr. Translated by Edmund Jephcott. Stanford, CA: Stanford University Press, 2002.

Husserl, Edmund. *Philosophy of Arithmetic: Psychological and Logical Investigations with Supplementary Texts from 1887–1901*. Translated by Dallas Willard. Dordrecht; Boston: Kluwer, 2003.

Ichikawa, Jonathan Jenkins, and Matthias Steup. "The Analysis of Knowledge." In Edward N. Zalta, ed., *The Stanford Encyclopedia of Philosophy* (Summer 2018 Edition), <https://plato.stanford.edu/archives/sum2018/entries/knowledge-analysis/>.

Kant, Immanuel. *Critique of the Power of Judgment*. Edited by Paul Guyer. Translated by Paul Guyer and Eric Matthews. Cambridge: Cambridge University Press, 2000.

Kirkham, Richard L. *Theories of Truth: A Critical Introduction*. Cambridge, MA: MIT Press, 1992.

Kok, John. "Vollenhoven and 'Scriptural Philosophy.'" *Philosophia Reformata* 53, no. 2 (1988): 101–42.
- *Vollenhoven: His Early Development*. Sioux Center, IA: Dordt College Press, 1992.
Kristeva, Julia. *Revolution in Poetic Language*. Translated by Margaret Waller. New York: Columbia University Press, 1984.
Kuipers, Ronald A. *Richard Rorty*. London: Bloomsbury, 2013.
Kuyper, Lester J. "Grace and Truth: An Old Testament Description of God, and Its Use in the Johannine Gospel." *Interpretation: A Journal of Bible and Theology* 18, no. 1 (1964): 3–19.
Langer, Susanne K. *Feeling and Form: A Theory of Art Developed from Philosophy in a New Key*. New York: Charles Scribner's Sons, 1953.
- *Philosophy in a New Key: A Study in the Symbolism of Reason, Rite, and Art*. 3rd ed. Cambridge, MA: Harvard University Press, 1957.
Lukács, Georg. "Reification and the Consciousness of the Proletariat." In *History and Class Consciousness: Studies in Marxist Dialectics*, translated by Rodney Livingstone, 83–222. Cambridge, MA: MIT Press, 1972.
Lynch, Michael P. *True to Life: Why Truth Matters*. Cambridge, MA: MIT Press, 2004.
- *Truth as One and Many*. Oxford: Clarendon Press, 2009.
- , ed. *The Nature of Truth: Classic and Contemporary Perspectives*. Cambridge, MA: MIT Press, 2001.
MacIntyre, Alasdair. *After Virtue: A Study in Moral Theory*. 2nd ed. Notre Dame, IN: University of Notre Dame Press, 1984.
Mariotti, Shannon L. *Adorno and Democracy: The American Years*. Lexington, KY: University Press of Kentucky, 2016.
Marx, Karl. *A Contribution to the Critique of Political Economy* (1859). Translated by W.W. Ryazanskaya. Edited by Maurice Dobb. New York: International Publishers, 1970.
Maxwell, Nicholas. *From Knowledge to Wisdom: A Revolution in the Aims and Methods of Science*. Oxford: Basil Blackwell, 1984.
McIntyre, Lee. *Post-Truth*. Cambridge, MA: MIT Press, 2018.
Medina, José, and David Wood, eds. *Truth: Engagements across Philosophical Traditions*. Malden, MA: Blackwell, 2005.
Mekkes, J.P.A. "Knowing." In *Jerusalem and Athens: Critical Discussions on the Theology and Apologetics of Cornelius Van Til*, edited by E.R. Geehan, 306–19. [Nutley, NJ]: Presbyterian and Reformed Publishing, 1971.
- "Methodology and Practice." In *The Idea of a Christian Philosophy: Essays in Honour of D.H.Th. Vollenhoven*, 77–83. Toronto: Wedge Publishing Foundation, 1973. [Reprint of *Philosophia Reformata* 38 (1973).]

Nielsen, Kai, and Hendrik Hart. *Search for Community in a Withering Tradition*. Lanham, MD: University Press of America, 1990.

Olthuis, James H. *Facts, Values and Ethics: A Confrontation with Twentieth Century British Moral Philosophy in Particular G.E. Moore*. 2nd ed. Assen: Van Gorcum, 1969.

– "Creatio Ex Amore." In *Transforming Philosophy and Religion: Love's Wisdom*, edited by Norman Wirzba and Bruce Ellis Benson, 155–70. Bloomington: Indiana University Press, 2008.

Oxford Dictionaries. "Post-Truth." https://www.oxforddictionaries.com/press/news/2016/12/11/WOTY-16; accessed 19 April 2017.

Parmenides. "Poem of Parmenides." In John Burnet, *Early Greek Philosophy*, 4th ed., 172–8. London: Adam & Charles Black, 1930.

Parry, Richard. "*Episteme* and *Techne*." In Edward N. Zalta, ed., *The Stanford Encyclopedia of Philosophy* (Fall 2014 Edition), <https://plato.stanford.edu/archives/fall2014/entries/episteme-techne/>.

Patterson, Hannah. "Introduction: Poetic Visions of America." In *The Cinema of Terrence Malick: Poetic Visions of America*, edited by Hannah Patterson, 1–12. London: Wallflower Press, 2003.

Pedersen, Nikolaj J.L.L., and Cory D. Wright, eds. *Truth and Pluralism: Current Debates*. Oxford: Oxford University Press, 2013.

Pieper, Josef. *Living the Truth: The Truth of All Things* and *Reality and the Good*. San Francisco: Ignatius Press, 1989.

Plantinga, Alvin. *Warrant: The Current Debate*. New York: Oxford University Press, 1993.

– *Warrant and Proper Function*. New York: Oxford University Press, 1993.

– *Warranted Christian Belief*. New York: Oxford University Press, 2000.

Popma, K.J. *Inleiding in de wijsbegeerte*. Kampen: J.H. Kok, 1956.

Putnam, Hilary. *Reason, Truth and History*. Cambridge: Cambridge University Press, 1981.

Quine, W.V. *Pursuit of Truth*. Cambridge, MA: Harvard University Press, 1990.

Rorty, Richard. *Truth and Progress: Philosophical Papers*, vol. 3. Cambridge: Cambridge University Press, 1998.

Russell, Bertrand. *The Principles of Mathematics* (1903). 2nd ed. New York: W.W. Norton, 1996.

Rybin, Steven. *Terrence Malick and the Thought of Film*. Lanham, MD: Lexington Books, 2012.

Ryle, Gilbert. *The Concept of Mind*. Chicago: The University of Chicago Press, 1949.

Scott, A.O. "Heaven, Texas and the Cosmic Whodunit." *New York Times*, 26

May 2011. http://movies.nytimes.com/2011/05/27/movies/the-tree-of-life-from-terrence-malick-review.html?_r=0; accessed 8 October 2012.

Seerveld, Calvin G. *Benedetto Croce's Earlier Aesthetic Theories and Literary Criticism: A Critical Philosophical Look at the Development during His Rationalistic Years.* Kampen: J.H. Kok, 1958.

– *A Christian Critique of Art and Literature.* Toronto: Association for Reformed Scientific Studies, 1968.

– "A Concept of Artistic Truth Prompted by Biblical Wisdom Literature." In *Truth Matters: Knowledge, Politics, Ethics, Religion,* edited by Lambert Zuidervaart, Allyson Carr, Matthew Klaassen, and Ronnie Shuker, 296–312. Montreal: McGill-Queen's University Press, 2013.

Smith, Huston. *The Religions of Man.* New York: Harper & Brothers, 1958.

– *Forgotten Truth: The Primordial Tradition.* New York: Harper & Row, 1976.

– *The World's Religions.* San Francisco: HarperSanFrancisco, 1991.

– *Why Religion Matters: The Fate of the Human Spirit in an Age of Disbelief.* San Francisco: HarperSanFrancisco, 2001.

Stich, Stephen P. *The Fragmentation of Reason: Preface to a Pragmatic Theory of Cognitive Evaluation.* Cambridge, MA: MIT Press, 1990.

Sweetman, Robert. "Why We Don't Join Institutions Anymore." First of two talks given in 2008 at *Another Brick in the Wall,* an ICS Worldview Conference. ICS Institutional Repository: http://hdl.handle.net/10756/304604.

– "Will This Church Have Children?" Second of two talks given in 2008 at *Another Brick in the Wall,* an ICS Worldview Conference. ICS Institutional Repository: http://hdl.handle.net/10756/304565.

– *Tracing the Lines: Spiritual Exercise and the Gesture of Christian Scholarship.* Eugene, OR: Wipf and Stock, 2016.

Taylor, Charles. *The Ethics of Authenticity.* Cambridge, MA: Harvard University Press, 1992.

Tol, Anthony. *Philosophy in the Making: D.H.Th. Vollenhoven and the Emergence of Reformed Philosophy.* Sioux Center, IA: Dordt College Press, 2010.

VanderVennen, Robert E. *A University for the People: A History of the Institute for Christian Studies.* Sioux Center, IA: Dordt College Press, 2008.

van Woudenberg, René. "Theorie van het kennen." In *Kennis en werkelijkheid: Tweede inleiding tot een Christelijke filosofie,* edited by R. van Woudenberg, 21–85. Amsterdam: Buijten & Schipperheijn, 1996.

– "Truths That Science Cannot Touch." *Philosophia Reformata* 76 (2011): 169–86.

Vollenhoven, Dirk H.T. *Logos en ratio: Beider verhouding in de geschiedenis der westersche kentheorie.* Kampen: J.H. Kok, 1926.

- *Hoofdlijnen der logica*. Kampen: J.H. Kok, 1948.
- *Calvinism and the Reformation of Philosophy* (1933). Excerpt in *Dirk H.T. Vollenhoven Reader*, edited and translated by John H. Kok, 21–65. Manuscript, 1998.
- *Isagôgè Philosophiae / Introduction to Philosophy*. Edited by John H. Kok and Anthony Tol. Sioux Center, IA: Dordt College Press, 2005.
- *Reformed Epistemology: The Relation of Logos and Ratio in the History of Western Epistemology*. Translated by Anthony Tol. Edited by John Kok. Sioux Center, IA: Dordt College Press, 2013.

Walsh, Brian J., Hendrik Hart, and Robert E. VanderVennen, eds. *An Ethos of Compassion and the Integrity of Creation*. Lanham, MD: University Press of America, 1995.

Weiskel, Thomas. *The Romantic Sublime: Studies in the Structure and Psychology of Transcendence*. Baltimore: Johns Hopkins University Press, 1976.

Wesselius, Janet Catherina. "A Responsible Philosophy: Feminist Resonances in Hendrik Hart's Reading of Objectivity." In *Philosophy as Responsibility: A Celebration of Hendrik Hart's Contribution to the Discipline*, edited by Ronald A. Kuipers and Janet Catherina Wesselius, 225–39. Lanham, MD: University Press of America, 2002.

Williams, Bernard Arthur Owen. *Truth & Truthfulness: An Essay in Genealogy*. Princeton, NJ: Princeton University Press, 2002.

Wilson, Rob. *American Sublime: The Genealogy of a Poetic Genre*. Madison: The University of Wisconsin Press, 1991.

Wolterstorff, Nicholas. *Justice in Love*. Grand Rapids, MI: Eerdmans, 2011.

Wright, Crispin. *Truth and Objectivity*. Cambridge, MA: Harvard University Press, 1992.
- "Truth: A Traditional Debate Reviewed." *Canadian Journal of Philosophy* Supplementary Volume 24 (1998): 31–74.
- "Minimalism, Deflationism, Pragmatism, Pluralism." In *The Nature of Truth: Classic and Contemporary Perspectives*, edited by Michael P. Lynch, 751–87. Cambridge, MA: MIT Press, 2001.

Zuidervaart, Lambert. "Kant's Critique of Beauty and Taste: Explorations into a Philosophical Aesthetics." Toronto: Master's thesis, Institute for Christian Studies, 1977.
- "Music." In *Shaping School Curriculum: A Biblical View*, edited by Geraldine J. Steensma and Harro W. Van Brummelen, 94–104. Terre Haute, IN: Signal, 1977.
- "Refractions: Truth in Adorno's Aesthetic Theory." Amsterdam: PhD diss., Vrije Universiteit, 1981.

Works Cited 251

- *Adorno's Aesthetic Theory: The Redemption of Illusion*. Cambridge, MA: MIT Press, 1991.
- "Consuming Visions." In *Dancing in the Dark: Youth, Popular Culture, and the Electronic Media*, co-authored by Quentin J. Schultze, Roy M. Anker, James D. Bratt, William D. Romanowski, John William Worst, and Lambert Zuidervaart, 111–45. Grand Rapids, MI: Eerdmans, 1991.
- "The Politics of Aesthetic Distance." In *Advocacy in the Classroom: Problems and Possibilities*, edited by Patricia Meyer Spacks, 232–7. New York: St Martin's Press, 1996.
- *Artistic Truth: Aesthetics, Discourse, and Imaginative Disclosure*. Cambridge: Cambridge University Press, 2004.
- *Social Philosophy after Adorno*. Cambridge: Cambridge University Press, 2007.
- "After Dooyeweerd: Truth in Reformational Philosophy." Manuscript, 2008. ICS Institutional Repository: http://ir.icscanada.edu/icsir/handle/10756/305241.
- *Art in Public: Politics, Economics, and a Democratic Culture*. Cambridge: Cambridge University Press, 2011.
- "How Not to Be an Anti-Realist: Habermas, Truth, and Justification." *Philosophia Reformata* 77, no. 1 (2012): 1–18.
- "Art, Religion, and the Sublime: After Hegel." *Owl of Minerva* 44, nos 1–2 (2012–13): 119–42.
- "Truth and Goodness Intersect." ICS *Perspective* 48, no. 2 (September 2014): 8–9.
- "Creating a Disturbance: Art, Social Ethics, and Relational Autonomy." *Germanic Review: Literature, Culture, Theory* 90, no. 4 (2015): 235–46.
- "Propositional and Existential Truth in Edmund Husserl's *Logical Investigations*." *Symposium: Canadian Journal of Continental Philosophy* 20, no. 1 (Spring 2016): 150–80.
- *Religion, Truth, and Social Transformation: Essays in Reformational Philosophy*. Montreal: McGill-Queen's University Press, 2016.
- *Art, Education, and Cultural Renewal: Essays in Reformational Philosophy*. Montreal: McGill-Queen's University Press, 2017.
- *Truth in Husserl, Heidegger, and the Frankfurt School: Critical Retrieval*. Cambridge, MA: MIT Press, 2017.
- "History and Transcendence in Adorno's Idea of Truth." In *The Routledge Companion to the Frankfurt School*, edited by Peter Gordon, Espen Hammer, and Axel Honneth, 121–34. New York: Routledge, 2018.
- "Adorno's Critique of Heidegger: The Temporality of Truth." In *The

Oxford Handbook of Adorno, edited by Henry Pickford and Martin Shuster. Oxford: Oxford University Press, forthcoming.

Zuidervaart, Lambert, Allyson Carr, Matthew Klaassen, and Ronnie Shuker, eds. *Truth Matters: Knowledge, Politics, Ethics, Religion*. Montreal: McGill-Queen's University Press, 2013.

Index

absolute spirit, 43, 52, 134
Adorno, Theodor, 3, 17, 18, 36, 96, 125, 127, 135, 146, 149–56, 161–3, 175–7, 180, 236n39, 238n62
aesthetics, 57, 62, 65–7, 115, 127–36, 148, 167–8, 221n20, 237n62
Alcoff, Linda Martín, 40
Alston, William, 49, 217n16
animals, 211n8, 223n2
Ansell, Nik, 121
Anselm, 43
anthropocentrism, 118–19
antithesis, the, 16–17, 117, 121, 124, 157
anti-truth, 201, 205
Arendt, Hannah, 3–4, 7–8, 10, 209n6
Arensberg, Mary, 141
Aristotle, 43
art, 51–2, 66–7, 73, 85–6, 96, 107–8, 122, 126, 130, 166–9, 189, 198, 210n19; in Hegel, 128–36; post-secular, 16, 17, 128, 143–5; and religion, 128–36; of the sublime, 16–17, 130–6, 140–4, 146; systemic pressures on, 96

Atanasescu, Adrian, 106–8
authentication, 50–1, 73, 111
authority, 88, 188–9, 194, 201, 232n9

Baghai, Farshid, 87, 98–9
beliefs, 32, 41–2, 71–2, 216n2, 228n52; and insight, 71–2, 198–9; justified true, 13, 47, 71, 224n9, 228n51; religious, 76–85, 226n26
Benjamin, Walter, 152–3
Blomberg, Doug, 13, 53–69, 72, 124, 219n4, 221n20, 222n47, 223n49
Burke, Donald, 135

Campbell, Richard, 211n6, 212n16
capitalism, 175–8; as economic system, 90–1, 96, 214n26
Carr, Allyson, 123–4, 171
Centre for Philosophy, Religion and Social Ethics (CPRSE), 103
Chaplin, Jonathan, 87–95
chesed, 21–3
Christianity, 111–12, 181–3; Kuyperian, 2–7, 90, 165, 183–4;

and philosophy, 20–3, 27–9,
154–9, 179, 203–6; and the left,
181–2; as wisdom tradition,
11–12, 20–4, 204, 212n11
Christian Reformed Church (CRC),
183–4
civil rights, 88
civil society, 14–15, 95–8, 101–2,
169, 175, 177
Cockburn, Bruce, 26–7
corroboration. *See under* justification
Costelloe, Timothy, 127
Crapo, Ruthanne, 87, 97–8
critical retrieval, 15–16, 69–70, 112
Critical Theory, 95–6, 127, 154,
161–3, 191–3, 205, 216n5
critique: architectonic, 14–15, 27,
90–6 101, 104, 175; faithful,
123–5; immanent, 15, 17,
112–14, 196; normative, 91, 174;
redemptive, 52, 126–7; social, 52,
87–95, 126, 174–7; with metacritical intent, 15, 17, 112–14, 156,
196
cynicism, 76, 176

Dahlhaus, Carl, 151
decontextualization, 198–200
deflationism, 33–4
deism, 116–17
DeMoor, Michael, 87, 100, 102, 117
DeRoo, Neal, 116–17
Derrida, Jacques, 240n8
Desmond, William, 135
Dettloff, Dean, ix–x, 118
Dewey, John, 189
dialectic, 155–6, 196, 236n38–9
differential transformation, 14,
17–18, 90–2, 97, 162, 177

differentiation, 7, 97, 143, 162; of
art and religion, 91, 131–2; and
normativity, 106–9; of truth,
42–3, 50
disclosure, 19, 52, 146, 198–9, 204;
dialectical, 145–6; faithful, 95;
imaginative, 52, 145–6; life-giving, 9, 28–9, 50, 192–3; worked,
75–6; worshipful, 52
disquotationalism, 33
dogmatism, 15, 111
Dooyeweerd, Herman, 6, 46, 69,
189, 225n18, 234n33; critical
retrieval of, 16–17, 92–3, 115–25;
on knowledge, 55–8, 61, 81,
220n13; *A New Critique of Theoretical Thought*, 55–6, 81, 160; on
theoretical thought, 5, 56, 59
Duck, Ruth, 22–3

Eagleton, Terry, 205, 214n32
Edwards, Douglas, 50
Elkins, James, 126–7, 133, 135, 144,
146
Ellul, Jacques, 182, 185
emeth, 21–3, 211n6
Enneson, Peter, 122–3, 234n33
epistemology, 4–5, 11–12; analytic/continental, 39–40, 228n52;
holistic/pluralist, 13–14, 31–52,
54–6, 69–87; reformational, 31,
46–7, 50, 53–71, 74, 86, 121–2
essentialism, 122–3
evil, 24–5, 52; societal, 14, 18, 26–8,
99–100, 117, 121, 136, 146,
175–7, 213n23, 214n28, 236n40
evolution, 93, 122
experience: lived, 122–3; mediated,
64–6; naïve/concrete, 57–60,
64–6, 222n47

facts, 49, 199–200; alternative, 10, 25, 200, 202; and values, 64–6, 190
factual accuracy. *See under* truth
faith, 77, 99; and reason, 78–83, 109–12
faithfulness, 11–12, 19, 22, 24–9, 45, 203–4, 211n6, 212n16
Feyer Salo, Jazz, 119–20
Foucault, Michel, 33–4, 174, 202, 216n6
Frankfurt, Harry, 26, 35, 213n25
Frankfurt School, 96, 152–4, 163, 178
Frege, Gottlob, 188, 190–1
Fulman, Ben, 87, 95–6

Gegenstand relation, 56—7, 73, 220n13, 222n44
God, 21–3, 28–9, 59–61, 77, 80, 85, 106, 136, 227n27; call of, 94–5, 121; in Hegel, 129–34, 136; knowledge of, 77–8, 80–2, 84–5, 105, 227n35
goodness, 24–7, 51–2, 176–8
Goudzwaard, Bob, 179
Guyer, Paul, 127

Habermas, Jürgen, 17, 107–8, 161–2, 232n9
Hadot, Pierre, 20, 211n4
Hampshire, Ben, 112, 114–15,
Harris, Joshua, 120, 213n18
Hart, Hendrik (Henk), 104–7, 109–11, 117, 123, 159–60, 215n37, 222n44; on knowledge, 53, 55–6, 63–4, 78–84, 147–8, 215n37, 220n13–14, 224n4–5, 227n35, 228n51
heart, 16, 116–20

Hebrew poetry, 131–2, 136
Hegel, G.W.F., 15–17, 43, 51–2, 127–36, 144–5, 189, 235n10
Heidegger, Martin, 191–3, 198, 204, 215n35
Herbert, George, 30
holistic pluralism: alethic, 12–13, 18–19, 31, 48, 50, 196–7; epistemological, 13–14, 53–61, 67–72, 86–7; of reformational philosophy, 7, 17, 53–61, 69–70, 86, 157–8, 197. *See also* truth theory: holistic alethic pluralism
hope, 14–15, 27–9, 98–100, 136, 205–6, 214n32
Husserl, Edmund, 121, 188, 190–1

identity politics, 98, 182
imagination, 57, 66–7, 108–9, 122
imaginative cogency, 62, 75, 108
imperialism, 190
insight, 49; and knowledge, 71–6; normative, 13, 59–64, 225n12; transformative, 113; and understanding, 59–61
Institute for Christian Studies (ICS), 6–7, 103, 147, 165–6, 182
institutions, 48, 66–8, 72–5, 83, 91, 97–8, 126, 146, 200, 218n29
integral curriculum, 53, 58–9, 65, 69
interconnected flourishing, 9–10, 12, 21–2, 97, 169, 179
intuition, 121–2
isomorphism, 18, 50, 70, 193

Jesus, 23, 28, 157
justice, 8–10, 12, 21–2, 51, 89–90, 94, 177, 180, 240n8
justification, 49–50, 228n51; and

corroboration, 49, 51; discursive, 40–2, 111

Kant, Immanuel, 128, 130, 189
King, Martin Luther, 88
Kirkham, Richard, 38–9
Klapwijk, Jacob, 119–20, 122
knowing, 220n14, 226n21; analytic, 53–5, 58, 61–4, 69–71, 78–9, 82, 84–6, 222n45, 226n24, 227n35; distantial, 13, 56–62, 64–7, 69, 74; economic, 57–8, 62–3; imaginative, 57, 66–7, 221n20; linguistic, 86, 229n57; and loving, 54–5; rational, 79; sensuous, 134; techno-cultural, 57–8; theoretical, 56–9. *See also* theoretical thought
knowledge, 13, 54–6, 220n14; artistic/scientific, 72–4, 148–9; bodily, 86, 229n55; compartmentalization of, 3–4, 7–8, 16, 126; and factual accuracy, 172–3; fiduciary, 78–81; and insight, 71–6; institutional embedding of, 46–8, 56, 62–4, 67, 73–4, 82–3; norm-relatedness of, 59–65, 76; propositional, 82–6; as relationship, 13, 60–1, 70–4, 77, 86, 224n3; religious, 57, 61, 77–82, 84–5, 224n4, 226n24; social domains of, 13–14, 46–8, 54, 70, 74–6, 82–3, 86, 91, 126, 224n5
Kok, John, 219n6, 222n45
Kuipers, Ron, 105–6, 210n13
Kuyper, Abraham, 5–6, 27, 161

Langer, Susanne K., 150
liberation theology, 181
Lie, the, 24–6, 29, 121, 213n23

life-giving disclosure. *See under* disclosure
logic, 188, 190
Lok, Peter, 117–18
love, 124, 142; call to, 21–3, 29–30, 60–1, 70, 94–5; of God, 23, 28–9; and knowing, 54–5; and truth, 22–3, 28–9; of wisdom, 20, 23
Lukács, Georg, 153–4
Lynch, Michael, 38, 39, 50

MacIntyre, Alasdair, 194
Malick, Terrence, 16, 127, 136, 140–2, 144; *The Tree of Life*, 16, 127–8, 136–44, 146, 237n49
Marxism, 152–3, 161–3, 178, 180
Marx, Karl, 178, 180, 189
Medina, José, 39
Mekkes, J.P.A., 54, 219n9
messianic condition, 21, 27, 179–80
modal theory, 57–9, 62–3, 66, 74, 78–9, 86, 92, 118–22, 159, 221n20, 225n18, 226n22, 228n52
mystery, 105–6

nature/freedom, 189–90
nature/grace, 137–8
new Earth, 99, 179
normativity, 9, 14, 40, 59–65, 76, 106–9, 180, 202, 223n49; and redirection, 14, 76, 90–1, 95–6, 99, 101–2, 177

Olthuis, James, 23, 62–3, 212n14, 222n44
opening process, 58
openness, 28, 52, 64–5
ordinary language, 43

Parmenides, 24, 203–4

Index

Patterson, Hannah, 141
Pederson, Miriam, 20
personhood, 93
phenomenology, 121–2, 188
philosophy, 27, 52, 114, 194–5; analytic/continental, 18–19, 39–40, 44, 168, 170, 187, 192, 197; of art, 122; and art/religion, 16–17, 43, 51–2, 133–5, 145–6; and Christianity, 20–3, 27–9, 154–9, 179, 203–6; and love, 20, 28, 52, 113, 124; of music, 148, 150–2; pedagogy of, 115, 159–60, 164–5, 223n21; reformational, ix, 5–8, 13, 15–17, 31, 52, 69–71, 86, 92, 103–25, 149, 156–60, 162, 179, 197, 215n37, 224n4, 224n9; social, 3, 5, 7, 192; as totality discipline, 15, 105–6; transformational, 98–100; as a way of life, 20–1, 52
Plantinga, Alvin, 224n9
Plato, 7, 8, 77, 173
pluralism, 97–8, 158. *See also* holistic pluralism
politics: American, 162–4, 175, 201–2; definition of, 8–9; democratic, 51, 91–2, 99–100, 103; of hope, 14–15, 98–100, 103; of the left, 181–2, 185–6; and religion, 14, 88–90, 97–8; of science, 14, 100–3, 200; as social domain of truth, 9–10; and truth, 3–11, 17–18, 25, 51, 87, 173–4, 200–1
Popma, K.J., 55, 71, 219n9, 225n11
populism, 162–4, 201–2
positivism, 172, 187–8
posthumanism, 117–18
postmodernity, 172–4, 202
post-truth, 3, 10–11, 17–19, 25–6, 172–4, 200–1, 213n25

power, 76, 174; and justice, 8–10; and truth, 3, 33–4, 51, 174, 202–3, 216n6
predicative self-disclosure, 73, 85, 199–200
propositional truth. *See under* truth
public deliberation, 101–2
public sphere, 88–9
Putnam, Hilary, 49

Quine, Willard, 33, 36, 216n3

radical contextualism, 33–4
rationality, 78–9, 109–12, 205
realism, 109–10, 234n33
redemptive art criticism, 16, 126–7
reformational philosophy. *See under* philosophy
reform/revolution, 17–18, 161–2, 178, 183
relativism, 35, 202
religion, 14, 51–2, 108–9, 114, 210n3; and art, 128–36; and politics, 88–90, 97–8; and reason, 76–85, 110–12
resourcefulness, 62, 90–1, 179–80
Rorty, Richard, 15, 33
Rudisill, Dan, 121
Russell, Bertrand, 188, 190–1, 193
Rybin, Steven, 140

Scheler, Max, 118–19
scholarship: Christian, 154–6, 179; serviceable, 165; socially ethical, 51, 102–3
science, 51, 73, 188–9, 199–201; normative integration of, 14, 100–2; and politics, 100–3
scientism, 32, 34
Scott, A.O., 137, 237n49

secularism, 89, 143
Seerveld, Calvin, 22, 24, 56–7, 62, 66–7, 148, 150, 155, 221n20, 225n18
Smith, Huston, 211n3
social critique. *See under* critique
social domains. *See under* knowledge; truth
societal evil. *See under* evil
societal macrostructures, 90, 177
societal principles, 9–10, 12, 14, 27–8, 50, 63, 95, 106–7, 193; as divine call/response, 94–5, 106; eschatological openness of, 28–9, 122; historical character of, 92–4, 123
solidarity, 16, 93–4; philosophical, 15, 112–13
spiritual crisis, 25, 203, 211n3
spiritual direction, 5, 7, 70, 98, 113, 116–17, 158, 226n24
state, the, 8, 88–9, 96, 160–1
stewardship, 62, 179–80. *See also* resourcefulness
Stich, Steven, 32, 216n2
Stockwell, Clinton, 87, 97
sublime, the, 16, 126–7; American, 141–2, 237n49, 237n53; art of the, 131–6, 140–4; in Hegel, 127–36; in Kant, 128, 130; postmodern, 142; postsecular, 143–4
suffering, 14, 51, 99, 125, 136–9, 146, 237n62
supratemporality, 116–17, 119–20
Sweetman, Bob, 90, 96, 112–13, 115, 122, 170, 210n2

Taubes, Jacob, 152–3
technology, 74–6, 85–6, 226n22

theological universalism, 16, 120–1
theoretical thought, 56–9, 61, 63–7, 69, 119–21
theory/practice, 56, 58, 63, 96
Thomas, Martin Luther, 163
transcendence, 118–19, 136, 140
Trinity, the, 111–12
Trump, Donald, 17, 25, 174, 200–3
truth, 31–3; in analytic philosophy, 40, 50, 187, 191–2, 194–5; and art, 15, 43, 45–6, 67, 108–10, 126, 128–9, 133–4, 144–5, 148–9, 167–8, 198; as assertoric correctness, 173; comprehensive, 133–5, 144–5; as dynamic correlation, 9, 18, 28–9, 50, 108, 192–3; existential, 42–6; and Judaeo-Christian wisdom, 11–12, 20–4, 203–4; factual, 4, 18, 25–6, 199–200, 213n25, 215n37; as factual accuracy, 10–11, 22, 25, 172–3; and friendship, 43–5; and goodness, 2–6, 29, 51, 232n15; and love, 21–3, 28–9, 212n14; and opinion, 4, 25, 32, 172–3, 202; philosophical criticism of, 31–4; and politics, 3–11, 17–18, 25, 51, 87, 173, 200; and power, 3, 33–4, 174, 202–3, 216n6; pre/postpropositional, 13–14, 46, 48, 50, 85–6, 229n57; propositional, 4, 12, 18, 40–6, 49–50, 52, 79–85, 144–5, 191–4, 197–9, 204, 217n10, 228n52; religious, 15, 43, 76–85, 108–12, 120, 134, 144–5; scientific, 18, 32, 47–8, 51, 100–2, 121, 191, 198–200, 218n29, 220n15, 225n16; in Scripture, 21–3, 27–9, 147–8, 211n8; social

domains of, 9–10, 14, 46–8, 50–2, 91, 100, 108–9; and the sublime, 133–6; and suffering, 125, 146; as a way of life, 11–12, 20–30, 46, 52, 211n4, 215n38. *See also* anti-truth; post-truth

truth theory, 4–5, 11, 31; alethic pluralist/monist, 38–9, 49–50, 197; alethic realist/anti-realist, 39, 41, 217n16; analytic/continental, 18, 39–40, 44; epistemic/non-epistemic, 41–2, 49; holistic alethic pluralism, 7, 9, 12–14, 17–19, 31, 48, 50–6, 67, 157–8, 169–70, 192–4, 196–7; Judaeo-Christian/Greek, 11–12, 19, 22, 24, 27–9, 203–5; monothetic/stereothetic, 44–6, 50; ontological/axiological concerns of, 12, 31, 36–41; post-anti/realist, 110.

Urban Institute for Contemporary Arts, 96, 167, 185–6

validity, 15, 49–50, 73–4, 108–10
values, 37, 39, 174
Van Dyk, Tricia, 122
van Woudenberg, René, 55, 86, 217n10, 218n29
Vollenhoven, Dirk, 6, 15, 46, 53–4, 63, 69–71, 149, 219n6, 222n45, 223n2, 226n22, 227n35
VU Amsterdam (Free University), 6

Weiskel, Thomas, 142–3
Wilson, Rob, 141, 237n53
Wittgenstein, Ludwig, 15, 36
wisdom, 11–12, 19–24, 26–30, 55–6, 65–6, 203–4, 212n11

Wolterstorff, Nicholas, xi–xii, 22
Wood, David, 39
work, 74–6
worship, 77, 80, 83
Wright, Crispin, 33, 50

Zuidervaart, Lambert: *Art, Education, and Cultural Renewal*, ix; *Art in Public*, 96, 101, 164, 168–9, 202; *Artistic Truth*, 166–8; *Religion, Truth, and Social Transformation*, ix, x, 14, 16, 87–125, 197, 199; *Social Philosophy after Adorno*, 169; *Truth in Husserl, Heidegger, and the Frankfurt School*, 197